Gay Plays: Volum

Round 2 by Eric Bentley, *Days of Cavafy* b'
A Vision of Love Revealed in Sleep, by Neil Bartlett,

A VISION OF LOVE REVEALED IN SLEEP – Neil Bartlett
'An unforgettable meditation on art, passion and persecution. . . . Here is a mix
– alternately disturbing and exhilarating – of parody, quips, torch songs and
personal testimony. *A Vision* was perhaps the single most audacious show of the
1980s.'
Jim Hiley, Listener

DAYS OF CAVAFY – Gerald Killingworth
'The scenes thrillingly conflate ancient civilisation and present experience into a
single moment.'
Irving Wardle, The Times

ROUND 2 – Eric Bentley
'This masterly transposition of the gaiety of Schnitzler's Vienna into the tragi-
comic gay life of New York, shows us the foibles of our universal search beyond
the thrill of encounter, towards the vision of pure love.'
Judith Malina, Director of The Living Theatre

WILD BLUE – Joe Pintauro
'Highly literate, brilliantly clear, and wonderfully operatic, Pintauro's voice is a
definite original'.
Studs Terkel

'*Gay Plays: Volume 4* reflects the rich diversity of both gay writing and gay
experience' (Peter Burton, *Gay Times*). Playwright Michael Wilcox has selected
the best of British and American gay writing: Neil Bartlett's startling and
brilliant *A Vision*; Gerald Killingworth's chamber piece on Constantine Cavafy; a
gay *La Ronde* set in 1970s New York by Eric Bentley; and Joe Pintauro's wild
and funny short pieces confronting themes of gay sexuality.

Michael Wilcox's plays include: *Accounts, Lent, Massage, Rents, Green Fingers* and
Time Windows. He has also written opera libretti for John Metcalf's *Tornrak*
(Welsh National Opera, 1991), Edward McGuire's *Cullercoats Tommy* (Northern
Stage, 1993), and, with Jeremy Sams, a new libretto for Chabrier's *The Reluctant
King* (Opera North, 1994). His autobiographical journal, *Outlaw in the Hills* is
published by Methuen. Michael is Literary Adviser to both Northern Stage and
Live Theatre companies.

Gay Plays: Volume Four

Round 2
Eric Bentley

Days of Cavafy
Gerald Killingworth

A Vision of Love Revealed in Sleep (Part Three)
Neil Bartlett

Wild Blue
Joe Pintauro

Edited and introduced by Michael Wilcox

Methuen Drama

Methuen New Theatrescripts

This volume first published in Great Britain in 1990
by Methuen Drama
an imprint of Reed Consumer Books Ltd
Michelin House, 81 Fulham Road, London SW3 6RB
and Auckland, Melbourne, Singapore and Toronto.
Distributed in the United States of America
by Heinemann
a division of Reed Elsevier Inc.
361 Hanover Street, Portsmouth, New Hampshire NH 03801 3959

A CIP catalogue record for this book may be obtained from the British Library.

ISBN 0-413-61890-0

Lyric to *In The Still of the Night* (Cole Porter) reproduced by kind permission of Warner Chappell Ltd.
Lyric to *For All We Know* (Sam Lewis) included by permission of Redwood Music Ltd.
Front cover: Neil Bartlett and Regina Fong in Gloria's production of *A Vision of Love Revealed in Sleep*. Photo: Mike Laye.

Printed and bound in Great Britain by
Clays Ltd, St Ives plc

Caution

Contents

Introduction

In Britain, the 1990s has started with a revival of Martin Sherman's **Bent** at the National Theatre, with gay actors Ian McKellen and Michael Cashman leading a fine cast. In his *Guardian* review, Michael Billington writes of 'a Britain in which the level of sexual intolerance is once again rising: "Pulpit Poufs" screams *The Sun*, while *The Times* magisterially decreed . . . that "It is not advisable for senior judicial appointments to be offered to practising homosexuals".' The latter reference is to an investigation into a number of Scottish judges that has resulted in one of them resigning, simply, we are led to believe, because he has been involved in some unspecified homosexual activity.

But consenting homosexual relations between males over the age of 21 in private is not a criminal offence, although it took Scotland, which has its own legal system, many years to come into line with English law in this matter. This affair is further evidence that, in spite of legal reform, homosexual men are second-class citizens. They can expect prejudice, insult, assault, and limited career prospects if they are open and honest about their sexuality, and fear, isolation, guilt and possible blackmail if they are not. (And after personal experience of both options, I have no doubt that the first is the one to go for!)

Billington continues, 'In such a climate, the revival of **Bent** takes on an extra importance . . . by taking Nazi Germany as its setting, it shows where the vicious persecution of people for their sexuality may ultimately lead.'

In the Introduction to **Gay Plays Three,** I wrote about the increasing homophobia in Britain. In the two years that have passed since then, intolerance and fear of homosexuality have grown steadily. Reports in Britain's leading gay magazine, *Gay Times*, suggest an increase in police harassment and entrapment of homosexuals in many parts of the country, as though the police are obeying some new protocol.

The Conservative Government, still led by Mrs Thatcher, seems to have backed away from its campaign to inform the public about AIDS and safe sex. Instead, stories are circulated in the tabloid press that it is impossible to catch AIDS from unprotected, vaginal intercourse, and that heterosexuals are not at risk from the HIV virus. The British Medical Association intends to protest to the Press Council about such wickedly inaccurate advice. But, whether out of ignorance, prejudice or some more sinister political motive, it appears that the Conservative Government is diverting from its original course, in which AIDS was portrayed in a controversial advertising campaign as being of universal concern, to isolating AIDS as being a crisis among homosexual males and IV drug abusers. If that is the case, the warnings of history that are dramatised so effectively in Martin Sherman's play, and which Michael Billington's review highlights, deserve the most urgent consideration.

If, as I believe, there is a right wing conspiracy in Britain that has on its agenda the re-criminalisation of male homosexuality, it is of the utmost importance that homosexuals 'come out' in massive numbers. Shame and fear are powerful weapons in the hands of evil-minded people, but they are weapons that closet homosexuals forge for those who wish them ill. That Scottish judge should not have offered his resignation, simply because he was gay. He should have 'come out' publicly, stood his ground and fought back. The idea that heterosexual judges are competent and worthy, whole homosexual ones are intrinsically undesirable, is as ludicrous and irrational as it is for any other profession. There are good and bad homosexuals, just as there are good and bad heterosexuals. Reality is as simple as that!

The continued publication of plays with gay themes, or depicting homosexual characters in not necessarily gay situations, has increasingly become a political act in such a climate. Just getting a new book accepted on the shelves with a Pink Triangle, or the Gay Men's Press logo, or the word 'Gay' on the cover is defiant. Visibility matters! But so, of course, do the contents of the plays themselves. In the four **Gay Plays** volumes, you can encounter homophobia and high camp on a nuclear submarine (**Submariners**), a gay, sheep-farming rugby football player and his closet coach (**Accounts**), a gay native American (**Bearclaw**), a schoolboy who uses Shakespeare for seduction (**Quaint Honour**), a phantom marksman (**Cracks**), a boxer who can only fight well when he is sexually aroused by his opponent (**Cock and Bull Story**), and the last boy in New York (**Terminal Bar**). The diversity and range of the plays collected in these volumes is surprising.

And there are further surprises in the present anthology. Who would have guessed that Eric Bentley is the author of **Round 2**? This gay **La Ronde** is set in New York in the 70s at a time when homosexuals were becoming increasingly visible and confident, but before the cruelty of AIDS. What is striking about this succession of sexual encounters is how very interesting even dull people become in such situations. Sex overturns, even if for a short time, the social and economic order. People reveal so much about themselves, shedding more than their clothes. Is there really such a thing as casual sex? There is so much to learn about humanity in even the briefest encounter.

Brief encounters with young and beautiful men play a part in Gerald Killingworth's **Days of Cavafy.** Biographical plays about the famous and the dead pose their own problems of credibility. The idea of witnessing a private meeting between Cavafy and E. M. Forster is intriguing, but even if it is extraordinarily well done, it is still fiction. Some years ago I wrote the first draft of a play about the French composer, Hector Berlioz. The trouble was (and remains) that famous people tend to know a lot of other famous people. Before I knew what was happening there was Liszt, Paganini, Cherubini, and Heaven knows who else, coming in and out of the story. Of course, I could only guess at what they said to each other and how they spoke (in English, of course!). The whole thing became laughable and I hid the hundred pages of script on my highest shelf where it has remained ever since. Nevertheless, I have had an eye on plays about T. E. Lawrence, Isherwood, Pasolini, Socrates and other luminaries for inclusion in this series, finding the genre irresistible. Killingworth's play has an excellent scene between Cavafy and a young man, which might have been part of **La Ronde,** and I thought it would be interesting to juxtapose it with Eric Bentley's play. I was also amused by the story of Forster taking the wrong door, while searching for Cavafy's apartment, and entering a brothel. There is something quaintly English about Killingworth's treatment of his subject, and in his literary dialogue. And you know from the outset that there is not the slightest chance of Killingworth's Cavafy getting into bed with his young Adonis. Would Cavafy have been so coy in reality? But literal 'reality' is not the intention of a biographical play. The subject is lending his or her name to a fiction, however skilful the playwright. But, if **Days of Cavafy** encourages people to explore Cavafy's poetry, it will have performed an invaluable service.

There is more biography in **A Vision of Love Revealed in Sleep** (Part Three). This time the subject is a little-known homosexual artist, Simeon Solomon. But Neil Bartlett and his company have approached their reality via a theatrical event rather than the word. What is published here isn't a playscript, and anyone reading through this transcript of an actual performance without first reading Neil Bartlett's introduction is likely to think that I, Neil and the rest of his company have all lost our marbles. But I was anxious to find a way of recording an aspect of gay theatre in the 1980s that has not been adequately preserved on film or video, and for which 'a script' doesn't really exist. Anyone who saw a performance of **A Vision of Love . . .**, or who even saw the poster with Neil standing naked, shaven and scarcely draped, is not going to forget the image. I predict that this poster will become one of the classic images of the past decade, and how frustrating not to be able to publish it here.

A Vision . . . only exists in performance and varies to a certain degree from one night to the next. If I described the artistes as stand-up drag queens (but not you, Neil!) that would be an inadequate description, and probably would put my life in danger. Let me play safe and say that the tradition from which this theatre comes is peculiarly British. Bette Bourne or Regina Fong wouldn't be seen dead on the stage of an American Burlesque. (Backstage, yes. On stage, no . . .) And if you want to find out more, follow up the reviews and magazine articles that are listed in the credits of the transcript, search out the remarkable photographs of the performance, and come to London to see Neil, Bette Bourne, Regina Fong and Ivan in action for yourselves!

Let's hurry back to the security of the scripted play in the form of Joe Pintauro's **Wild Blue.** Or plays, for here is a collection of short scripts, each of which could stand on its own feet, but together provide a concentrated and varied experience. What is apparent at once is that Pintauro, none of whose plays have I ever had the opportunity of seeing performed, writes superb dialogue. This has been a feature of all the American playwrights included in these anthologies. So many of the scripts I receive from British writers are over-burdened with literacy, producing dialogue that may work in a novel, but which is death in the theatre.

Short plays can be very frustrating. We enter and leave the action wanting to know so much more. What happened next to Nicky and Uncle Chick? But elsewhere, we know quite enough. I'd had enough of Wendell, who has just fucked his transexual son without knowing it. I'm sure that the Priest (another father) followed the Penitent to Chicago, but am happy to leave it at that. And I certainly have had enough of Mr Rosen (yet another father!) whose attitude to tragedy is tiresomely self-centred. Yet I am glad to have encountered all of them, however briefly. Uncle Wayne is the man I should love to know and **Lenten Puddings** is a perfect short play.

As with Timothy Mason and Paul Selig, the other young American dramatists whose work is still almost unknown in Europe, one can only admire Pintauro's original talent and wait expectantly for his next play. And let no one imagine that these scripts, collected under that most unsatisfactory banner **Gay Plays,** are written by a minority for a minority audience.

Michael Wilcox, January 1990

Round 2
or *New York in the 70s*

a Schnitzler variation

Eric Bentley

For Maxim

Weltspiel, das herrische,
Mischt Sein und Schein –
Das Ewig-Närrische
Mischt uns – hinein!

Eric Bentley was born in Bolton, Lancashire in 1916 and became an American citizen in 1948. He began as a scholar, went on to become a drama critic and translator and then became a playwright, with his best known play being **Are You Now Or Have You Ever Been**. Three volumes of his plays are in print in the United States: **Rallying Cries** (Northwestern University Press); **Monstrous Martyrdoms** (Prometheus Books) and **The Kleist Variations** (Southern Illinois University Press). **Round 2** is his first play to be published in his native England.

Preface

A word, but not of apology

Gay sex was a taboo subject before the 70s and bids fair to become a taboo subject again in the 90s. For the 80s was the time of the Great Plague. The word sex could now be used only if the word safe preceded it. There were people who considered me heartless because I wrote **Round 2** in the 80s, a play about gay sex that never mentions AIDS. Indeed, what takes place in the play could not have taken place before 1970 or much after 1980. What of it? Is AIDS forever? I cannot believe it. Have we no memory; are the 70s already forgotten? I cannot believe it. Do they lack interest – these mores – for those too young to remember? I cannot believe that.

And the author of this play, where has he been these last few years? Someone asked that. I must reply: not hiding from AIDS. I wrote the play for an admired colleague to direct but, sadly enough, he died of AIDS before having a chance to do so. Losing him was the worst but, by that token, the deepest experience I had in the 80s.

For the non-American reader or spectator, let me add that all the locales of my scenes are actual, though not all have survived into the late 80s. One exception: the ice cream parlor with a private dining room in the back is an invention. Too good to be true, yes.

Eric Bentley, New York City, 14 September 1989

1. The Hustler and the Soldier

Times Square. The titles on the movie marquees are of the 70s. Late evening. Sidewalk. In the doorway of an Adult Bookstore, a Black **Hustler** *is standing. A very handsome* **Soldier** *walks by, smoking a cigar.*

Hustler (*in an undertone, close to the* **Soldier**'*s ear*) Lookin' to score?

Soldier Ha?

Hustler You're gorgeous. Bargain rates for guys like you.

Soldier You makin' a pass, faggot?

Hustler Ladies' man, huh? (*Pause.*) Takes all sorts to make a world. (**Soldier** *turns away, looks in store window.*) Ten inches, ten bucks.

Pause. **Soldier** *continues to study store window.*

Soldier Like, where?

Hustler How 'bout your place?

Soldier My place is Fort Dix.

Hustler You stayin' in a hotel 'round here?

Soldier Nah. Got no money anyhow.

Hustler The army don't pay? (**Soldier** *stares at him.*) I don't need no money.

Soldier Oh, no? What's your racket? Coke?

Hustler I gotta get money – from civilians. Not from guys in uniform.

Soldier Patriotic, huh?

Hustler You're gorgeous, Gorgeous.

Soldier You're not bad lookin' yourself. How old are ya?

Hustler Eighteen. You?

Soldier Twenny-five.

Hustler Perfect age! I'd like to be twenny-five for life.

Soldier So where do we go?

Hustler My place, I guess.

Soldier Where's that?

Hustler One thirty-fifth street.

Soldier A hundred blocks away? Harlem at that.

He again starts to go.

Hustler My folks don't mind. (*Pause.*) Lots of white guys like it there.

Soldier I gotta get back to Fort Dix.

Hustler How long you been in the army?

Soldier Too long. How 'bout some place 'round here?

Hustler Wanna pay for a hotel?

Soldier Nah.

Hustler Tell you what. Come tomorrah. Uptown. I'll give you the address.

Soldier Now that shows real trust, don't it? *If* the address is correct. Okay, give it to me.

Hustler *does not.*

Hustler You'll be a no show.

Soldier So some white guys *don't* like it?

Hustler There's a no show once in a while.

Soldier I said okay.

Hustler Tell you what. There's a place on Eighth Avenue.

Soldier What street?

Hustler 44th. Two blocks from here. Come to the corner, I'll show ya. (*They walk, then stop.* **Hustler** *points.*) There!

Soldier How d'we get in?

Hustler The street door's open.

Soldier And then?

Hustler I'll show ya.

Again, they walk.

Soldier (*as they enter a dimly lit building*) Can't see a fuckin' thing.

Hustler Hold on to me, there's no rail on the stairs.

Soldier If I'm dead, I'm dead.

Hustler You're real morbid.

Soldier Kill or get killed. That's war.

Hustler Everythin's gonna be okay. I love ya, know what I mean?

Soldier No. What?

Hustler You remind me of someone.

Soldier I heard that before someplace.

Hustler I could use someone like you. For a boyfriend. A real lover!

Soldier I'd make you too jealous.

Hustler I could handle that.

Soldier Think so, ha?

Hustler Keep your voice down.

Soldier Who would be in here?

Hustler We don't wanna meet *nobody*, that's the thing.

Soldier Okay, let's do it, let's do it.

Hustler There's a better place next floor up. That floor got a railing.

Soldier (*pushing his groin out*) Feel this.

Hustler My God, you're hard as iron. But if we do it here, you're gonna fall right off.

Soldier (*pushing* **Hustler** *down on his knees*) Get goin', get goin'.

Hustler Against the wall then. Lean back against the wall. (**Soldier** *does so.*)

*　　*　　*

Hustler We shoulda gone up on the next floor.

Soldier (*buttoning his fly*) One floor's like another. When are you gonna get up?

Hustler There's no rush. Lemme –

Soldier Gotta get back to Fort Dix. I'm late awready.

Hustler (*getting up*) What's your name, baby?

Soldier Whadda you want my name for?

Hustler Because I love ya, remember? I'll tell you mine: Hyacinth.

Soldier A fuckin' flower.

Hustler Anyway, George – you look like a George –

Soldier Anyway, what? And I'm not a George!

Hustler I seen your I.D.

Soldier Sly, huh? Suppose it's not *my* I.D.?

Hustler Can you loan me ten bucks?

Soldier What d'ya think *I* am? So long. (*He starts off down the stairs.*)

Hustler (*calling after him*) Cunt! Motherfucker!

2. The Soldier and the Art Student

Night. On the sidewalk outside the Underground, a disco near Union Square. The **Soldier** *is pulling the* **Art Student** *out of the disco. Seventies disco music is heard throughout the scene.*

Art Student Why did you keep wanting to leave? (*The* **Soldier** *gives an embarrassed laugh.*) Don't you like to dance?

Soldier (*holding him close, and slow-dancing to the music*) Sure.

Art Student This is not dancing, it's sex.

Soldier (*stopping the dance*) I don't even know your name. Did someone in there call you Kevin?

Art Student So there was a Kevin caught your eye?

Soldier Okay, that was *him*. They called you – Desmond?

Art Student This is a dangerous block. Full of fag bashers.

Soldier You're under the protection of the armed forces, Desmond!

He pulls the student with him along the block.

Art Student Where are we going? I can't see an inch in front of my nose.

Soldier (*using a cigarette lighter*) How 'bout now?

Art Student You're a looker, aren't you?

Soldier You like me?

Art Student You were the best looking guy in the whole place.

Soldier You're not bad yourself.

Art Student But Kevin was the one you danced with most of the time.

Soldier That's because I knew him awready.

Art Student And you thought I was Kevin?

Soldier I was just kiddin'. Did you see my buddy?

Art Student The other guy in uniform?

Soldier Yeah. Kevin's dancin' with him.

Art Student He's pretty fresh. The other guy in uniform.

Soldier Did he try somethin' on you? I told him you were *my* property.

Art Student Well, he didn't listen. And I'm not your property.

Soldier Hey, look, I meant that as a compliment.

Art Student United States property. I'm honored. Maybe.

Soldier And I knew you were Desmond.

Art Student You don't have a name?

Soldier Top secret.

Art Student I'm going back in.

Soldier (*stopping him*) My name's George.

Art Student As in Washington. I like that.

Soldier So keep movin'.

They do so.

Art Student Can't see a thing. (*It's dark but he sees something.*) Hey, no. They're not doin' it right there, are they? In the parking lot?

Soldier (*pointing to another section of the lot*) And that?

Art Student (*seeing something else*) My God, it's an orgy.

Soldier Nah. They mind their own business.

Art Student Let's go back.

Soldier Lemme touch you first. Just lemme touch ya.

Art Student *allows* **Soldier** *to touch him.*

Art Student My God but not like that. My God. We're still on the sidewalk.

Soldier (*pulling him into the darkness*) Not here we're not.

*   *   *

Art Student *steps into the light of the streetlamp.*

Soldier (*from the dark*) Hey, where you goin'?

Art Student That was great.

Soldier So where you goin'?

Art Student Back in, I guess. Where are you?

Soldier Waitin' for you.

Art Student You wanna do it again? Right away?

Soldier Come – see. (**Art Student** *hesitates.*) Come – see.

Art Student *moves back into the darkness.*

*   *   *

Soldier *steps into the light of the streetlamp.*

Soldier You're the affectionate type.

Art Student (*following him eagerly*) That was . . . real nice.

Soldier Let's get back in there.

Art Student (*trying to embrace him*) What's the hurry? (**Soldier** *pulls away*.) Why d'ya walk away?

Soldier To get this damn cigar lit.

He gets his cigar lit and enjoys the first puff.

Art Student (*hurt*) You like cigars, huh? D'you like me?

Soldier (*laughs*) Three guesses! Let's get back in there.

Art Student Why?

Soldier And why stick around in a parking lot, for God's sake? This is a rough block.

Art Student Do you *like* me?

Soldier I picked you, didn't I? I haven't had sex with no one else, have I?

Art Student Then hold me in your arms.

Soldier Okay. (*As he takes hold of him, the music comes up louder.*) Just listen to the music!

Art Student You'd rather dance?

Soldier. Yeah. Let's get back in.

Art Student I'm gonna have to leave. I've an exam tomorrow.

Soldier Where at?

Art Student Parson's School of Design.

Soldier Sounds like it has 'class'. Design, huh?

Art Student Will you walk me to the subway? This section's dangerous.

Soldier Where's the nearest stop?

Art Student Union Square.

Soldier Oh, that's on my way ... But not now. I got a late pass at Dix. Come back in for a while.

Art Student Kevin's in there, isn't he?

Soldier The jealousy bit!

Art Student So it *is* Kevin.

Soldier Bullshit.

Art Student Okay, dance all night with *me*, and I'll come back in!

The music has stopped. A new tune starts here.

Soldier Hear that? This I can't miss. (*He sings along for a bar or two.*) Okay, I'll walk you to Union Square. Later. If you wanna wait. If not, goo' night.

Art Student Good night. No, wait a minute, George. OK, I'll wait.

Soldier Get yourself a drink, Desmond. Or something stronger. I'll pick you up at the bar.

Art Student (*left alone*) So I'm an M. As in S and M. But he *is* gorgeous.

3. The Art Student and the Young Lawyer

Warm summer afternoon. An Upper East Side apartment. In the bedroom he gets in return for houseboy services, the **Art Student,** *in a cotton sweater and short shorts, sits writing a letter to the* **Soldier.**

Art Student (*reading*) 'Dearest George: how is Dix? No, I did *not* say, How *are* Dix! I enclose five high quality cigars. Crumbs from the rich man's table. The rich man's my new boss, a lawyer. Works out of his apartment where yours truly is houseboy. Strictly professional, of course. I answered his ad in the *Village Voice*. He's gay, but the ad said, in so many words, "This is not a sex ad" and anyway, George, I'm yours now.

> I dream of your bod:
> It rhymes with God.

Poetry! Your lover to all eternity and keep your hands off that Private First Class, Desmond.'

A buzzer rings. The **Art Student** *gets up and goes to the next room, the living room, where the* **Young Lawyer,** *in shirt sleeves and slacks, is busy mastering his new word processor.*

You buzzed?

Young Lawyer Did I? Oh yes. Desmond, right? Now what was it? Oh yes, would you help me with the Venetian blinds. I can't get them to come down.

Art Student *lowers the blinds, which present no problem.*

Well, thanks.

Art Student Is that a computer?

He looks over **Young Lawyer***'s shoulder.*

Young Lawyer IBM Composer. Computer with a word processing program. An invention that makes the 70s, the 70s.

Art Student *leaves.* **Young Lawyer** *works away at word processing. Then presses a button, and the buzzer rings in* **Art Student***'s room.* **Art Student** *returns.*

Art Student Yes?

Young Lawyer Oh, Desmond, yes (*Again* **Young Lawyer** *has been interrupted at work*), is there any brandy – in the liquor cabinet?

Art Student Let's see. (*The cabinet is near the word processor.*) No. No liquor at all.

Young Lawyer Oh, well, you'd better leave me to it.

Art Student *leaves. Same business.*

Art Student Yes?

Young Lawyer Get me some iced water, would you?

Art Student (*looking in the icebox*) There's some in the icebox. Where shall I put it?

Young Lawyer Give it to me. (*Their fingers touch on the glass. For a split second they make eye contact.*) Well, well, I *must* get on with this.

Art Student *withdraws.* **Young Lawyer** *works on, briefly, then buzzes.*

Art Student (*minus his sweater. He is wearing a pink tank top*) Here I am.

Young Lawyer Again? Oh yes. I keep forgetting why I buzzed you in the first place.

Art Student Why *was* that?

Young Lawyer Oh yes, to say I was expecting someone. To give me my lesson. How to use this thing. (*He points to the processor.*)

Art Student I didn't know lawyers used computers.

Young Lawyer They use secretaries. This miracle of modern science will save me all those salaries . . . The guy's name is Schuller. He should've been here long ago.

Art Student I see.

Young Lawyer He hasn't been here already, has he?

Art Student No.

Young Lawyer Are you sure? Would you know him?

Art Student No one has been by. (*Lingering in the doorway.*) Shall I go now, sir?

Young Lawyer Yes. No. Desmond, about that 'sir' business. This is not the Victorian age. Didn't I tell you to call me Alex?

Art Student No, but I will . . . Alex.

Young Lawyer This is your third day, isn't it? I must've said something about it?

Art Student Well, we haven't really talked since you interviewed me for the job.

Young Lawyer And I didn't say: call me Alex?

Art Student No. You just said, let's keep this professionally correct.

Young Lawyer Is that how I put it?

Art Student In the *Village Voice* you said: 'this is not a sex ad'. It just happened, you explained later, that you didn't really want a girl on the premises.

Young Lawyer Too much responsibility. In New York.

Art Student Is there something else I should've remembered?

Young Lawyer No, that's about it. Sex on the job is a mess. So, since we're both grown men . . . (*He stops.*)

Art Student Yes?

Young Lawyer Well, you get the general idea. (*Pause.* **Young Lawyer** *still tinkering with the machine,* **Art Student** *lingering.*) Look, Desmond, are you flirting with me?

Art Student Flirting?

Young Lawyer How about that shirt?

Art Student Too pink?

Young Lawyer You *are* gay, aren't you?

Art Student 'This is not a sex ad.'

Young Lawyer I know you *are*.

Art Student Do I hide it?

Young Lawyer I don't mean that. I mean there are men in your life.

Art Student Men, plural?

Young Lawyer Or man, singular.

Art Student Do you peep through keyholes, Alex?

Young Lawyer No, you leave doors open, Desmond.

Art Student That door of yours is not *left* open. It will not close.

Young Lawyer I saw what I saw.

Art Student You're a voyeur, Alex!

Young Lawyer And what are you?

Art Student Me?

Young Lawyer You're staying. In . . . *my* room.

Art Student You don't want me to?

Young Lawyer Well, Desmond, I should confess this: *I'm* gay.

Art Student That's cool.

Young Lawyer And I find you . . . shall I say attractive?

Art Student I think you shall. And, gee, thanks.

Young Lawyer You're still there.

Art Student Should I leave?

Young Lawyer Yes. (**Art Student** *starts to do so.*) Desmond!

Art Student (*turning*) Yes, Alex?

Young Lawyer Who was the guy?

Art Student The guy?

Young Lawyer I saw him. With my own eyes.

Art Student Ah yes, Alex, the voyeur. Who saw what he saw.

Young Lawyer You and –

Art Student (*firmly*) My lover, Alex. That was my lover.

Young Lawyer You have a lover? You're going steady!

Art Student And that's wrong?

Young Lawyer No, no, I like couples very much. And of course they should be faithful.

Art Student And you are a single, Alex?

Young Lawyer (*nodding*) Not for the world would I break up a couple. The world is my Singles Bar.

Art Student You *confine* yourself to singles?

Young Lawyer (*nodding again*) And the occasional double.

Art Student You go in for threesomes?

Young Lawyer No, no, no. Desmond! Don't you recall what someone or other said about marriage?

Art Student I'm not too familiar with someone or other.

Young Lawyer Marriage is a cage: those who are in want to get out, those who are out want to get in.

Art Student And you enjoy catching those who want to get out!

Young Lawyer How did you guess?

Art Student The way you said: You have a lover?

Young Lawyer How *did* I say it?

Art Student Like it was very much your business.

Young Lawyer I shouldn't love my fellow men?

Art Student Do you love your fellow women?

Young Lawyer Desmond, you *are* flirting with me.

Art Student No, I'm not.

Young Lawyer The pink tank top. The hanging around. The way you look at me.

Art Student My heart belongs to another. I told you that.

Young Lawyer Then why did you remove your sweater?

Art Student I was too warm. And I thought you could take it in your stride.

Young Lawyer Desmond, you may leave.

Art Student I know that. (*Pause*.) I know I may leave.

Young Lawyer Then do it for God's sake.

Art Student You mean: do it or else?

Young Lawyer Yes, do it. Or else.

Art Student Or else what?

Young Lawyer Or else, I . . . I may do something I'll regret later.

Art Student As long as it's not something *I'll* regret later.

Young Lawyer Huh? But you would. You'd feel all the guilt of . . . adultery.

Art Student How d'you know?

Young Lawyer This all began with you declaring you had a lover.

Art Student This all began with you watching me make love.

Young Lawyer Then you repeatedly said your heart belonged to another.

Art Student I said that *once*. Besides . . .

Young Lawyer Ah, so there's a 'besides'?

Art Student It wasn't my heart you saw through that open door.

Young Lawyer Now you *are* making a pass. Desmond, you have me totally confused.

Art Student You've never heard of an open relationship?

Young Lawyer Huh? What's that?

Art Student George and I have an open relationship.

Young Lawyer I'm losing my self control. (*Silence*.) And you're not going to your room. (*Silence*.) Desmond, if this keeps up, I just may break the rules.

Art Student 'Oh, sir!'

Young Lawyer Oh, *Alex*.

Young Lawyer *moves across the room and removes* **Art Student***'s tank top:* **Art Student** *calmly lets him do so.*

Art Student (*continuing the talk*) Yes, of course: 'Alex'. You're certainly Alex – now.

They stand looking at one another.

Young Lawyer You let me do it.

Art Student What if Mr Schuller rings the bell?

Young Lawyer Let him ring. He'll think I'm out.

Art Student (*gently*) Now I don't want to cause you –

Young Lawyer (*fervently*) Oh please, please –

* * *

The door bell is ringing. They are getting their clothes back on.

Young Lawyer Jesus Christ, he'll rouse the whole neighborhood! D'you think he was ringing all along and we just didn't hear?

Art Student No, no, I was listening for him.

Young Lawyer Look through the peephole.

Art Student I just wanted to say: I like you, Alex.

Young Lawyer Please, go!

Art Student *goes.* **Young Lawyer** *pulls the blinds up. Light floods in.*

Art Student (*at the peephole*) No one there now, but I suppose it was Mr Schuller.

Young Lawyer Thanks. That's all for now – Desmond.

Art Student What!?

Young Lawyer I told you from the first. That was *not* a sex ad. Besides –

Art Student Now *you* have a 'besides' – ?

Young Lawyer (*severely*). You have a relationship.

Art Student An open relationship. And ... not really as close as I made out ... actually, I've only seen the guy twice ...

Young Lawyer (*still severe*) That is none of my business. I don't break up relationships whatever they are!

Art Student (*crestfallen*) I'd like to ... make a relationship ... with you.

Young Lawyer Desmond! I have made a fool of myself and I apologize. Now, all will be as it was.

Art Student Ha? I *can* keep the job?

Young Lawyer Just keep *to* the job. Your job. And I'll keep to mine. Oh, Desmond,

I'm really sorry about this. (*Silence.*) But, look, I did say: that will be all.

Art Student You're not consistent ... Alex.

Young Lawyer I was right the first time. Our relationship is going to be entirely correct from now on.

Art Student But –

The bell starts ringing again.

Young Lawyer Desmond, I am going to let Mr Schuller in. Please go to your room!

Young Lawyer *leaves the room.* **Art Student** *looks quickly about him, spots a cigar box, takes a handful of cigars and, shaking his head, goes back to his room.*

4. The Young Lawyer and the Businessman

The same setting as 3. When he has finished donning a business suit, **Young Lawyer** *tidies up the living room so that it looks, when he's finished, like an office, dominated by the word processor. He places books and papers prominently. The bell rings. He lets in a young black man, also in a business suit.*

Young Lawyer Michael!

Businessman Alex! (*They shake hands first, then switch to a cordial, slightly embarrassed embrace.*) Well, I came!

Young Lawyer I knew you would.

Businessman I told myself I wouldn't.

Young Lawyer And right on time too. Make yourself comfortable.

Businessman (*sitting in the chair* **Young Lawyer** *indicates*) Is this really your law office?

Young Lawyer Doesn't it look like it?

Businessman This is an apartment house. In a high-class residential neighborhood.

Young Lawyer (*waving his hand around the room*) Law office. And that's a word processor. (**Businessman** *looks it over.*) America's new toy. It'll revolutionize even lawyering.

Businessman No bed?

Young Lawyer In a law office? Michael! I always tell the truth! Gin and tonic?

Businessman Thanks. It's funny, isn't it. Since we're both gay, you'd think –

Young Lawyer But – you're in a certain situation and I accept it.

Businessman A certain situation. Known as marriage. To a guy. But married. D'you believe in gay marriages? We do. Obviously. So, um –

Young Lawyer I have to respect that fact. As I did when we talked. As I do now.

Businessman Just like straights, gay people can be . . . just friends, after all. (**Young Lawyer** *hands* **Businessman** *his drink.*) Thanks.

Young Lawyer Not just 'after all' but, as you said, 'above all'. Cheers! (*They drink.*)

Businessman Cheers! Friends above all. And *just* friends.

Young Lawyer (*sitting, now, to chat*) According to Plato, it's the greatest relationship there is, friendship. So we're denying ourselves nothing. We're even giving ourselves a present.

Businessman Don't make it sound like my lover is the unlucky one.

Young Lawyer He's lucky in his own way. We're lucky in ours. Well, aren't we?

Businessman Absolutely. That's why I'm here. To come here otherwise would be . . . playing with fire.

Young Lawyer And no one would want to . . . play with fire. We've all done it – too often – but that's how we know mustn't do it. Right?

Businessman Right. (*Pause.*) One of your neighbors saw me ring your bell.

Young Lawyer Yes?

Businessman I hope he doesn't know Michael. My lover's called Michael, too.

Young Lawyer Michael and Michael! One of my neighbors might know you both, recognize one Michael, and report back to the other?

Businessman Yes.

Young Lawyer Report back what? That you rang a door bell?

Businessman He's very jealous. I mean he would be. If he had reason to be.

Young Lawyer But he hasn't. You're paranoid, Michael.

Businessman He has my promise. Absolute fidelity.

Young Lawyer You can't tell him someone's just a friend even when it's true?

Businessman Maybe I could. I'm not sure. But I won't. For his sake. Don't want to bug him.

Young Lawyer So the just-friends-routine is for me only!

Businessman Just-friends-routine? It's the truth, isn't it?

Young Lawyer That's what I said. It's the truth. But just for me?

Businessman For the two of us. (*They both drink.*) It's hot in here.

Young Lawyer Take your coat off.

Businessman What? Oh, sure. (*He puts his jacket on the back of a chair and sits down again.*) Cheers!

Young Lawyer Cheers! (*They both drink.* **Young Lawyer** *kicks off his moccasins.*) Take your shoes off, Michael! Be comfortable! (**Businessman** *looks dubious.*) Among friends? (*Pause.*) In Japan they all take their shoes off. (**Businessman** *kicks off his moccasins*.)

Businessman I must leave.

Young Lawyer In your socks?

Businessman Don't you remember, I finally agreed to come to your office – if it is just your office – and if we could just be friends – and if I could leave in five minutes.

Young Lawyer Fine. All those conditions are met. You *can* leave. Friends of mine are free to leave at any time. This is America!

Pause.

Businessman This room is stifling.

Young Lawyer You are wearing a vest.

Businessman *takes the vest off, places it on the jacket, and sits again.*

Businessman What time is it?

Young Lawyer You are also wearing a watch.

Businessman (*consulting same*) Six o'clock on the nose. I should've been at my sister's an hour ago. (*He stands.*)

Young Lawyer You can see your sister any time.

Businessman I *must* leave. (*But* **Young Lawyer** *has got up and gone to the door.*) You are blocking the doorway!

Young Lawyer Ah, now we're getting somewhere.

Businessman What?

Young Lawyer What you just said.

Businessman (*sitting again*) Alex, you are breaking your promise.

Young Lawyer Which one? You make me promise so many things!

Businessman Above all –

Young Lawyer And 'after all' –

Businessman You promised to be good.

Young Lawyer Me and Queen Victoria.

Businessman You know what I mean.

Young Lawyer Queen Victoria knew what she meant. Finish your drink.

Businessman (*picking up the glass*) Oh, God, Alex, why did you get me into this?

Young Lawyer (*leaving the door*) D'you really wanna know?

Businessman Of course I do.

Young Lawyer (*sitting facing* **Businessman** *again, his own glass in hand*) Even if I have to be very bad to tell you?

Businessman Tell me. Tell me the worst.

Young Lawyer Even though you know damn well what I'm gonna say.

Businessman I don't. I swear I don't.

Young Lawyer You're a liar, Michael. That should give *me* a certain licence. But I'm not even lying. I *thought* it would be possible for us just to be friends. I was mistaken.

Businessman No!

Young Lawyer (*singing*) 'Falling in love again, never wanted to . . .'

Businessman No, no, we must keep love out of this –

Young Lawyer Ha? It's a deal. I'll settle for naked lust.

Businessman I can't bear it.

Young Lawyer Substitute a euphemism: lechery, lubricity, lasciviousness, debauchery, profligacy . . . What's the noun for dissolute?

Businessman Dissolution? My God. (*He undoes buttons on his shirt.*)

Young Lawyer It's *that* hot? I'll open a window. (*He gets up and does so.*)

Businessman Alex, Alex, you don't know me! I was going to be a priest. Till I met *him*. I was in the Seminary . . .

Young Lawyer Really? You need another drink. (*He pours another drink for both.*) Is it true that seminarians carry on something terrible?

Businessman *We* didn't.

Young Lawyer No orgies? No visits from Cardinal Spellman?

Businessman Alex, what I'm trying to tell you is: you and I only met yesterday.

Young Lawyer We only talked yesterday. We'd *met* before that.

Businessman Eye contact maybe. At the Opera. In the lobby.

Young Lawyer (*ready with the drinks*) The nice thing about those great big lobbies is that everyone can lose their companion-of-a-lifetime in them. Cheers!

Businessman Only for a moment. Cheers!

Young Lawyer (*seated again*) *Our* eyes had met even before that.

Businessman New York is all eyes!

Young Lawyer Eyes that *avoid* eye contact.

Businessman Eyes that stare hatred. At gays. At Blacks. Not to mention gay Blacks.

Young Lawyer Whereas we . . . you remember now?

Businessman (*slowly*) In the Nickel Bar on West 72nd Street?

Young Lawyer So you do remember? You with your lily white lover. 'Spouse' I should say. I could tell he was a spouse. He was between us, wasn't he?

Businessman You looked right across him.

Young Lawyer Man of distinction, your spouse. Silver hair. The Brooks Brothers look. What does he do?

Businessman He's in real estate. With me. Semi-retired. I do the work, he –

Young Lawyer Puts up the dough?

Businessman Alex!

Young Lawyer I'm only jealous. Where d'you live – Sutton Place?

Businessman We have a brownstone in Harlem.

Young Lawyer Oh, among the natives?

Businessman He has a thing for Blacks.

Young Lawyer Do you have a thing for Whites?

Businessman It's stifling in here. (**Young Lawyer** *jumps up to consult the thermostat.*) OK, I'm a snow queen.

Young Lawyer The temperature's down to 65.

Businessman I gotta lie down.

Young Lawyer Lie down? Did you say lie down?

Businessman Yes. I gotta lie down.

Young Lawyer Great! The Big Lie can now be exposed. This *is* my apartment, Michael, and I *don't* sleep on the floor. (*He presses a button, and a wall bed descends swiftly from the wall to the floor.* **Businessman** *gasps.*) I even have a houseboy in the spare bedroom.

Businessman I can't handle this.

Young Lawyer Try.

Businessman Have there been men in that bed before me?

Young Lawyer That bed has been there for years.

Businessman I'm getting my just deserts.

Young Lawyer How so?

Businessman The wages of sin –

Young Lawyer Is death! You *need* to lie down. (*He beckons to* **Businessman,** *who allows himself to be placed on his back on the bed.*) Now close your eyes and listen to me. (*Hypnotized,* **Businessman** *does so.*) I lied to you – on one small point – to make one big point clear: you turn me on. (**Businessman** *opens his eyes in panic.*) Close your eyes. (**Businessman** *does so.*) Be glad that you have that effect on people. On this person. Ten years from now you won't. 'For faggots are as roses whose fair flower/Being once displayed doth fade that very hour.'

Businessman (*with eyes closed*) The way you put things.

Young Lawyer I turn *you* on, too, Michael. (**Businessman** *opens his eyes to protest.*) Close your eyes. For this is the secret you have carried from opera house to gay bar and from the gay bar to this office, sorry, bedroom, which makes no real difference, Michael; what you can do in a bedroom, you could also do in an office.

Businessman I'm shivering now.

Young Lawyer That's as it should be. (*He starts to take his clothes off.*) I'm going to warm you up.

*   *   *

Both are in bed unclothed.

Young Lawyer Now, how did *that* happen?

Businessman You couldn't get it up, Alex.

Young Lawyer I know I couldn't get it up, Michael. I asked how did it happen.

Businessman It happens to the best of people sometimes.

Young Lawyer It doesn't bother you?

Businessman It should bother *me*? *I* came.

Young Lawyer Bitch. OK. Now tell your friendly *New York Post* reporter how it feels to be an adulterer.

Businessman Super-bitch. But then I *was* bullshitting. I've done this before, Alex. I mean, at least once.

Young Lawyer So now we get the truth. And I put all that effort into –

Businessman Seducing me. I *had* to be seduced, you see.

Young Lawyer By a eunuch?

Businessman Oh, come on. It did bother me – that you were –

Young Lawyer Impotent.

Businessman Talking someone into sex is one thing, Alex. Having sex is another.

Young Lawyer Yes, Daddy.

Businessman Active in one role, maybe you wanna be passive in the other.

Young Lawyer My God, you've been reading those ads in the gay papers: Top Man Wanted.

Businessman I'm not talking body. I'm talking soul.

Young Lawyer You want to be the active . . . soul?

Businessman I'm saying you were hyper-active as seducer –

Young Lawyer And you were hyper-passive –

Businessman (*shaking his head*) Just coy. To bring out the seducer in you.

Young Lawyer And if we switch roles –

Businessman Me active, you passive – maybe I'd warm *you* up.

Silence. **Young Lawyer** *just lies there.* **Businessman** *takes him in his arms.*

*   *   *

They are getting dressed during this conversation.

Businessman Maybe it takes a married man.

Young Lawyer A seminarian. That was sacramental sex. Holy communion.

Businessman Was it all right?

Young Lawyer It was an all-time high.

Businessman This time I *must* go.

Young Lawyer Oh, let your sister wait.

Businessman It's much too late for my sister's. I must go straight home.

Young Lawyer To *him*?

Businessman You're damn right. What time *is* it?

Young Lawyer The watch was all yours.

Businessman You took it off me. You took everything off me.

Young Lawyer Touché. (*Finding the watch*.) Eight o'clock.

Businessman Eight o'clock! There'll be hell to pay.

Young Lawyer Not that you're gonna tell him?

Businessman But *what* am I gonna tell him?

Young Lawyer You got stuck in the Lexington Avenue subway.

Businessman He knows I don't use the subways. He won't *let* me use the subways.

Young Lawyer You'll think of something. You have a rich fantasy life.

Businessman How would *you* know?

Young Lawyer As your lover.

Businessman I have two lovers now?

Young Lawyer One lover, one spouse. When does your lover see you next?

Businessman Never!

Young Lawyer After that all-time high?

Businessman *Because* of that all-time high.

Young Lawyer Here's your shirt.

Businessman (*shuddering*) This escapade could cost me my neck.

Young Lawyer Why?

Businessman He's gonna ask where I've been.

Young Lawyer You've been at your sister's, silly.

Businessman I'm a bad liar.

Young Lawyer Learn from your lover.

Businessman If only you were just a liar.

Young Lawyer What am I?

Businessman A bachelor. Probably sleeping with half New York.

Young Lawyer Please!

Businessman At least with your houseboy. Houseboys are bed boys.

Young Lawyer No sex. I put that in the ad.

Businessman (*sighing*) Alex, what will it be like if, say, ten years from now, we should meet again, you and me? Bump into one another in an airport or someplace?

Young Lawyer Come off it. You'll be at the Nickel Bar tomorrow night.

Businessman I will not.

Young Lawyer Then you'll be here. Day after tomorrow.

Businessman What? Can't we discuss that – at the Nickel Bar tomorrow?

Young Lawyer So you will be there.

Businessman But with *him*.

Young Lawyer *That* won't work.

Businessman How'd you like to be our lawyer? We just about had it with old Lester, our present legal eagle.

Young Lawyer I'm not in real estate.

Businessman Be practical. I'm not about to leave Michael for you.

Young Lawyer Spouse before lover every time.

Businessman Then again: how can one hold on to the lover for a while without losing the spouse?

Young Lawyer Introduce lover to spouse as 'our new lawyer'?

Businessman Our *possible* new lawyer. Even if he says no, he'll have met you. From then on, you're family.

Young Lawyer Now wait a minute. This marriage of yours. You deceive him. So I suppose he deceives you?

Businessman He does *not*.

Young Lawyer Does he know about you?

Businessman Of course not.

Young Lawyer Then how do you know about him?

Businessman I know him, that's all. Through and through. He wants to settle down, and he *has* settled down.

Young Lawyer But does he think *you* wanna settle down?

Businessman Obviously he does.

Young Lawyer Then he's stupid. Only men over fifty settle down.

Businessman Maybe he doesn't know that.

Young Lawyer Or maybe it's you that's stupid, and he has you good and fooled.

Businessman Ha?

Young Lawyer Maybe he does know about you.

Businessman If he did, he'd raise Cain.

Young Lawyer If he could afford to. But if he couldn't?

Businessman He'd *pretend* not to know.

Young Lawyer So is that what you're doing? Pretending not to know about him?

Pause.

Businessman Look, I just want you to realize that when we've done this, you and I, a few times, that will be that. Michael-and-Michael is forever.

Young Lawyer (*feebly*) Didn't you hear me say I love you?

Businessman No. *That's* what I can't afford to do: hear you saying that sort of thing. Kiss me goodbye.

Young Lawyer Au revoir: you'll be back. A few times. Which is better than no times.

Businessman *kisses* **Young Lawyer** *on the lips. The latter makes a feeble attempt to make it a long kiss.*

Businessman You're very cute, you know that?

He leaves. **Young Lawyer** *lifts up the bed and replaces it in the wall.*

Young Lawyer (*sadly*) So who said I'd never make it with a married man?

5. The Businessman and the Lover

Bedroom of a brownstone in Harlem. Elegant in Victorian style. Late evening. **Businessman** *in bed reading. Enter his* **Lover** *in bathrobe. He is white, sixty-ish, somewhat distinguished.*

Businessman (*without looking up*) Stopped work, Michael?

Lover Yes, I'm tired, Michael. Besides . . .

Businessman Yes?

Lover I was lonely, Michael. For you.

Businessman Is that true, Michael?

Lover Can you doubt it? Can you doubt *me*? Don't read tonight.

Businessman (*closing the book*) What's up?

Lover (*fervently*) I love you!

Businessman (*routinely*) I love *you*.

Lover I'm *in* love with you.

Businessman Ah yes. One might forget it sometimes.

Lover One has to forget it sometimes.

Businessman Huh?

Lover If one didn't forget it *some*times, it wouldn't be true other times.

Businessman Ah yes, our life style.

Lover Our *modus vivendi*. It's provided a score of love affairs with each other.

Businessman A score is twenny?

Lover If we'd just tried to prolong Affair Number One indefinitely, we'd have been all through in six months.

Businessman Five.

Lover Five and a half. Isn't everyone we know all through by now?

Businessman All through, twenny times over.

Lover By now, you and I would have had nineteen other lovers each.

Businessman Yeah. But for your great invention.

Lover Repeated re-marriage. After periods of being just friends.

Businessman The let's-just-be-friends routine.

Lover Not routine. It's a necessary phase. What you seminarians call a Retreat. After Retreat, Return. Re-marriage. One honeymoon after another!

Businessman You couldn't have Number Twenny-One on your mind right now?

Lover How could you guess? Frankly, Michael, I can't wait to be your lover – your spouse – once again. This system works like a charm.

Businessman Provided I fit in.

Lover You always fit in.

Businessman But supposing, one day, it's just a suppose, supposing one day I wasn't ready at the moment chosen by you. What happens at that moment in the remote future when one day, just by chance, I don't fit in?

Lover You'll always fit in.

Businessman Fit in what? It sounds so anatomical. (*Pause.*) Sorry.

Lover You naughty thing. You're irresistible.

Businessman That's the kinda remark a guy likes to hear.

Lover My innocent little seminarian!

Businessman My guilty old capitalist!

Lover My generation will never get over its guilt feelings.

Businessman How d'ya mean?

Lover The whole gay thing being taboo, we had to pick up sex where we could find it.

Businessman And where could you find it?

Lover I've told you a hundred times.

Businessman I like hearing it.

Lover Subway johns. Turkish baths. The shower room at the Y. The men's room at Bloomingdale's. Or Hunter College, the ninth floor. D'you realize even now what we had to resort to?

Businessman And who?

Lover Whom.

Businessman Sure I realize. But tell me. I do like hearing it. Who did you have to resort to?

Lover Whom. We had to resort to hustlers. Young men driven to whoring by poverty, I suppose.

Businessman I love the way you say 'poverty, I suppose'! From on high. Rich bastard.

Lover Michael! Being what you call rich doesn't stop me feeling . . . compassion.

Businessman Do they need it?

Lover Hustlers?

Businessman In the seminary, I got to envying people who *have* the pleasures we did without. Especially if they could make a living at it.

Lover Michael!

Businessman Michael! I ask you, as the expert. You *used* hustlers and, as you say, I didn't.

Lover The big thing is that since *we* joined forces, we exclude other men. *In* fact and *on* principle.

Businessman Which means it's quite harmless for you to regale me with your, um, pre-marital amours.

Lover There was no *amour* about it. Just lust. With high risk of venereal disease.

Businessman Which you got. Repeatedly.

Lover May it be a warning to you, my dear Michael!

Businessman Right you are, my dear Michael. But you've never told me about the fun part. There must've been a fun part.

Lover There wasn't.

Businessman Not even for *them*.

Lover Least of all for them. Where's the fun in certainly being poor and probably getting VD? But let's start up that honeymoon, Mike, please! I'm horny as hell!

Businessman One question first. Were *all* those boyfriends –

Lover Sex partners –

Businessman Okay, were *all* those sex partners hustlers? Were they all even promiscuous?

Lover What are you getting at?

Businessman Didn't you ever have the experience of sleeping with a, well, with a monogamous person, a real life 'spouse'?

Lover A gay married man – cheating on his lover – with me?

Businessman Exactly.

Lover I'd have to decline such a proposition. It would make me an adulterer.

Businessman *Did* you decline it? Begin again. If *I* had such an experience, would I be having an experience you never had?

Lover What a funny question! But yes, there was one guy with a lover – before I met you of course –

Businessman Where is he now?

Lover Where? Oh. Oh, you know what. He's dead. I sometimes think such people always die young –

Businessman Lovers?

Lover Lovers who cheat on, um –

Businessman Their lovers?

Lover Adulterers.

Businessman Drop dead? Just like that?

Lover Fast or slow, yes, they die –

Businessman Fast or slow, we all die. What are you doing over there?

Lover I'm about to turn the light out. (*And he has his hand on the switch.*)

Businessman So you did have the experience. Now tell me –

Lover Let the dead bury their dead, Michael.

Businessman He didn't bury you. What did you make of it? I bet you had a ball.

Lover The memory of all that is completely *blacked* out by –

Businessman Your black seminarian?

Lover (*nodding*) And I'm all excited because we're back together again. Honeymooning yet again. Husband! Wife! Black Beauty! Throw back the bedclothes!

The overhead light goes out.

*   *   *

They are still in bed. Bedside light.

Lover Lost in thought, Michael?

Businessman Sort of.

Lover Penny for them.

Businessman (*singing*)

> 'Night and you and blue Hawaii
> The night is heavenly
> And you are heaven to me . . .'

Lover (*who has joined in the song*) Waikiki Beach. Our first honeymoon.

Businessman That's how it should be – all the time.

Lover Only it can't be. Read history. Read fiction. Just live.

Businessman It was that way tonight.

Lover First night of a honeymoon. First night of our twenty-first honeymoon.

Businessman Tell you what, Michael. Let's drop those just-let's-be-friends periods.

Lover What?

Businessman Just drop 'em. Beginning now! Let's not have our twenty-first let's-be-friends period!

Lover We're not *gonna* have it. Yet.

Businessman But the time will come.

Lover Life is life. And we have the best 'arrangement' possible. We're the happiest couple in the world!

Businessman One teeny weeny question. Very personal. In the friendship periods, Michael, does your eye wander – once in a while?

Lover I thought we disposed of that question long ago. *You* learned the answer in the seminary. Self control. Mind on higher things. *I* learned it in the world. Work. Lose oneself in work.

Businessman In theory.

Lover And practice. So your eye wanders. Must *you* wander with it?

Businessman Well, do you wander with it?

Lover Who did *you* meet today?

Businessman What?!

Lover You've met someone. I can tell.

Businessman Only a lawyer. Someone I thought might handle our real estate.

Lover Was he gorgeous?

Businessman He was . . . okay.

Lover Young?

Businessman My age.

Lover I'd rather stay with old Lester.

Businessman I'll introduce you to Alex anyway.

Lover He doesn't have a last name?

Businessman You're changing the subject.

Lover From what?

Businessman When your eye wanders, do you wander with it?

Lover I lose myself in work. (*Pause.*) All I want is to settle down. (*Pause.*) With you here, what else *would* I want?

Businessman With your thing for Blacks and all. Younger Blacks.

Lover And you're the perfect younger Black.

Businessman Then again you had the hots for teenagers. White teenagers.

Lover Before the Flood.

Businessman How d'you feel today when a beautiful white teenager crosses your path?

Lover You're teasing me. Because *you* met a lawyer who was young and . . . okay.

Businessman I give up.

Lover What?

Businessman I'm sleepy. We did have sex.

Lover And wasn't it great? A successful marriage in a beautiful home – we have what America wants – we're a success. Till death do us part. Fidelity till Hell freezes over. We made it, didn't we, Michael? (**Businessman** *is beginning to snore gently.*) My God, he's asleep. (*To himself.*) But we did make it. Didn't we?

6. The Lover and the Teenager

A private dining room in the rear of the Lavender Lounge in SoHo. The door is open. The **Lover** *is on a sofa sipping wine. At a small table sits the* **Teenager** *eating a large banana split.*

Teenager Mm!

Lover Sounds good.

Teenager Mm!

Lover Like another?

Teenager (*shaking his head*) This is my second after all.

Lover Your glass is empty. (*He fills it.*)

Teenager No more wine or –

Lover Or what?

Teenager I'll get really drunk, sir.

Lover You must call me Randy.

Teenager Is that your name?

Lover Of course.

Teenager Mine's Tommy.

Lover Hi, Tommy. If that's *your* name.

Teenager Why wouldn't it be?

Lover Then: Hi, Tommy.

Teenager Funny to say 'Hi' after all this! (*He motions towards his plate, now empty.*)

Lover 'All this' being a banana split?

Teenager Two banana splits. In . . . a place like this. Guess you think I'm pretty cheap.

Lover What?

Teenager Letting you pick me up on the sidewalk.

Lover I didn't 'pick you up'.

Teenager Well, we got to talkin', an' you said, 'Let's go to an ice cream parlor'. This is not an ice cream parlor.

Lover This, you see, is more appropriate to my situation in life.

Teenager Which is what?

Lover I'm what they call a man of means.

Teenager Means means money? Well, this place is 'appropriate' to sump'n else.

Lover I beg your pardon?

Teenager This place is gay.

Lover You know the neighborhood?

Teenager I can read.

Lover Ha?

Teenager It's called the Lavender Lounge, for Pete's sake.

Lover Ah yes.

Teenager But don't worry. Some of my best friends are gay.

Lover How about yourself?

Teenager An' how about *yourself*? Are you a pederast?

Lover Wow.

Teenager A paedo*phile*? Bringin' me here an' all?

Lover Since you ask: no.

Teenager You just happen to like *me*?

Lover That's more like it.

Teenager Not a married man by any chance?

Lover Oh, no.

Teenager Or 'married' to a guy?

Lover (*nervously*) No, no. Just a lonely bachelor looking for love. L.O.V.E.

Teenager I've heard of it.

Lover And you're gay or you wouldn't have come here with me.

Teenager Why not? It's cold out. (*Pause.*) An' I didn' know about these private rooms. (*Pause.*) So I'm gay. What else is new? I *think* I'm gay. I don't find myself goin' for girls.

Lover You like older guys?

Teenager You're an older guy and I've come here with you, haven't I?

Lover When did you catch on I was following you?

Teenager Lotsa guys follow me.

Lover What do you say to them?

Teenager Nut'n.

Lover So I'm privileged.

Teenager You don't scare me. Sump'n tells me you're harmless and, after all, in New York, that's Topic A.

Lover You can take care of yourself, then?

Teenager I hope so. And, right now *I'm* privileged, livin' off your ice cream.

Lover Not to mention my banana.

Teenager Don't talk dirty.

Lover Since you're so sophisticated, couldn't we talk dirty? Together? – unless you want more ice cream?

Teenager No, thanks. (*Pause.*) I never talk dirty. Don't dig it.

Lover Like to talk serious then?

Teenager Sure. Though I thought I'd be going soon. I like you, of course, or I wouldn't have come. Wouldn't have spoken to you on the street. But I gotta get back home. (*He stands up.*)

Lover Sit down, Tommy. (**Teenager** *hesitates*.) The door's wide open. Those that want *can* leave.

Teenager (*sitting*) Well, just for a minute.

Lover Look, Tommy, am I grabbing your balls? Ripping your clothes off?

Teenager 'Course not. But don't talk like that.

Lover Then tell me about yourself.

Teenager Whadda you wanna know?

Lover You're gay. You like older guys. Are you . . . experienced?

Teenager Nah. Just explorin'. I lied to you, Randy. I did know about this place. I hang out on the block. 'Cause my kinda *guys* hang out on the block.

Lover Well! I'd say you're pretty damned experienced for – how old are you?

Teenager Fifteen.

Lover You're jail bait, Tommy, you know that?

Teenager Sure I know that. An' *I* could be sent to reform school.

Lover So you gotta be very careful.

Teenager I *am* very careful, didn't you notice?

Lover How many . . . older guys have you . . . been with?

Teenager Millions.

Lover Seriously?

Teenager Nah. Just a couple. Nine or ten.

Lover One night stands?

Teenager One *hour* stands. Ten minute stands. Do it and run.

Lover You wanted more?

Teenager With one I did. You remind me of him, you know that?

Lover Really? That's very significant, Tommy. And rather wonderful. I remind you of someone. In what way?

Teenager Oh, I dunno. The eyes, I guess. The way you smile.

Lover That's very interesting. Even uncanny.

Teenager It is? Uncanny?

Lover (*heavily*) Because *you* remind *me* of someone.

Teenager And that's significant too? Who may *he* be?

Lover Someone your age.

Teenager Your boyfriend? You must introduce me.

Lover I can't, Tommy. He's dead.

Teenager Dead? At my age?

Lover The good die young. That's a saying.

Teenager A saying that makes me glad I'm bad. Sorry: I don't want to hurt your feelings, Randy.

Lover What was *he* called? The guy you liked.

Teenager I never found out.

Lover You . . . went all the way with him and never found out his name?

Teenager I found out he was married. And faithful.

Lover Except that night.

Teenager Evening. There was my mother to think of.

Lover You live with your mother?

Teenager (*nodding*) She teaches at Queen's College. That's where my Dad – my late Dad – used to teach –

Lover What d'you tell her when you get home late?

Teenager She don't ask. (*Pause.*) You're pretty nosy, you know that?

Lover I'm interested in you.

Teenager She knows I'm gay, my Mom. She says my life is mine to live.

Lover Sounds terrific, your Mom. Your life is yours to live. And I'm interested in you.

Teenager You guys sure know what you want. Me, I decided that night, *after* that night, not to be in such a hurry. Learn to take my time. Get hurt less.

Lover You got hurt – already?

Teenager Are you kiddin'? It *always* hurts. Afterwards.

Lover After – sex?

Teenager Yeah. They all want it. But, when they've had it, they don't want *you*.

Lover And that hurts, eh, Tommy? How lucky you are to meet me!

Teenager Don't say you love me.

Lover Love's what I'm looking for, I told you that!

Teenager It's too fast.

Lover Love at first sight? It happens. It has happened since the world began.

Teenager It doesn't last.

Lover (*earnestly*) Tell me about the guy I remind you of, Tommy.

Teenager (*hand to head*) Your wine's getting to me, Randy. (*Pause.*) He was the same *age* as you, too. How old *are* you, thirty?

Lover (*who is obviously quite a lot older, rotates his hand*) Give or take, um –

Teenager Now I *must* go. (*He gets up with an effort. It's no good. He sinks down again.*) Did you put something in that wine?

Lover Certainly not. (*Pause.*) Ready now?

Teenager The waiter can come in at any moment.

Lover No waiter's gonna come in here. Not in your lifetime.

Teenager Well, at least shut the door. You've worn me down, Randy boy, you've worn me down.

*   *   *

The **Teenager** *is spread out on the couch with his eyes closed. The* **Lover** *is pacing the room, smoking. Silence.*

Lover Done it again. One day Michael will get wind of these things and leave me . . . And who *is* this young punk? The creatures one resorts to! How'd I get mixed up with a fifteen-year-old?

Teenager (*without opening his eyes*) You did put something in that wine.

Lover (*nervously*) What's that? What did you say, Tommy?

Teenager (*opening his eyes and not seeing* **Lover** *at first*) Where are you, Randy? Oh there. Why so far away? Come over here. (**Lover** *sits gingerly on the end of the sofa.*) You like me, don't you?

Lover Isn't that rather obvious?

Teenager What did you put in the wine? Huh? Because, otherwise, I would never . . . you know . . .

Lover But you did. Because I reminded you of . . . him.

Teenager Because you got me drunk.

Lover Anyway I didn't believe that story.

Teenager Why not?

Lover Gay people always lie. Fabricate. Fantasize. The one guy. The one night. 'You remind me of someone!' 'The eyes, the eyes!'

Teenager The good die young and all that. He reminded you of me.

Lover Okay. *I* lied. *You* lied.

Teenager Only I didn't.

Lover Prove it.

Teenager How'd I prove it? Don't nag me.

Lover Cigarette? But you're too young, aren't you?

Teenager Yes.

Lover My God! D'you realize what time it is?

Teenager What time is it?

Lover Twenty five to twelve.

Teenager Why did you want me to know?

Lover How about your mother? Or is she a lie too?

Teenager You want me to go?

Lover Now that's not fair. You told me yourself that –

Teenager Hey, you're different now.

Lover I'm not different at all. At my age a man can't change – not in half an hour!

Teenager I did know about the private dining rooms. But I never went to one. Till tonight. That should show *something*.

Lover You know: I think we should have an arrangement, you and I.

Teenager Arrangement?

Lover Come here – at certain times, I don't *always* have time – or somewhere else if you don't like this place – what d'you think?

Teenager You still want me – after, um –

Lover I'm looking for love, I told you that.

Teenager But then you wanted me out of here. And when I woke up just now, you were mumbling to yourself that –

Lover Post-coital discouragement.

Teenager Post wha-a-t?

Lover It doesn't last. When shall I see you next?

Teenager Well, um –

Lover Now I don't live in the city.

Teenager You commute?

Lover No, no, I live . . . in the country.

Teenager Like where?

Lover Does it matter?

Teenager Don't worry, I won't come out there and surprise you!

Lover You can come out as much as you want! I live in Westchester.

Teenager (*sceptically*) Yeah?

Lover A lot of people live in Westchester!

Teenager I recognize the symptoms: you're married. And you probably live about two blocks from here.

Lover Well, I'm not exactly married. What made you think I was?

Teenager You don't live in town and don't always have the time.

Lover You're smart.

Teenager Experienced. You said I was. And take this: you're not 'exactly' married. You're *inexactly* married?

Lover I didn't say that.

Teenager It means you have a lover. You're married to a *guy*.

Lover Now don't start feeling bad because you think you've broken into a marriage.

Teenager That wouldn't make me feel bad. Married guys *want* their marriages broken into. Where is your lover right now? (*Tauntingly.*) Somewhere like this? Or at the Baths?

Lover Cut it out! That's in really bad taste.

Teenager I thought you didn't have a lover?

Lover Whether I have a lover or not, such remarks are –

Teenager Randy!

Lover Tommy!

Teenager You're mad at me. Don't be. So you're not married and you don't have a lover. Can we be friends?

Lover You're a terrific guy, you know that? Let me hold you. Just for a second. (*He not only holds him but runs his hands over him urgently.*)

Teenager Oh, no, not again, it *is* late –

Lover Okay, sit down. I won't touch you. (*And now he doesn't.*) We must have a serious talk. Tommy, I want to see you again. And again. And again.

Teenager I'll believe that when I see it.

Lover Tommy, you're forgetting –

Teenager You're lookin' for love – ?

Lover OK. I'm not looking for love. I do have a lover, and I love him.

Teenager Does he know you sleep around?

Lover I don't.

Teenager Ha?

Lover Well, not much.

Teenager 'Again and again and again.'

Lover That's three times.

Teenager I suppose he does likewise 'again and again and again'. Three times.

Lover No, he doesn't.

Teenager He *says* he doesn't.

Lover I *know* he doesn't.

Teenager How can you be sure?

Lover I just am.

Teenager Really?

Lover Even if I weren't, I'd pretend I was.

Teenager Well! In *that* case –

Lover Look. Can we change the subject?

Teenager Sure. I've been coming to certain conclusions.

Lover You *are* a big boy.

Teenager I guess I *am* lookin' for love.

Lover What?

Teenager OK, I like older guys. I enjoy sex. With you, fr'instance. But I want more. I gotta find someone to *give* me more.

Lover Looking for Mr Right?

Teenager What's wrong with Mr Right? You have your Mr Right and aren't about to give him up for the likes of me.

Lover I didn't call you the likes of you.

Teenager You're sweet. (*Pause*.) But I'm gonna split.

Lover Forever?

Teenager It *is* a long time. But you can take care of *yourself*. Should I wish you good hunting? Or a happy marriage?

Lover Oh, both, both, by all means.

Teenager 'Bye, then.

Lover Just like that?

Teenager Like this. (*Walks over to him, kisses him on the lips*.) 'Bye again.

He leaves. The **Lover** *watches him go, then walks to the door.*

Lover Waiter! My check!

7. The Teenager and the Writer

Spacious studio apartment on West End Avenue done up to look Gothic: even the one window we see has a paper maché Gothic arch in front of it. Desk. Papers. It is rather dark. The **Teenager** *and the* **Writer** *come in. The* **Writer** *carefully locks the door behind them. There is enough light for us to see that the* **Teenager** *is wowed by the Gothic effect.*

Writer Well, such is my modest pad. The throne room, if you will. It's the only room actually. Now kiss me. (*He snatches at the* **Teenager** *in an enthusiastic embrace. Letting him go*.) Phew! I've waited for that! Through three long hours of Central Park!

Teenager It's so dark in here.

Writer Gothic gloom. Romantic, ha?

Teenager Can we have some light now?

Writer No. My interior decorator expressly forbids it. Officially, we don't even *have* light.

Teenager But you're a writer, aren't you? When you write –

Writer Oh, if I work at night, I may smuggle in a flashlight. There may even be a little switch – behind the arras. (*He points to a drape*.) But when I play, I play in the dark! Or by candlelight. I have long slender church candles. Lewd, huh? Another little kiss. (*He again kisses* **Teenager** *on the lips.* **Teenager** *accepts but does not react*.)

Teenager Now I gotta split. Thanks for showin' me your pad. It's great.

Writer We only just arrived.

Teenager Like I said. I can only stay a minute.

Writer Oh, look. (*He looks at his rug which* **Teenager** *is standing on*.) You must take your shoes off.

Teenager For one minute?

Writer For my one and only Persian rug. Gift of the Shah.

Teenager You know the Shah of . . . is that Iran?

Writer Gift of the Shah to . . . a friend of mine. With Persian music to match. (*He plays a tape of* In a Persian Market *by Ketelby. The music continues softly behind the following dialogue*.) Lie down, my pet, while I recite a poem. One of my own. (**Teenager** *turns in surprise*.) Yeah, you gotta lie down for this. It's a Persian custom. (**Teenager** *lounges on a divan*.) Flat on your back. With your eyes closed. (**Teenager** *obeys*.)

Teenager (*from the position indicated*) Did you say a poem of your own?

Writer (*lighting a candle*) Is that what I said?

Teenager I thought you wrote plays?

Writer I, er –

Teenager You're not famous, are you? You said, one of my own.

Writer Maybe I was mistaken!

Teenager What?

Writer If a poem is good, who cares who wrote it?

Teenager No one, I guess.

Writer You don't know what I'm talking about, do you?

Teenager Maybe not. (*Looks at the divan.*) I could doze right off on this thing.

Writer (*seated and writing by candlelight in a notebook*) '. . . has no idea what I'm talking about. *Sancta simplicitas!*'

Teenager (*overhearing this last phrase*) That's not English, is it?

Writer Not quite.

Teenager I bet it's derogatory. About me.

Writer *Au contraire.* It celebrates your divine simplicity.

Teenager In other words, I'm dumb.

Writer That's all right. You're beautiful. And young.

Teenager And you have the brains. And maturity.

Writer 'But the myrtle and ivy . . .' How old did you say you were?

Teenager Fifteen.

Writer 'The myrtle and ivy of sweet fifteen/Are worth all the laurels that ever have been.' (**Teenager***'s eyes are closed.*) Did that put you to sleep?

Teenager No. Was that your poem?

Writer That was Lord Byron's poem. My translation.

Teenager I'm waitin' to hear *your* poem.

Writer The anonymous poem.

Teenager Okay. Shoot.

Writer (*stroking his hair*) I'm basking in your presence.

Teenager You're ruining my hair-do.

Writer (*again writing*) 'After a day in the spring sunshine, we take refuge, now, in the Gothic twilight of West End Avenue, wrapped in its cryptic shadows as in a – As in a what?

Teenager Are you asking me?

Writer I'm in the throes of creation.

Teenager (*whose eyes have been closed*) Here and now?

Writer Of course. I'm improvising. At your feet.

Teenager You're at my head. I liked your poem.

Writer You shouldn't have. It was bad. And it wasn't my poem. (*He scribbles away.*)

Teenager What are you doing now?

Writer Writing about you.

Teenager I'm gonna be in a book?

Writer In a play. With luck. With inspiration. I don't just tape-record people, you understand. I transpose. I transform. I transfigure.

Teenager You've lost me.

Writer Then how about a little something to eat . . . to drink . . . ?

Teenager I'm hungry.

Writer Be thirsty, do you mind? If it's food we need, I'll have to run out and get it at the deli.

Teenager Any ice cream in the freezer? You do have a fridge?

Writer Hidden away someplace, maybe –

Teenager And a couple of bananas?

Writer (*shaking his head*) Look, I'll run out to the deli.

Teenager (*getting up*) Forget it. I gotta go home.

Writer No, no, no, no, no! When we're . . . ready to leave, we'll have supper out. There's a great Mexican place one block away.

Teenager You and me? We'd get good an' stared at.

Writer This is the West Side!

Teenager The West Side would consider you a child molester.

Writer Oh, there are places for people in . . . our position . . .

Teenager Kids with older guys?

Writer And I bet you know all about it, too. You're the type.

Teenager What type?

Writer The type an older guy takes to, oh, a private room in the back of some gay bar.

Teenager (*challenged*) Come to think of it, I *was* taken to some such place once.

Writer Who was the lucky guy?

Teenager (*defiant*) My Mom took me there for my birthday.

Writer You sure tell tall stories. I can't see you in this light but I bet you're blushing. (*Moves close to feel his cheeks.*) Yes, I can *feel* the hot blood in your cheeks. In any case, you're so pretty, I can see you in the dark.

Teenager It's someone else you see, I bet.

Writer Actually, I can't remember, now, what you look like!

Teenager Thanks!

Writer (*very seriously*) It's very interesting. And rather spooky. Consider. (*He writes.*) 'If I can't visualize your face, it means I've forgotten you.' Now say something! And I'll improvise.

Teenager What?

Writer Thanks. (*He improvises without writing.*) 'You said: "what," and I did not recognize your voice! I *have* forgotten you! We are a thousand miles apart. A thousand

years apart. Yet I only have to light a candle, you return, and I remember you . . .' Corny, huh?

Teenager I kinda liked that too.

Writer You're adorable. May I kiss you?

Teenager You already have.

Writer Where are your lips?

Teenager Just above my chin. No, not below my neck. There!

They kiss.

Writer Something you said in Central Park really touched me.

Teenager 'I love you, I love you, I love you . . .'

Writer Yes. Dare I believe it?

Teenager Depends how much courage you got.

Writer Well, do you say that to all the guys?

Teenager All the guys on earth?

Writer Two or three dozen you might have met.

Teenager Nah.

Writer But you said there *was* one.

Teenager He was married.

Writer Oh yes. And faithful.

Teenager Except that one time.

Writer I don't want you thinking about him.

Teenager You brought him up.

Writer Look, are you going to have sex with me?

Teenager Not just like that. No.

Writer You aren't on your way out?

Teenager As a matter of fact, I am. (*He gets up.*)

Writer At least let me *see* you before you go . . .

Teenager See me?

Writer Hold it. I wanna show you something.

He takes a photo album from a drawer and gives it to **Teenager.**

Teenager (*inspecting the contents, taking his time before speaking*) Naked boys, huh? But in real good taste.

Writer Classical taste. Neo-Greek poses, see that? (*As* **Teenager** *is flipping through, he points to a picture.*)

Teenager Who took these pictures? (**Writer** *points to himself.*) You? All of them? (**Writer** *nods.*) Hey, you said you were a playwright! And a poet!

Writer Photography's my hobby.

Teenager I can certainly see why.

Writer Well, would you object?

Teenager To being photographed like *that*? – Jesus! (*He points at the pictures.*) Think I don't dare? I don't have time. You know that.

Writer Just one shot. It'll take all of thirty seconds.

Teenager Thirty seconds to do, yeah. Then in your album forever. Then magazines. Marilyn Monroe calendars . . . My Mom would pass out.

Writer (*showing his camera, which just happens to be handy*) It's a polaroid. If I give *you* the picture, you got the negative too.

Teenager (*suspicious*) Then what's in it for you?

Writer Seeing you. In all your glory.

Teenager Stark naked? I wear bikini underwear. It's *very* photogenic!

Writer I dare you!

Slowly, **Teenager** *starts to strip.*

*   *   *

The studio is now brightly lit – by electricity. The

Writer *is getting dressed. Lying on the divan, the* **Teenager** *is naked.*

Teenager You still haven't taken my picture.

Writer That was terrific sex, first things first. What's your name, by the way?

Teenager Tommy. What's yours?

Writer Robert.

Teenager So now we know each other.

Writer In the Biblical sense, even.

Teenager I like you as it turns out. May I know your last name?

Writer I call myself Robert Rich.

Teenager Call yourself?

Writer I write under that name, you've probably seen it around?

Teenager I guess I should have. In *TV Guide*?

Writer The *Village Voice*. The *New York Times* once in a while.

Teenager Far out. Would I have seen your stuff on the tube?

Writer If you watch Public Television. Or local cable channels.

Teenager I'll sure look out for it on Channel J.

Writer The boy who never heard of Robert Rich! Have you ever been to a theatre, Tommy?

Teenager You mean, not the movies? No.

Writer I have a play in preview all this week.

Teenager On Broadway?

Writer Off-Off Broadway. You must come see it with me.

Teenager Like I said – we'd get stared at.

Writer I could get you a ticket by yourself.

Teenager Is it funny?

Writer (*nodding*) Mademoiselle Charlot's in it.

Teenager I've heard of him.

Writer Her!

Teenager (*grimacing*) A real screwball.

Writer (*reaching for his camera*) Pull that face again. I'll take a picture.

Teenager Of my *face*?! I got undressed for that?

Writer That face. (**Teenager** *pulls the face again. The camera flashes.*) You can get dressed now.

Teenager (*getting dressed during the following dialogue*) Have I been manipulated, would you say?

Writer Depends. Did you like it?

Teenager Sure.

Writer Then you weren't. Hey, look at this picture.

The polaroid picture comes clear as they watch it.

Teenager He reminds me of someone.

Writer Me too. May I keep it?

Teenager It's not a nude, so okay.

Writer When you told me you loved me –

Teenager In Central Park?

Writer Yeah, did you notice anything strange?

Teenager Yeah. *You* didn't say you loved *me*.

Writer (*nodding gravely*) I say it now. It took till now!

Teenager Till we'd had sex? (**Writer** *shakes his head.*) Till you'd taken my picture? A head shot?!

Writer Till you found out I was Robert Rich.

Teenager I don't get it.

Writer You hadn't known. You hadn't loved Robert Rich. You had loved *me*. For myself alone. I might have been a gas station attendant. You'd have loved me just the same . . .

Teenager Only I was kidding.

Writer I was suspicious! Let me admit it now. All the boys want to sleep with Robert Rich.

Teenager (*grinning*) He offers them such 'terrific sex'.

Writer Stop a minute. You're not a Star Fucker, are you?

Teenager What's that?

Writer No, of course not. Tommy, forget everything I just said. Forget you ever heard of Robert Rich.

Teenager You forgot me. I gotta forget you now?

Writer Hold in your memory the *me* you have known all these years –

Teenager We met today in Central Park.

Writer And you said, 'I love you, I love you, I love you'. That makes it years.

Teenager Sorry.

Writer I'm not a playwright. I'm not a poet. I'm not a photographer. I'm just a guy who . . . plays piano . . . in a piano bar.

Teenager (*intrigued*) *Can* you play the piano?

Writer Certainly.

Teenager I like *that* idea. The piano bar.

Writer Tommy, can you take a couple of weeks off? Sometime soon?

Teenager Off school!?

Writer You're still in school? How about summer?

Teenager What would I tell Mom? What did you have in mind?

Writer A vacation with you. In a Caribbean paradise. Palm trees. A beach for two. You've seen the ads in the subway. We'll become one with nature.

Teenager And afterwards?

Writer Death ends all.

Teenager Not just yet, I hope.

Writer When the bell tolls, it tolls for thee.

Teenager You're saying that now? The day we met?

Writer (*pacing the room*) Tommy? Is that you? Are you still there?

Teenager Can't you see me now I have my clothes on?

Writer Put your shoes on, Tommy. (**Teenager** *does so while* **Writer** *continues.*) And tell me something.

Teenager What?

Writer Are you happy?

Teenager How d'ya mean?

Writer When you confront the world, Tommy – your life, your death – are you happy?

Teenager Things could be better.

Writer You misunderstand. No, I haven't forgotten what you told me in the Park. Your Mom's a widow. Queen's College doesn't pay her enough. But, setting all that aside, do you feel alive? *Are* you alive? Are you *real*?

Teenager Got a comb?

Writer (*takes a comb over to* **Teenager**) You are *so* beautiful! (*He embraces him.*)

Teenager Your hands are all over the place.

Writer Stay a while. I'll go out and get that food and then –

Teenager Robert, it really is too late.

Writer Only nine o'clock.

Teenager Which is too late.

Writer When shall I see you, Thomas? May I call you Thomas? It'll give you stature.

Teenager OK, so you're horny. But does it have to be with me? If you're not sure I'm real.

Writer You take me too seriously. I'm a writer. Words are a game to me.

Teenager Even the words, 'I love you etcetera'.

Writer Which doesn't mean I don't love you. Or couldn't.

Teenager Love *just* me?

Writer Who else?

Teenager There's no one else in your life? Lover or whatever?

Writer Did I say *that*?

Teenager I'm asking.

Writer All Greenwich Village knows about me and . . . well, have you heard of D'Annunzio and Duse?

Teenager No.

Writer Richard Burton and Elizabeth Taylor?

Teenager Sure.

Writer Well, that's us, today: Robert Rich and –

Teenager So you *are* Robert Rich?

Writer Robert Rich and Mademoiselle Charlot. To sleep with *anyone* else is to betray her.

Teenager But you just slept with me.

Writer Oh, I'm not *complaining*. On the contrary. I get my kicks that way.

Teenager From betraying somebody?

Writer From betraying a great man. Or woman. Don't look so crestfallen, Thomas. Sex isn't sex unless someone's being deceived.

Teenager Then, if you and I were going steady, you'd be deceiving me?

Writer No, no. You aren't the type.

Teenager The type you deceive?

Writer You're the type I deceive *with*. And you loved it. You said it was terrific sex.

Teenager *You* said it was terrific sex. And anyway, I didn't know. So *I* was deceived.

Writer Whadda you want? To change the world?

Teenager I enjoyed what we did but, um –

Writer You wanna be Beatrice to my Dante. 'Love is not love/Which alters when it alteration finds/And bends, with the remover, to remove . . .'

Teenager Robert! Shut up a minute. (*Silence.*) Do you like me?

Writer Yes.

Teenager So, if this . . . liking grew, one day, to be more, you could consider giving her up – for me?

Writer (*vehemently*) But she stimulates my appetite for you! (**Teenager** *recoils*.) I shouldn't have said that.

Teenager But it was true?

Writer I'm a cruel son of a bitch, and I take that back. What's *really* real, Tommy? The present moment, huh? Well, right now there is just you. And it's just you I'd like to make another date with.

Teenager Some summer in the Caribbean?

Writer Right now. Just stay a while . . .

Teenager No, no, you know I gotta split.

Writer Tomorrow.

Teenager It's Saturday. I gotta help Mom with the shopping.

Writer Sunday then. After the matinée. I'll get you a ticket for the show and see you afterwards. The play by Robert Rich, remember?

Teenager I can't see you afterwards.

Writer Later that evening –

Teenager Not ever. We just aren't . . . for each other.

Writer I was tactless. I apologize.

Teenager You are you. I'm different, I guess. Dante and Beatrice? Don't know much about *them*. How about David and Jonathan?

Writer No role for me in *that* partnership.

Teenager Can I still use the ticket?

Writer Of course. It'll be in the box office in my name.

Teenager Robert Rich?

Writer (*nods; a pause, then*) And thanks for everything, kid. Hey, this is the nicest goodbye ever! Thank you!

Teenager (*turning to go*) Thank *you*, Mr Rich.

8. The Writer and the Actress

*Dressing room of Mademoiselle Charlot in an Off-Off Broadway theatre on Washington Square. The **Actress**, in an evening gown and full make-up, is on her knees before a small crucifix. The door opens and the **Writer**'s head pops in.*

Writer Half-hour, Charles. (*He sees that the **Actress** is on her knees*.) What, in God's name, are you up to?

Actress In God's name is right. I'm praying.

Writer You don't even believe in God.

Actress *Believe* in God? I practically own Him. Spent my whole childhood on my knees in the churches of San Juan. Sundays anyway. Kneel with me. Pray for inspiration.

Writer We pray standing. We who spent our Saturdays in the synagogues of Brooklyn.

Actress What are my options? Aerobics? Yoga? Transcendental Meditation? (*He has knelt down to cuddle with her.*) Don't do that. It's blasphemous.

Writer Tell God on me.

Actress I was just telling him all about you.

Writer Did he comment?

Actress He said I'd be a big hit tonight – if only your play holds up.

Writer If the play's a hit, it'll hold us both up for months, and you know it.

Actress That's why we must both pray our hearts out. (*Kneeling still, he pinches her backside.*) Are you out of your mind? At half hour? On the opening night of a play that, whatever its modest merits, cannot possibly succeed, except as a vehicle for the talents of Mademoiselle Charlot, the greatest female impersonator East of Japan? All there's time for is a little prayer. A little God music.

Writer On the opening night of – what was it? –

Actress How would *I* know?

Writer You were known to be fucking Bernie Blossom ten minutes before curtain time.

Actress Are you still jealous of Bernie Blossom? He's in San Francisco.

Writer I'm citing historic precedent.

Actress I *worshipped* that guy.

Writer You told me.

Actress I'm sorry. I can leave if I bore you.

Writer Leave and go where? In that outfit? At half hour?

Actress Then *you* can leave. It *is* more suitable.

Writer Look. I know we are Burton and Taylor –

Actress D'Annunzio and Duse –

Writer Accept the adoration of your author, damn it. Never mind the Author of your being.

Actress I accept all the adoration I can get. Now leave me to my prayers! I'll pray for *you*.

Writer You're kicking me out?

Actress Yeah.

Writer Rejecting my . . . little suggestion?

Actress How can I fool around with all this on? (*Pause.*) Oh, very well, tell the stage manager, we go up ten minutes late tonight and not to disturb me till *quarter* hour.

Writer So you will –

Actress Be back in three minutes and keep out of the other dressing rooms.

Writer I'll be on MacDougal Street studying the masses.

Actress They're worth *two* minutes anyway. You have your notebook on you?

Writer You bet. (*He displays it.*)

Actress Keep your hands off the boy in the box office.

Writer *leaves. The lights dim. When they come up,* **Actress** *is revealed as a youngish man, slightly bald, in a bikini. A knock on the door.*

Actress (*grandly*) Who is it?

Writer Three guesses. (**Actress** *opens the door.*) It's a boy!

Actress Lock the door. No, first put the Do Not Disturb sign out.

Writer (*shakes his head*) Then all MacDougal Street will be in on it.

Actress (*finger and thumb together*) You're right. Just lock up.

Writer Off with that bikini.

Actress The boy is a gentleman. Sit down beside him, and tell him the secret of eternal youth.

Writer (*beside her as bidden*) And what else?

Actress Tell him who you are cheating on at this very moment, *mon cher*.

Writer I'm not cheating on anyone at this very moment, *ma chère*.

Actress Well, don't fret about it. I am, too.

Writer You are, too, what?

Actress Cheating.

Writer I'll bet.

Actress On whom?

Writer It's anyone's guess.

Actress What's *your* guess?

Writer Oh, our dear, sweet producer?

Actress How would he have the time for me? He has every boy in the cast coming and going.

Writer Our leading man?

Actress Lenny? He's a flaming straight, didn't ya know? Prowls the *Village* in search of that endangered species, the straight female.

Writer Bernie Blossom?

Actress Don't be rude. I haven't seen him in five years.

Writer I give up.

Actress Okay. Shall we dance?

Writer It's now or never.

Actress What's *that*? That funny little sound? Listen! The crickets are chirping in the park!

Writer Crickets on Washington Square?

Actress Why not? There's grass, there's trees. If you want romance, you got to have romantic atmosphere. Hark!

Writer Who says 'hark' in the Nineteen Seventies?

Actress (*severely*) We drag queens all say 'hark' when we're on our high horse.

Writer You're not a drag queen, you're a female impersonator.

Actress A Kabuki Queen.

Writer That's why we all love you.

Actress I suppose you'd like to have an affair with me, Mr Rich?

Writer I thought you might realize that sooner or later, Mademoiselle Charlot.

Actress You'd all like to have an affair with me, you men. You men-men.

Writer But at this moment in time the odds are rather strongly in my favor.

Actress All right, Cricket. I'm going to call you Cricket from now on.

Writer So you got your cricket after all.

Actress Who are you cheating on? Right now. There must be *someone*.

Writer A little blond teenager that tracks older guys. His mother teaches at Queen's College. How about you?

Actress How *about* me? I haven't looked at anything but your damned script for months.

Writer And the Virgin Mary. (*He points to the statuette.*)

Actress She won't even do it with Joseph.

Writer That leaves – ??

Actress That leaves nobody.

Writer In your past.

Actress Or present.

Writer How about the future?

Actress That doesn't make sense.

Writer Someone you haven't yet met. But you're already planning to cheat on him.

Actress Cricket, you are talking rot, and we only have ten minutes left.

Writer My God, you're right. Listen. Concentrate. There is a man somewhere. The one man in the world that's meant for

you. Do you see him – in your mind's eye?
Don't answer. You've gone to work on him.
Ts, ts, ts, you are cheating on him already!

Actress (*weakly*) Already? With who?

Writer With who? Who but me, Charlie
darling? Me, me, me! (*He starts to move in.*)

*   *   *

Both are beginning to dress. **Actress**'s make-up
*has not been smudged. She will now put her female
attire back on.*

Actress Well, that's better than acting in
damn silly plays, don't you think?

Writer Depends on the damn silly play, I
should suppose, wouldn't you?

Actress I know which play you're thinking
of!

Writer Surprise, surprise.

Actress Seriously, it's a very great play.
You're a genius, Robert.

Writer Thanks (*He lights a cigarette.*) Why
did you cancel the preview two nights ago?
There was nothing wrong with you.

Actress Oh, just to annoy *you.*

Writer What had I done to deserve it?

Actress You're so fucking conceited!

Writer That's what you think.

Actress That's what everyone thinks.
Everyone who is anyone.

Writer Really?

Actress But I told them –

Writer Everyone who is anyone?

Actress Yes. I said: a man like that has
every right to be conceited!

Writer And what did everyone who is
anyone reply?

Actress How would I know? We're not even
on speaking terms. Me and everyone who is
anyone.

Writer I see.

Actress They all want me taken care of.
You know: shot. By someone in the Mafia.
But they will never succeed. I'm hiring
bodyguards. Gorgeous bodyguards. (*She is
still getting dressed and continues to do so till the end
of the scene.* **Writer** *is dressed again by now.*)

Writer Don't think about those people. Just
bear in mind I love you, Charlie. Do you love
me?

Actress Haven't I just proved it?

Writer Things like that can't be proved.

Actress Mother of God! What more do you
want?

Writer Do you love all the guys you've had
sex with?

Actress Just one, of course.

Writer Well, thanks. You get a little kiss for
that.

Actress I was referring to Bernie Blossom.

Writer No. Not tonight! Not right after we –
Then what am I to you, if it's Bernie Blossom
you're always thinking of?

Actress A whim.

Pause.

Writer Well, it's nice to know.

Actress I think you're quite proud of
yourself at that.

Writer How so?

Actress Of your amorous exploits, shall we
say? One of them in particular. I can see it in
your face.

Writer You're seeing stars.

Actress And hearing crickets. Do you hear
them now?

Writer Yeah, I hear them.

Actress Well, that's not crickets, my dear.
(*Shouting.*) There are no crickets on
Washington Square. That's frogs.

Writer There are no frogs on Washington Square. Frogs croak.

Actress I know frogs croak.

Writer What I hear is chirping.

Actress You're pigheaded. Kiss me. (*They kiss.*) Frog!

Writer Don't call me that.

Actress What *should* I call you? Cricket?

Writer I have a name.

Actress A boring name if ever there was one.

Writer (*simmering*) I am asking you to call me by my name.

Actress Robert. There! I've called little Robert by his darling little name. Kiss me. (*He does so.*) Satisfied now – frog? (*A trilling laugh.*)

Writer I should take to drink.

Actress Coke is the thing these days.

Writer On Off-Off Broadway earnings?

Actress Steal it. Bernie does.

Writer Bernie! Again! (*Pause.*) He actually *steals*?

Actress By the by, you still haven't said a word about last night's preview.

Writer I didn't see last night's preview.

Actress I suppose that's your idea of a joke.

Writer Not a bit. You cancelled the preview before that. You were sick. How could I guess you'd make such a quick recovery?

Actress Well, you missed something.

Writer Like what? A great play? A landmark in the history of American drama?

Actress I was sensational. People turned pale.

Writer You could see the audience?

Actress Our flaming straight leading man said to me: Darling, you are a goddess.

Writer And so sick one day before.

Actress Know what made me sick? My *yearning* for you.

Writer You cancelled that preview to spite me. You admitted as much.

Actress Such a thing as a grand passion is beyond your ken, I suppose. I was running a fever for days on end. My temperature was 105.

Writer Quite a temperature – just for a whim.

Actress How dare you call it a whim, my feeling for you? (*Very loudly.*) I'm dying for love of the guy, and he calls it a whim!

Writer And Bernie Blossom?

Actress (*shrieking*) Don't keep bringing *him* up! The man is a common thief!

9. The Actress and the VIP

*The **Actress**'s small but campy loft in SoHo. It is late morning. The bed is made but the **Actress** has not yet dressed. In just a robe, and without make-up, she is propped up on pillows, reading the morning papers which, in New York, are three: the* Times, *the* News *and the* Post.

*A ring at the door. The **Actress** runs to open it and lets in the **VIP**, a middle-aged man, bald, in an expensive, well-pressed three-piece suit.*

Actress The spy that came in from the cold! This is an honor, your honor!

VIP The honor is mine, my dear. I'm not the Mayor of New York by the way. Just a member of your audience last night. You were superb.

*The **Actress** offers her hand to be kissed. He kisses it.*

Actress You're so kind. I know your face, of

course, from the papers. And the tube. What a thrill to see you in the, shall we say, flesh? In my little . . . boudoir. May I touch? (*With mock reverence, she dares to touch his sleeve.*)

VIP Am I real? I've often wondered.

Actress You're a philosopher. I thought of you as a statesman.

VIP Let's say a public servant. With a large office in City Hall. At heart a student of reality. You were real last night.

Actress Oh, I'm real *now*.

VIP I certainly hope so.

He looks her over, a new sight to him, without the costume and make-up.

Actress Do sit down. (**VIP** *does so.* **Actress** *flits about.*) I'm so nervous, this being Top Secret and all. Your man 'briefed' me – is that the word? – yeah, *briefed* me about you on the phone. Your name must never be spoken, etcetera.

VIP Meaning: don't give me banner headlines in *The Daily News*. I pass as straight.

Actress Well, you're up front anyway, Mister –?

VIP Call me Henry.

Actress Prince Hal!

VIP If you wish. But don't worry about *me*. They told me you weren't well. Nothing serious, I trust?

Actress I was dying. Call *me* Charles, Charlie or, when we're on camera, Mademoiselle Charlot.

VIP Dying? Not really?

Actress Very really. But then the show must go on, as some great Queen once remarked.

VIP And *how* it went on! Last night was tremendous and this morning – but I see you have the papers.

Actress Nothing in the *Post*. Nothing in the *News*. And Mel Gussow in the *Times*. So we're a hit.

VIP A smash.

Actress And your roses came in ahead of Gussow. What a critic!

VIP You deserve more.

Actress Shall I be *getting* more? (*He looks nervous.*) I mean more flowers, more triumphs, more *gloire*! The *gloire* – of a star!

VIP 'Mademoiselle Charlot' in lights across the sky.

Actress Did you recognize me (*Pointing at her present get-up.*) this morning?

VIP I took you in. This you. It makes Mademoiselle Charlot all the more wondrous a creation. How you handled those gowns! And the spike heels!

Actress That became . . . real for you, did it? How about this? The real little Lord Fauntleroy? Or a mirage of same?

VIP A real mirage of same. I like boys too, by the way.

Actress Even old boys – with thinning hair and a bald patch? (*She shows* **VIP** *her bald patch.*)

VIP You're still boyish enough.

Actress And, on stage, girlish enough.

VIP The original hermaphrodite – Hermes *and* Aphrodite!

Actress Gender fuck. Pardon the expression.

VIP Androgyny is the word, I believe.

Actress Oh, I know, I know, my admirers write books about it.

VIP *I* should understand. What brought *me* here was –

Actress Oh, I can't guess! And maybe it should not be spoken!

VIP It's easily guessed. I came to solve the mystery. Learn your secret.

Actress I'm a Sphinx, Henry? They *were* bisexual, weren't they, those little ol' Sphinxes?

VIP For the moment, yes, you're my Sphinx.

Actress How about the boy in the box office?

VIP How about him?

Actress For the moment, you like *him*, don't you? The town is talking.

VIP I've spoken with him.

Actress Did you . . . solve *his* riddle?

VIP Oh, *he's* a Sphinx without a secret. Maybe *that's* why nothing came of it.

Actress I may be without a secret too.

VIP Then that will be that, won't it?

Actress But I *could* be the blue bird of happiness. In drag. That could be my secret. Wanna know the secret of happiness?

VIP I've hunted it at times.

Actress And love? Dear old love? You must have searched high and low for that one?

VIP Very high. And very low.

Actress But then you heard of Mademoiselle Charlot!

VIP Yes. Though I'd never seen you till last night. In my job one doesn't get to the theatre, especially not the, um . . .

Actress *Avant garde* theatre? *We* called ourselves The Rear Guard, believe it or not, till some third rate graffiti artist scrawled Charlot's Rear End across the front door . . .

VIP I realized last night what I've been missing.

Actress Fun.

VIP And maybe . . . another dimension . . . But Lulu says I think too much.

Actress Lulu is quite a name.

VIP She's my best friend.

Actress Your fag hag?

VIP That is not an expression I approve of.

Actress I shall never use it again.

VIP Lulu says politicians shouldn't think.

Actress Lulu must be a real pain in the ass.

VIP No, no, our work is mindless. And predictable. All these long meetings. You know exactly what everyone's going to say. So what's in your head? Day dreams. Questions. Like: what does it all mean?

Actress Here you can let it all hang out.

VIP Do you like people, Mademoiselle? Do you find it possible to like people?

Actress Certainly not. I loathe them. Which is why you find me alone in a deserted apartment.

VIP You live by yourself?

Actress 'Far from the madding crowd's ignoble strife.' They taught us that at City College. A loft in SoHo can be as far from that mad, bad crowd as Antarctica. And much farther than Puerto Rico.

VIP You're a misanthrope at heart?

Actress The original misanthrope in the play.

VIP So am I. Misanthropic, I mean. Is that what draws me to art, Mam'selle? Are artists all misanthropic at heart?

Actress When they have a heart.

VIP Unlike politicians, they know why they're alive.

Actress I haven't a clue why I'm alive.

VIP You're alive because you have talent. Talent brings recognition.

Actress And recognition brings . . . happiness?

VIP (*shaking his head*) Happiness is a butterfly. Now you see it, now you don't.

Actress How about love? Can you catch *that* in your butterfly net?

VIP Even less than happiness. There are the well-known intoxications, the much-touted ecstasies. Love duets! Love deaths! When the cauldron simmers down, what's left?

Actress *You* tell *me*.

VIP Are our young people wrong to accept the intoxication and achieve ecstasy if and as they can? For us today, there is only a present. What is our parents' world, our past? Two world wars, a depression, and a holocaust! We must forget our past. As for our children's world, the future, the population explosion, the polluted environment, the coming holocausts, the coming wars, who dare give them a thought?

Actress Our 'public servants' maybe?

VIP Oh, no. We, above all, need . . . distraction.

Actress Ah yes. In the West Indies. Or was it Martha's Vineyard? It's all here in the *Post*. Or is that just the straights?

VIP No, no. When *I* have a morning off – it *is* still morning? –

Actress Oh, it is.

VIP Who knows where I may find myself?

Actress I'm learning.

VIP I'm learning, too. And politicians don't learn.

Actress You're a *great* politician I've heard.

VIP A contradiction in terms, my dear.

Actress A great lover, then. My John Barrymore. Would you like to take your clothes off? (*He looks startled.*) Your coat? (*She takes his coat off him.*)

VIP (*sitting down again*) What were we talking about?

Actress Everything. Happiness! Dear old love!

VIP If you can imagine you're in love there'll always be someone to imagine *he* loves *you*.

Actress There's always a boy at the box office. (*She tweaks his ear.*)

VIP Charlie!

Actress The story is all over the Village. You two are a number!

VIP First I heard of it.

Actress Well, you did make out, didn't you?

VIP The *National Enquirer* no doubt says I fought a duel on his behalf and was shot dead.

Actress The *National Enquirer* is a liar. You are faithful to me!

VIP What?

Actress Oh yes. You were faithful to me even before we met. Come closer. (*He sits on the edge of the bed.*) The boy in the box office belongs to that forgettable past. (*She strokes his head.*) My Prince has a teeny weeny bald patch too.

VIP Your Prince is all bald patch.

Actress I knew you were coming, by the way.

VIP When you got the briefing from my assistant?

Actress Before that.

VIP Before that, I hadn't decided to come.

Actress You were in the front row last night. I played the whole show to just you, saw your face at curtain call, and said to myself: that man will stop by in the morning.

VIP 'Won't you come into my parlor,' said the spider to the fly.

Actress Exactly. So do something undignified like unbuttoning your . . . collar.

VIP All right. (*And he does so.*)

Actress Monsieur Henri, aren't you ever horny? I mean, you did set this date up. Or did you think it'd be a philosophy seminar?

VIP No.

Actress Then kiss me this minute. (*He administers a long, soft kiss, then returns to his chair.*) So why'd you stop?

VIP I didn't 'stop'.

Actress Henry – Hal – you are a *poseur*.

VIP How so?

Actress There's hardly a man in the Village who wouldn't be happy to be in your shoes.

VIP *I'm* happy to be in my shoes.

Actress So happiness does exist! How about love? Don't you love me, Princeling?

VIP One might say so.

Actress One might? Then one should. Then one does. Say it. Say: 'I worship you, Charlot'.

VIP I worship you, Charlot.

Actress So ask me a favor. Let your imagination run riot. What do you want most in all the world?

VIP Permission to return tonight.

Actress What?! I'm playing tonight.

VIP After the theatre.

Actress That's all you want? Nothing else?

VIP Everything else. But after the theatre.

Actress You are a goddamned *poseur*, Monsieur Henri.

VIP Mademoiselle Charlot, you are frank. Let me be frank. Yes, I'm often 'horny'. What fun to use a word like that! I find you attractive – to put it mildly –

Actress You put everything mildly, your highness.

VIP We're going to make love. Maybe that's putting it mildly? But why not at leisure, my dear? At an hour when there are no rings from doorbell or phone?

Actress There'll be no rings from doorbell or phone, idiot. I've taken care of that!

VIP Sex in the morning is simply not my thing.

Actress That's an insult!

VIP It's a compliment, Mademoiselle: one shouldn't eat a girl like you for breakfast.

Actress Now that's pretty raunchy.

VIP D'you want to hear what I have in mind?

Actress Yeah, what do you have in mind, your highness?

VIP I'll be in the back seat, waiting. Not my limousine. A yellow cab. Not outside the theatre. Two blocks down. Then somewhere chic for a little supper –

Actress Champagne, the whole bit? Me still in drag or what?

VIP Whichever you like. I like you both ways. I like you all ways.

Actress Hey, now we're gettin' somewhere.

VIP After which, events will take their natural course. It will be rather beautiful.

Actress Gee, it's hot in here. (*All of a sudden he kisses her passionately.*) Henry! That is not on your program.

VIP I have no program.

Actress But it *is* hot.

VIP It is *not* hot. That's an old gay gag to get people into bed.

Actress So what's wrong with old gay gags? Take your clothes off.

VIP I guess I have one last scruple.

Actress Scruple?!

VIP Mr Robert Rich . . . aren't you and he – ?

Actress (*shrugging*) What if we are?

VIP You don't mind? What about him?

Actress Robert? He'll love it. Hearing about you . . .

VIP You'll tell him?!

Actress He's been inventing lovers for me to deceive him with. You're real, aren't you?

VIP Comparatively speaking.

Actress (*walking over to the Venetian blinds and pulling them down. As* **VIP** *takes his clothes off.*) Antony and Cleopatra. Tristan and Isolde. Or are you my Romeo? And are we both thirteen again? Anything is possible. Finish undressing, your highness. (*She peeps behind the blinds.*) Night falls over SoHo. This is gonna be a beaut.

*   *   *

VIP *is dressing.* **Actress** *is still in bed.*

Actress So sex in the morning is simply not your thing. *Poseur!*

VIP You're a little devil.

Actress And you're a wonder lover – especially before breakfast.

VIP You're the wonder lover.

Actress And now I should strangle you. Aren't there insects that do that sort of thing – after sex?

VIP Oh yes, the –

Actress And fairy tales about princesses who do it to lovers who learn their fatal secret?

VIP Yes, indeed, there's one that –

Actress And how about the prince who learns that the princess has no secret?

VIP Oh, that would only mean –

Actress That her secret was just fucking? By whatever name? A fuck by any other name? Antony. Tristan. Romeo. I know what became of them.

VIP They came to a sticky end.

Actress Which gives me my cue right now.

VIP For what?

Actress This line, darling: 'I shall never see you again.' That's if it's a play. In real life, gay guys are silent. They take down your phone number and fade away.

VIP Why wouldn't you want to see me again?

Actress That's not what I said.

VIP You mean I won't be back.

Actress I'm not whatever it is you're looking for.

VIP Maybe no one is.

Actress So I'm no one.

VIP I didn't say that. I apologize. And I didn't say I wouldn't be back . . .

Actress So come back tonight. *Then* say goodbye.

VIP Does that make sense?

Actress You suggested it. Yellow cab. After the show. Two blocks down the street.

VIP I see. Well, how about the day after tomorrow?

Actress By then you'll have forgotten me. Moved on.

VIP To what? To whom?

Actress (*street smart*) Whatsa matter, Mister? Can't do it twice in one day?

VIP It's no problem physically, Charlie, but let's look at the spiritual side –

Actress I *never* look at the spiritual side!

VIP I can't separate the two sides.

Actress If that's philosophy, keep it for your fag hag – what's her name again?

VIP Lulu. And she isn't a fag hag. Look, Charles, if we don't see eye to eye –

Actress We'll be eyeball to eyeball. Here! Tonight!

VIP You insist I come in the yellow cab and – ?

Actress We'll cut the supper and the ridin' around. I'll be back at 11.30 sharp. And you'll be waitin' for me, OK?

VIP It's a crazy little plan.

Actress One last fuck and goodbye. What's crazy about it?

VIP So desperate. And the way you word it.

Actress Wanna call it off? Say g'bye right now? (*Silence.*) Which is *more* 'desperate': goodbye with a fuck attached, or goodbye and nothin' attached, just nothin' and nothin'?

VIP I guess we see eye to eye on that one.

Actress You'll come? (*He nods.*) Lookin' at the *less* spiritual side, huh? You know, Mr VIP, Mr Philosopher, Mr Spiritualist, in your own style you are a very great seducer! Can you deny it?

VIP I only meant –

Actress Save it for tonight!

VIP Tonight?

Actress Eleven-thirty! Sharp!

He leaves. **Actress** *is still in bed.*

Mademoiselle Charlot conquers the Establishment

10. The VIP and the Hustler

A double 'room' at the Ansonia Baths on upper Broadway. Morning, about six. Such rooms have partitions rather than walls and no furniture other than a double bed and a chair. No washbasin, no pictures or ornaments. The **Hustler** *is asleep under the bedclothes. The* **VIP** *is partially dressed and on top of the bedclothes, just opening his eyes.*

VIP 'Where am I?' As the heroine says in the melodrama. Broadway and 73rd. The Ansonia Baths. Foolish to come here and risk being seen. I must stop doing these things. (*Looking around.*) And, my God, *he's* still there, probably glad of as good a place as this to sleep. I paid him for his trouble. Though, actually, we didn't do anything. I was too drunk. I must stop drinking or move from the Ansonia to the Riverside Funeral Home. Rather nice, to think one can spend the night at the side of some young fellow like this, just peacefully sleep, then kiss him goodbye. Haven't had such a satisfying feeling in quite a while. I must consult Lulu about it. Good boy, that kid. A kind face now, in repose. Not like on the street, brutal, macho. No one is a hustler in his sleep. Sleep's a big democrat. Like his brother, Death. *Did* we do something, he and I? Nah. Not a thing.

He has finished dressing and is ready to leave. Evidently the **Hustler** *has followed the last part of this, though he is still more than half asleep.*

Hustler Hey, you leavin'?

VIP Oh, hi. Yeah. I gave you fifty bucks last night, remember?

Hustler *checks that he still has it.*

Hustler Oh, yeh, thanks. Don't want nothin' else? (*Silence.*) I'll sleep some more if that's OK?

VIP I've had all I want, thanks. What a thing to be able to say: I've had all I want. May I hold you for a minute?

Hustler Hold me all you want.

VIP *goes to* **Hustler**'*s side of the bed and puts an arm round him.*

VIP What's your name, honey?

Hustler Hyacinth. What's yours, baby?

VIP (*impulsively*) Narcissus! Narcissus and Hyacinth! What a pair we make!

Hustler For real? Nar-ciss-us?

VIP (*the smile fading*) No. In mere reality, things are different, aren't they? In mere reality, one is called Henry.

Hustler You're a big shot, I know.

VIP What gives you *that* impression?

Hustler Your clothes. And, on the street, you look over your shoulder all the time . . .

VIP I'm a middle-sized shot. A little shot, really. How old are you, Hyacinth?

Hustler Eighteen.

VIP May I ask how long you've been –

Hustler In the business? Two years.

VIP You started early.

Hustler Better than too late.

VIP I'm just a student. Of life and such. Tell me something, my dear Hyacinth. Have you ever known . . . love?

Hustler Ha? Oh yeh. Once. I *think*.

VIP Tell me about it.

Hustler I really grooved on this guy. Never thought of askin' him for money. Went to sleep in his arms . . . (*He hesitates.*)

VIP Yes?

Hustler When I woke up, he was gone.

VIP Forever?

Hustler (*nodding*) *He* was gone. And so was my wallet.

VIP Oh dear, oh dear. You're unhappy, aren't you, Hyacinth?

Hustler Ha?

VIP Have you *ever* known happiness?

Hustler (*defensive*) I'm doin' awright. Did'n' you just give me fifty bucks for . . .

He boggles at bad language in front of a **VIP**.

VIP For nothing. Nothing at all.

Hustler Nah, doan put me down. *That* was more than . . . a shoe shine, ha? Two years

ago I was gettin' fifty *cents* for shinin' shoes.

VIP You should put *me* down. I pass the time in dreams and idle talk while you struggle for survival.

Hustler I'm doin' awright.

VIP What do you plan for later?

Hustler Huh?

VIP When you're too old for . . . this.

Hustler Whadda they say? 'Sufficient to the day . . .'

VIP (*to himself*) '. . . is the evil thereof.' My view exactly. To find people to agree with me I have to come to the Ansonia Baths?

Hustler How's that?

VIP I'll bother you with another question, Hyacinth, if I may.

Hustler Go ahead.

VIP Is sex still enjoyable when you . . . (*He hesitates.*)

Hustler Do it with everybody? But I don't. I'm choosy. I chose you.

VIP I thought I chose you.

Hustler You're supposed to think that . . .

VIP It's all done with mirrors – ?

Hustler I choose my guys. Sure, I'll talk with any guy that talks to me. Then – in five minutes – I know if I'm gonna choose him. Chose you in three minutes.

VIP What did you see in me?

Hustler You're rich. And that counts. Then again, you're real sweet – *under* all that.

VIP There's a lot of mutual respect here.

Hustler Yeh. You an' me could go places. In another world.

VIP My, how strongly you remind me of somebody.

Hustler Oh, please, not that one!

VIP I know it's a cliché, Hyacinth, but once in a long while it's true. You have the face of a very wonderful person I once knew. May I kiss your eyes?

Hustler Why? Then again: why not?

VIP In memory of him. The eyes are identical. (*He kisses* **Hustler**'s *eyes*.) And now goodbye.

Hustler 'Bye, Henry.

VIP One last thing, Hyacinth. Were you surprised?

Hustler At what?

VIP That we . . . did nothing. That I didn't ask you to.

Hustler Lotsa guys don't dig morning sex.

VIP We must do this again sometime.

Hustler Any time. You'll find me . . . where you found me last night . . . where *I* found *you*. If you don't, ask the bartender for Hyacinth.

VIP (*to himself*) I spend the night with a hustler and all I do is kiss his eyes because he *truly* reminds me of someone! Hyacinth, does this happen often?

Hustler What?

VIP A guy picks you up, pays you, and then doesn't ask for a thing.

Hustler That has *never* happened. Not in this world.

VIP Don't take offence. I didn't mean I wasn't attracted.

Hustler You sure *were* attracted – last night.

VIP I am now.

Hustler Not like last night.

VIP Last night I just flopped down on that bed.

Hustler Yeah, with me underneath ya.

VIP With you underneath me?

Hustler Sure. You don't remember?

VIP Well, um, not exactly, but, um . . . Oh dear, is that how it was?

Hustler You must've been really sozzled to forget. You're very good in bed!

VIP Oh dear . . . Oh dear . . . I did pay you?

Hustler (*letting himself doze off again*) Fifty smackers. Thanks.

VIP *leaves the little room and walks down the corridor.*

VIP Nice idea, though, to have . . . just kissed his eyes, there's beauty in it, beauty's the next best thing to love, my dear Lulu, and with love comes the blue bird of happiness . . . there was *some* resemblance . . .

Days of Cavafy

Gerald Killingworth

Gerald Killingworth was born in Peterborough and read English at Cambridge. **Days of Cavafy** was his fourth play to be produced on the London 'fringe', but has since been followed by his free adaptation of Apuleius's **The Golden Ass** (The Old Red Lion 1992). His other plays are **Abroad** (Prince of Wales Theatre Club, 1983 and The Old Red Lion, 1984), **Sunspot Sonata** (The Old Red Lion, 1984) and **Nightbirds** (Finborough Theatre Club, 1986). His four years of teaching English in Greece not only provided the inspiration for **Days of Cavafy** and **The Golden Ass** but also for **Welcome Wanderer**, a play depicting a modern version of the homecoming of Odysseus, and **Lefsina**, a children's novel dealing with the ancient Eleusinian Mysteries. As well as plays, Gerald writes novels for adults and children.

Preface

The most and least enthusiastic of the reviews of **Days of Cavafy** were, oddly, those in the gay press. The two reviewers who were unhappy with the play took me to task for failing to present Cavafy's homosexuality in the one and only way in which they had decided it should be presented. I thought that this dissension would be a good starting point for a brief discussion of the specifically gay thread in my play. One particularly splenetic reviewer insisted that Cavafy was an 'early gay hero'. This is simply not the case. He would never have conceived of himself as a banner waver, as a flaunter of that side of his life which was furtively entered at nightfall or was committed to paper and not generally circulated. Thank God, for us, that the words he so movingly wrote were the very truth of the man and that we can now brandish them in a way in which their author never dared. In the very last scene of the play, talking of the walls of inhibition behind which he has been sheltering, he says, 'I daren't come out.' In our modern parlance, he never did 'come out'. He spoke from his heart about his loves, of male beauty, but the words were whispered, not bawled through a megaphone.

My play is an act of homage to a writer whose work I came to love during my four years teaching English in Athens. I never dreamt for one moment of hijacking Cavafy and using him to make a point of my own about 'the problem', 'gay rights' or whatever. Unavoidably, my choice of action and language within the play will make the Cavafy an audience sees *my* Cavafy, but my aim was to recreate on stage a man, a poetic vision, an atmosphere that I felt enthusiastic enough about to want to share with an audience. The basic point was that I hoped he would be judged for what he was and not for what I made him out to be. It was important, therefore, to approach him from many sides and not to squeeze him through a mould of my making. Paradoxically, I was trying to be self-effacing in a play which contains only one complete poem and no actual remarks that Cavafy made. It is replete with echoes from the poems, particularly in the erotic scene, but it contains an enormous amount of my own invention of the sort of things that *could well have happened* to Cavafy or that he *could well have thought or said*. One critic insisted that I should have had E. M. Forster and Cavafy sitting discussing the merits of the men of Alexandria. The only retort one can make to this sort of 'criticism' is, 'Grow up!' because our poet would never, never, never have behaved in this way. Perhaps I should have had them drooling over the 1917 equivalent of *Zipper*.

The homosexuality in Cavafy's work is hugely important; who would want to deny this? Certainly not me. However, if Constantine Cavafy were alive and we asked him to encapsulate his poems, his first adjective would not be 'gay'. The fundamentals, the general human issues he deals with are those of failure, of the transience of achievement and beauty and of the frequent wretchedness of desire. They are relevant to us all but they happen, in this instance, to be approached through the medium of a homosexual sensibility. This gives them their distinct colouring because he was particularly susceptible to the poignancy of fine looking young men condemned to lives, deaths and unhappiness which their physical charms suggested were unfair. Many poems are simply sympathetically ironic or sad and in no way gay (think of *Ithaca* or *Waiting for the Barbarians*); others talk of young men and not of sex. The contemporary poems are the most explicitly sexual ones and often just have a date for the title – *Days of 1903*, *Days of 1908* and so on. These suggested the title of the play itself as I was concerned to show Cavafy in all his days – days at home, at work, in love. At first I thought I could show all that I wanted of the man in four scenes, but the material fell more naturally into six fairly self-contained units with Cavafy as our guide and commentator linking them.

A key word I would use in describing how I manipulated the gay material is 'context'. I wanted to show as many facets of the poet as I could and to point the contrast between his outer and inner lives and between his public and personal ones. Outwardly he was a restrained, sometimes petty, minor civil servant. Inwardly he strode the Hellenistic Near East conversing freely with men and gods. The erotic encounters he describes need not necessarily have been personal experiences. You need to see the man in various settings fully to appreciate these contrasts.

No commentary on the first production of the play would be complete without a deep appreciation of the subtlety, variety and sheer magnitude of Tim Hardy's portrayal of Cavafy and of Alison Skilbeck's intelligence and perception in the direction. The delight of finding colleagues who tune in at once to the wavelength of your writing is a highpoint in any artistic collaboration. Watching Tim *be* Cavafy on stage, or listening as Alison described the play to prospective members of the cast at the auditions told me it could not be in safer hands. Nor should I forget our young man in the cinnamon-brown suit, Mark Frankel, who memorably stood for all Cavafy's doomed youths.

Gerald Killingworth

Production Note

The play as printed here reflects in its setting, stage directions and doublings, the production which ran at the Finborough and King's Head Theatre Clubs. We found this the cheapest and most efficient way of presenting the play but, obviously, the setting could be as opulent as a director would like, and there need be no doubling at all. It is, however, very important that the actor playing The Young Man should *only* play Sarpedon and Caesarion in the masque and no other character elsewhere in the play as I have made this figure a recurrent dream and source of inspiration for the poet. He should look like a Greek god in shabby clothes and cause a stir when he appears for the first time in Act Two. For the doublings, other combinations are, of course, perfectly possible, but a minimum cast of eight is required.

The events in this play do not take place in strict chronological order. Rather, it consists of a number of scenes in which we see aspects of Cavafy's life – family, work, friends, literary acquaintances, love affairs. In the very last scene of all, when we know the poet well, it is time to enter the private world of his poetic imagination and to meet some of the historical, mythological, forgotten figures who were so real to him. Cavafy's age changes during the course of the play and he may be younger in a later scene than in an earlier one. Linking the scenes, as a commentator, is the poet aged 54 as he was in 1917.

For the convenience of the reader, I have indicated dates and the ages of the particular characters. The audience would be given no such indication other than in the obvious age of the characters as portrayed by the actors.

The setting is Alexandria – various locations throughout the city. Our production was a very effectively stark one, set against four draped ochre and gold curtains and a marbled black back wall. Ex-hospital sheets make wonderful theatrical curtains!

Days of Cavafy was first presented at the Finborough Theatre Club, London, on 17 May 1989, with the following cast:

Constantine Cavafy	Tim Hardy
Haricleia Cavafy/The Empress Irene	Marina McConnell
Paul Cavafy/Stephanos/ Horse One/Ptolemy (*son of Cleopatra*)**/ Onlooker One/Snob Two/Man One**	William Relton
Mohammed El Said/Alexander (*Cavafy's friend*)**/Onlooker Three/Snob One/Man Two**	Ashley Russell
Ibrahim Mukhtar/Vassili/Alexander (*son of Cleopatra*)**/Snob Three/Man Three**	Ben Wheatley
Hamid/Dimitris/Horse Two/ The Man from Commagene/Onlooker Two	Rodney Matthew
E. M. Forster/Pericles/Zeus/ The Toppled King	James Woolley
The Young Man/Sarpedon/Caesarion	Mark Frankel

Directed by   Alison Skilbeck
Designed by   Rachel Lawson
Lighting Design by   Richard Rafter
Music and sound by   Mark Greaves

On 20 June 1989, **Days of Cavafy** transferred to the King's Head Theatre Club, London, where the part of Haricleia Cavafy was played by Carol Macready.

Act One

The sound of wind and a flute. Most of the stage is in darkness. To one side, downstage, is a trestle table in a pool of light. On the table is a line of bundles of poems held together by butterfly clips. There is also a small coffee cup. At the very edge of the stage next to the table is a hat stand with the coats and hat **Cavafy** *will wear at various times during the play.*

Cavafy, *aged 54, stands at the table in his shirtsleeves busy with the papers and oblivious of the audience. He takes a poem from another unclipped pile and adds it to one of the bundles. He repeats this with other poems and other bundles. At last he looks up at the audience.*

Cavafy (*to the audience*) Each folder has a name. (*He points to the folders as he mentions the names of the recipients.*) My brothers Paul and John, my niece, Alexander Singopoulos a dear friend, a few admirers abroad. This is my special room called 'The Bindery' where I bind my poems into these folders. Excuse me. (*He takes a sip of his coffee and adds a few more poems to the bundles.*) This one is called *The Tomb of Iasis.* (*He reads some of the poem aloud.*) 'I, Iasis, lie here – I was famous for my handsome face in this great city.' (**Cavafy** *becomes reflective.*) 'This great city.' (*He adopts a confidential tone.*) In your travels around the Mediterranean, you have seen undistinguished little seaports exactly like Alexandria. In the Levant or Syria you noticed the same untidy buildings with no claims to grace, the same cafés whose debris offended you, the same loungers. Always loungers. 'What are they doing?' you asked in your disapproving English way. (*He sips his coffee.*) Excuse me. I missed out my great friend from boyhood Pericles Anastassiades. (*He adds another sheet to the bundle.*) Yes. 'What are they doing!' The coffee in their cups is thick and cold like the mud at the very beginning of the world. (*He picks up his own coffee cup and stares into it.*) There's no better brain-food than half an inch of mud. (*He*

drinks.) Believe me. 'Idlers', you think. 'Wranglers.' With their gestures and imprecations in smoky Greek or slum Arabic.

But I'm an Alexandrian. I see something quite different. I'm not bursting from my hotel to the museum or taking a madcap English constitutional along the admittedly smelly Corniche. I stand still and with a half closure of my eyes. (*He demonstrates this.*) Ah. (*He breathes in.*) I inhale the real Alexandria, the spiritual city, the dream. I'm not standing at a corner of the dowdy Rue Lepsius any more. It's the Canopic Street linking the Gate of the Sun and the Gate of the Moon. Try it with me. Breathe in. Let the ancient pavement sprout through the carpet. Because its walls are no longer solid, that doesn't mean they have gone away. Touch them with the finest part of you.

He relaxes and looks at them for a while smiling.

Three centuries before Christ, a wild boy from Macedonia blew through here. 'Build me a city!' he cried and was gone. 'Build me a city. Here and here.' It was that easy in those days. Did you know Alexander had a tic, by the way? His head was put on at an angle. (*He demonstrates.*) So perhaps, when he said, 'Here and here,' he meant, 'There and there.' Just a thought. Fate's sense of humour has always amused me.

Alexander intended to come back, of course, but he never did. Tempests like him blow forwards only. He didn't see a single stone laid on top of another. I cast my inner eyes over his city for him. You know all about the lighthouse, don't you, that possibly had a telescope on top – fifteen hundred years before Signor Galileo started fiddling about with a length of tubing? The two wondrous libraries and Alexander the boy hero's glass coffin which might or might not be in the unexplored cellars of the Mosque of the Prophet Daniel? Enough. Let me introduce you to some real people. 'Real' in *your* sense.

Flashes of light, darkness, the sound of explosions.

The British bombardment of 1882. (*More flashes and explosions.*) The British are *very* 'real'. (*A final flash and explosion.*) Wherever they go. They were bombarding everyone at that time. Bang, bang, bang and the frail and lovely minaret by the harbour became a cloud of powder in the July air. The Cavafys were amongst the last Europeans to leave but in October we were home and mother was back in the swing of Alexandrian society.

Lights up for next scene.

After a Khedivial Ball (c.1890)

Dance music.

The scene is the Cavafys' drawing room in the early hours of the morning. **Haricleia Cavafy** – *the poet's mother – aged 55, enters with her son* **Paul,** *aged 30. There is a predominance of reds and purples in the furnishings of the room, with oriental cushions and rugs, over-gilded ornaments and tables inlaid with mother of pearl.* **Paul** *is very attentive to his mother who sits down wearily.* **Cavafy,** *aged 25, puts on an evening jacket while* **Paul** *helps his mother into a chair or onto a divan. Both* **Paul** *and* **Cavafy** *are homosexual and the occasional knowing glance between them should hint at this.* **Paul** *is otherwise very dapper, the epitome of mondain and certainly not camp.*

Paul (*to his mother*) Did you enjoy yourself, o fat one?

Haricleia A cup of coffee, please, Paul. No, a sip of boiled water. Coffee will not improve my headache. My veins are going 'gnous, gnous, gnous'.

Cavafy But did you enjoy yourself?

Haricleia The Khedive of Egypt offered me his arm.

Cavafy We saw you.

Paul All Alexandria saw you.

Haricleia Financially the Cavafys may have seen better days, but we know who we are. The Khedive of Egypt knows who we are. Socially, we still matter a good deal.

Paul (*giving her the water in a red glass*) You didn't say this to the people at the ball, did you?

Haricleia I *felt* it. My father was an aristocrat who handled diamonds.

Cavafy I pray, mother, that you never feel out loud in high society.

Haricleia Every day I thank my saints that I am not a member of one of the nouveaux families in Alexandria, always chasing the British for the honours they scatter like icing sugar. '*Sir* Kimon Antoniades', what a silly sounding mixture of names. Promise me, my sons, that you will never run after them just to be called a 'Sir'.

Paul We shouldn't bite the hand that made us British subjects.

Haricleia I am talking of two different things, Paul, as well you know. Being British subjects doesn't mean that we have to go on our knees to the gypsies they send over with their army of occupation. They are not of our class. Decidedly.

Cavafy Arrogant and ignorant. They strut around as if *they* built the pyramids.

Paul Their women are, if anything, worse than the men. Have you seen them at table?

Haricleia I was horrified. All those little sweetmeats gone in an instant. I thought, 'How lovely. My dear little Constantine with his sweet tooth would love one of those.' But no. The English ladies did not allow it. Whoosh and the plates were empty. It hurts my veins now to remember it.

Paul I believe they fast before they come out to evening parties.

Haricleia I trust they saw the Khedive bowing his head to hear what I was saying.

Paul Don't worry, imperious fat one, *all* Alexandria saw you.

Cavafy The Pavlides and the Antoniades saw you.

Haricleia I am sure the Khedive didn't see *them*. All tinsel and bustle though they were. A woman's bustle should make her shape more interesting, not turn her into a . . .

Paul A Bedouin tent?

Haricleia (*clapping her hands in delight at the comparison*) Yes. He walks very fast, you know.

Cavafy Who does?

Haricleia The Khedive.

Paul He swept you along in a great gesture of approval.

Haricleia But look. (*She pulls up her skirt to reveal her shoes.*)

Cavafy Mother, how naughty, flaunting your ankles at your impressionable sons. Save them for his majesty.

Haricleia I mean look at my shoes. My heels. You men should try sweeping along on heels that high. Any moment I felt I should topple. (*She slips off her shoes with great relief.*)

Paul Imagine it.

Haricleia Lying on the floor at his feet.

Cavafy Saying, 'I wonder whether I could trouble your majesty to set me upright again, I seem to have fallen off my shoes.'

Paul I think you managed it like Queen Victoria.

Haricleia I hope that I dress a little more interestingly. A great lady, indeed, but there's no need to look as if you're in mourning for the whole world. There are black clothes and black clothes. She is advised to wear the wrong sort.

Paul You should be her Lady-in-Waiting.

Haricleia The Khedive asked me what I thought of his champagne.

Paul That wasn't very fair.

Cavafy Why?

Paul If mother criticised it, he might think her ill-mannered and make up his mind that in future she should drink her own champagne at her own ball, and not his.

Cavafy And if she praised it?

Paul Let me see. She might appear insincere or, worse, patronizing, as if, for an Egyptian, he had done quite well, but the choosing of wine is best left to a European.

Cavafy You exaggerate.

Haricleia Oh no. Paul's an expert in these matters. He's the most mondain man in Alexandria. Everyone says so. He's too mondain and successful for his poor old mother.

Paul *has heard all this before and is mildly irritated by it.*

When he escorts me to the Casino or The Sporting Club, he soon makes it clear he wants to be on his own. I'm abandoned, heartlessly.

Paul What *was* your reply to the Khedive?

Haricleia I don't remember now. My headache is coming back. (*She puts her hands to her temples.*) My veins are howling.

Paul Mother.

Haricleia Perhaps I didn't say anything.

Paul You refused to answer a question put to you by the Khedive in person. That's almost treasonable.

Haricleia I said I always enjoyed his balls. I expected that he had the most enjoyable balls in the world.

Cavafy *and* **Paul** *exchange smirks.*

Haricleia Why are you boys looking at each other? Was I offensive?

Paul No, mother, you were very tactful. When in doubt, sidestep the question. That way no one can put a black cross against your name.

Haricleia I shouldn't like to think of him sitting in his palace scoring through my name. Imagine it. I'd die of shame. 'Mrs Haricleia Cavafy behaved very badly and is no longer to be invited or even mentioned.' Score. Score. And then he'd order his secretary to tear out the page and rip it into tiny pieces. Oh. (*She puts her hand on her heart.*)

Cavafy Paul, you're cruel to tease mother in this way. She's clutching her heart now.

Haricleia A little flutter, no more.

Cavafy Just because you always have a glib answer or a smirk for every smart social event, you forget that the rest of us are amateurs overflowing with worry on such occasions.

Paul How are you feeling, little fat one?

Haricleia My headache is twisting my eyes. Pour me a little more water please, Paul. (*She gives her glass to* **Paul** *and as he crosses the room she seizes* **Cavafy**'s *arm.*) Constantine, that wasn't my answer at all.

Cavafy It isn't important. Paul's being grand and a know-all.

Haricleia (*seeing that* **Paul** *is coming back and that she needs to speak quickly*) I said, 'The champagne is quite nice'.

Cavafy Don't worry. (*He pats her hand.*)

Paul *hands her the glass of water.*

Haricleia (*unable to contain her worry*) One shouldn't say, 'Quite nice' to a Khedive. One should say, 'Perfect' or 'Blissfully wonderful'.

Cavafy Paul, you *always* have to be the expert don't you!

Haricleia My sons, don't quarrel! I was very proud of you both tonight. Handing coffee and ices to some quite intolerable ladies. Always smiling. Always smiling. What would they do without you both? Whenever Paul joined a gathering and found them glum, he soon had everyone laughing.

Cavafy He seems to have left his charm behind him in the ballroom, then.

Paul Don't pout, Constantine. It's the mannerism of a girl.

Haricleia I know how you both love gossip, even if Paul pretends to be above it. So . . .

Cavafy So?

Haricleia I'm going to tell you what I heard about the Makroyannis family.

Paul Father in cotton, a son drowned, two daughters: one flighty and the other knock-kneed.

Cavafy Thus spake the social encyclopaedia of the town.

Haricleia Mother and daughters have decided that a certain British officer . . .

Paul One Captain Markham.

Haricleia Oh, Paul, you know!

Cavafy Don't let him spoil your story. Carry on, mother.

Haricleia (*huffily*) Paul probably knows ten times as many details as I do. He'll keep interrupting to correct me.

Cavafy No he won't. Will you, Paul?

Paul I'm going to smoke a cigarette and relax my practised smile.

Cavafy Good. Continue, mother. (*Cajolingly.*) Please.

Haricleia Madame Makroyannis and her daughters have decided that Captain Markham would be an ideal catch for Eugenia, the one Paul said was knock-kneed.

Cavafy How did Captain Markham react to this news that he had been chosen?

Haricleia With dismay, I suppose. They have heard that his father has a large business in Liverpool and they follow him everywhere. It's costing them a fortune in dresses for her. If he goes to the Casino, she pops up. If he's invited to a reception, the family gets wind. He'd probably rather rush out into the desert and fight savages. She isn't at all pretty, or charming, or accomplished or interesting. Imagine dropping your fan near the same man three times.

Cavafy (*giving* **Paul** *a meaningful look*) Throwing herself at a British officer. Disgraceful, isn't it, Paul?

Paul Utterly.

Haricleia And now for some gossip nearer home. You, Paul Cavafy, are getting a *worldwide* reputation.

Cavafy *and* **Paul** *exchange an alarmed look.*

As a ladies' man!

Sighs of relief from the brothers. **Paul** *makes a dismissive gesture.*

Paul (*anxious to preserve his reputation*) I always have the fullest dance card, it's true.

Cavafy He's revelling in the accusation.

Haricleia And he needn't pretend to me that he hasn't seen more than one pair of lacy drawers.

Cavafy (*in mock horror*) Mother, for shame!

Haricleia Don't imagine that your mother doesn't know how they talk about you as the giddiest bachelor of all. What I want to know is – now don't purse your lips at me, Paul. I want to know when you are going to marry one of the hundreds of young ladies whose eyes widen when you come into a room. You are invited everywhere . . .

Cavafy Like an expensive table decoration.

Paul Perhaps the young ladies' eyes widen with horror. They may know of my unpleasant personal habits.

Haricleia You are being vulgar and selfish. When you are married and *out of the way*, Constantine will come into his own. You make him into a bridesmaid.

Cavafy This is champagne talking. It wasn't your high heels that made you unsteady.

Haricleia Paul is so successfully mondain he pushes you into the shadows.

Cavafy I am very happy in the shadows.

Haricleia No one can be happy in the shadows.

Cavafy This one can. I am as much in the light as I desire and I can observe the world's goings on from a distance.

Haricleia Paul *is* the world's goings on. (*She re-arranges* **Paul**'*s hair, much to his irritation.*)

Cavafy That is his choice, not mine. And look what happens. You say everyone gossips about him. I shall make sure I am *never* the subject of gossip.

Paul Sensible fellow.

Haricleia I shall sleep late tomorrow.

Cavafy You should be in bed.

Haricleia I thought the pain in my head might ease if I sat for a while, but it hasn't.

Paul We'll help you.

Cavafy *and* **Paul** *take one of* **Haricleia**'*s arms each and help her up out of her chair. They kiss her hands and she sighs with satisfaction. They escort her into the darkness at the side of the stage.*

Haricleia My shoes, Paul. My handbag.

Paul *picks them up from beside her chair and hands them to her. Just before she exits she lightly slaps his face for being a naughty boy and teasing her. When she has disappeared, they return centre stage.*

Cavafy So, my brother Paul is the most notorious ladies' man.

Paul How can I help it, being so charming?

Cavafy What a *useful* reputation.

Paul Poor Captain Markham, so heroically acned and laid siege to by a knock-kneed girl. Let me give you a brotherly piece of advice, Constantine.

Cavafy What's that?

Paul When you drop your fan for a British

officer, choose a better prize than Captain Markham.

They dissolve into laughter. **Paul** *walks to the side of the stage and, before disappearing, he exchanges a last, sad look with* **Cavafy. Cavafy** *removes his evening coat and returns to the bindery table which is the only point of light on the stage.*

Cavafy at his bindery table again, aged 54

Cavafy My poems are full of endings and disasters. Some disasters happened at home and were, to be frank, embarrassing for all of us. In 1889 my brother Aristides deserted his wife and absconded to Marseilles. The dowry was lost and her family threatened criminal proceedings. Then in 1908 Paul took his financial disorder too much to heart and caught a boat for England and the South of France. (*Slowly and sadly.*) Never to return. He had been so mondain, so popular. He could not bear to live in a city where shame made him hang his head.

The greatest disaster in the history of the world occurred on November the 8th, 641. Hellenic Alexandria fell. Amr the Arab conqueror sent back a despatch to the Caliph of Baghdad saying, 'I have taken a city of which I can only say that it contains 4000 palaces, 4000 baths, 400 theatres, 1200 greengrocers and 40,000 Jews'.

Empires rise and fall, pillars soar skywards and crumble, wheels turn and, my goodness, the time, the time . . . (*He rushes from the stage.*)

The lights go down on the trestle table and up on **Cavafy**'s *place of work, the setting that occupies the centre and back of the stage.*

Cavafy at work, 1917, aged 54

The setting, an office in the Department of Irrigation, should be kept as simple as possible: on one side of the stage a desk for the Egyptian clerks; on the other side **Cavafy**'s *desk in a part of the stage designated the inner office; hat pegs or a hatstand. The safe, which contains the clerks' papers for the day, may be imagined offstage. The two young Egyptian clerks,* **Mohammed El Said** *and* **Ibrahim Mukhtar,** *are waiting sleepily at their desk for* **Cavafy** *who is always late.* **El Said** *has his feet on the desk.*

El Said This is the kind of work I enjoy best – wearing out the heels of my shoes and smiling at the locked safe which contains my papers for the day. If the Englishman sees that we cannot get into the safe, we shall have to tell more lies to protect Mr Cavafy.

Mukhtar It is the privilege of Europeans to be late and to kick us when *we* are late.

El Said Now I shall take the sleep I deserve. (*He closes his eyes and crosses his arms on his chest.*) Nudge me if you hear footsteps.

There is a sound offstage. The two clerks jerk into life and sit very straight-backed at the desk. **Hamid, Cavafy**'s *servant, enters breathlessly.*

Hamid I have the key to the safe. I have the key.

El Said We know you have the key to the safe, Hamid. Every day you bring the key in advance of poor Mr Cavafy who cannot be expected to get up at the hour humble Egyptians do. (*He takes the key with an irritated flourish and goes into the wings to unlock the safe.*)

Mukhtar (*anxious that* **El Said**'s *remarks might be repeated*) Tell Mr Cavafy that we shall happily undertake the usual precautions.

Hamid He is expected very soon.

El Said *returns with the papers for the day.*

El Said (*ironically*) Of course.

Exit **Hamid.** *The two clerks spread out their papers.*

El Said He will be sitting in his taxi drumming his fingers. (*Mimicking a mincing, precise voice.*) 'Will it be today they discover I was still flat on my back snoring when I should have been writing correspondence.'

Mukhtar And only we know that he could snore and snore because his English masters are just one minute earlier than he is. What it is to conquer the world and never have to be on time.

El Said What it is to know a secret that would stop your chief worrying –

Both And not to tell him!

They laugh and then busy themselves sorting through the papers again.

Enter **Hamid** *with a panama hat.*

El Said (*without looking up*) You had forgotten the hat.

Hamid Yes, I had forgotten the hat.

Mukhtar We will deal with the matter.

El Said As always.

Hamid It is a new hat. Please take care with it.

El Said Go home now, Hamid.

Hamid *leaves.*

El Said Taking the 'new hat', I smack it reasonably carefully onto its hook. Then I admire it and think, 'How many dinners would this Greek man's hat have bought me?' And when our English master says, 'Has Mr Cavafy arrived?' I reply, 'Mais oui.' for being of a conquered race I have absorbed several languages. 'Mais oui. Mr Cavafy arrived many hours ago and is about the British Empire's business. Is that not his new hat on the hat peg?'

Cavafy *passes across the front of the stage and speaks to the audience. He is not part of the scene at the office yet. As he speaks,* **El Said** *and* **Mukhtar** *continue to busy themselves with the papers.* **Cavafy** *wears a jacket and perhaps carries a cane.*

Cavafy In April 1892 I obtained a post in the Third Circle of the Irrigation Department and stayed there for ever. The European office above a pâtisserie near Ramleh station. The third circle of Dante's Hell, by the way, is the last resting place of the gluttonous. Their punishment is to lie in the mire with an eternal storm of hail, snow and tainted water blowing above them. (*Perhaps looking in the direction of the clerks.*) The vicious mouths of Cerberus tear them apart from time to time. To the Third Circle!

He enters the office and becomes part of the scene.

Good morning Mr El Said, Mr Mukhtar.

Both (*standing to attention*) Good morning Mr Cavafy.

El Said I hope the taxi jolted your European buttocks.

Cavafy (*handing* **El Said** *his cane*) No Arabic in the office, please.

El Said It is a saying we have. 'May your day begin sweet.'

Mukhtar 'And grow sweeter.'

Cavafy 'Sweet'. Yes. Has the boy been up from the pâtisserie yet?

Mukhtar Not yet.

Cavafy When he does, I shall have a coffee and one of their most freshly-made cakes to nibble with it.

El Said *and* **Mukhtar** *sit behind their desk and work at their papers.* **Cavafy** *mimes opening the door of his inner office. He sits at the desk and takes out papers which he arranges carefully over his desk top. He is obviously making himself look busy.*

A very English voice is played over the tannoy to the audience.

Voice Mr Constantine Cavafy. Though formerly a British subject, he was Greek born and could not expect promotion.

Cavafy *looks up briefly.*

El Said *goes to* **Cavafy** *'s office with a letter in his hand. He mimes knocking on the door and enters.*

Cavafy I am very busy as you can see.

El Said As I can see, Mr Cavafy. There is a letter for your approval.

Cavafy Is this your letter without punctuation?

El Said Without one particular comma.

Cavafy Without an important comma *and* a full stop.

El Said I know nothing of the full stop. It was not mentioned.

Cavafy Too many clerks know nothing of the full stop. Where would the literature of the world be without that flick of the pen that looks almost like a blemish?

El Said I have added the comma.

Cavafy Please return to your desk and add the full stop.

El Said *returns to his desk. The sound of a chicken is heard.*

Cavafy Was that another proverb in Arabic?

Mukhtar It was the sound of a chicken.

Cavafy I thought it was a chicken.

Hamid *enters with a prop wriggling chicken. From time to time he gives it a violent jerk as if it is very alive.*

Hamid I must show Mr Cavafy the shopping.

He walks across the stage and into **Cavafy**'s *office.*

This is your supper, sir. Supper that will be.

The chicken jerks and squawks.

Cavafy Hold it still.

Cavafy *examines the chicken meticulously to see whether it is plump and healthy. Suddenly he pulls a few feathers from it. Loud squawking. He waves them under* **Hamid**'s *nose as he speaks fairly severely to him and then puts the feather in his breast pocket.*

I shall keep these until my supper is served. If you take this creature back to the market and exchange it for a cheaper one and keep the profit, I shall know.

Hamid (*aggrieved*) It was the best chicken in the market. I chose it for you.

Cavafy These feathers had better match those taken from the bird I have for my supper. I have a very good eye in these matters. Did you pay the price the rogue wanted?

Hamid Oh, less sir. Much less.

The chicken struggles again and appears about to leap onto **Cavafy**'s *desk.*

Cavafy Hold its legs and its neck. It's a chicken, not a set of bagpipes.

Hamid (*cunningly*) Would the Sir like to show me how?

Cavafy The Sir would not. Take it away before it rains any more feathers.

Hamid Thank you, Sir. (*He bows and walks to the door of* **Cavafy**'s *office. There he stops and looks back at* **Cavafy**.) That was a very good joke about the bagpipes, Sir. (*He pumps the chicken under his arm as if it were bagpipes. Then he leaves the office to a great sound of squawking, exchanging a conspiratorial look with* **Mukhtar** *on the way out.*)

The very English male voice is heard over the tannoy again.

Voice Mr Cavafy!

Cavafy *jumps up at the sound of the voice, walks forward a few paces and replies nervously to a space above the front of the stage.*

Cavafy Yes, Sir?

Voice Mr Cavafy, you are not giving satisfaction.

Cavafy I shall try to give you satisfaction, Sir. I shall try to give you satisfaction. (*He backs away from the voice and stands leaning against his desk.*) Must I wait all morning for my full stop!

El Said *jumps up from his desk and brings the letter into* **Cavafy**'s *office. He wants to hand it over then and there but* **Cavafy** *insists on sitting behind his desk again before he will accept it.* **Cavafy** *examines the letter very carefully.*

El Said If Mr Cavafy does not wish to read the entire letter again, the full stop is in the line before the last.

Cavafy (*looking up sharply*) There may be other mistakes.

El Said It is not an important letter and between us we have read it perhaps six times.

Cavafy Mr El Said, let us read it sixteen times if we are to be sure it is satisfactory. It is a matter of pride to me that no letter leaves this office with imperfect English. There. (*He hands the letter back.*) It may be delivered now.

El Said If I may be permitted to raise another point.

Cavafy The letter is satisfactory now.

El Said It is not the letter.

Mukhtar (*coming forward with a paper*) A man in the Arabic office had an accident, perhaps on Tuesday.

El Said You know these imbecile tram drivers.

Mukhtar They never let you step both feet on the ground before they ring that accursed bell. He needs good treatment in hospital and we have taken it upon ourselves to make a small charitable collection on his behalf. Perhaps Mr Cavafy . . .

Cavafy Mr Cavafy sends the unfortunate man his good wishes, of course, but there are many equally pressing demands on my purse. I regret . . . (*He makes a gesture with his hands. The two clerks linger, to* **Cavafy**'s *annoyance.*) Do tell the man that I send him my good wishes. Now, as you can see, my desk has a pyramid of papers. For an hour I shall lock the door so as to avoid disturbance.

He ushers the clerks out of the office and mimes locking the door behind them.

El Said (*angrily but quietly outside the door*) May you slip from a tram and damage your European buttocks!

The English voice comes over the tannoy again.

Voice Mr Cavafy!

Cavafy *sits to attention in his chair.*

Voice With reference to your report on the messenger Khaled Al Falahy. In English we say, 'A tall man,' not 'A *long* man'.

Cavafy *clenches his fists and glares. He takes a cigarette case from his jacket and removes a cigarette. Then he takes a pair of scissors from the desk drawer and carefully cuts the cigarette in half. He returns the other half to the cigarette case which he puts back in his pocket. He pushes the cigarette into a holder, lights it and takes one or two puffs luxuriously. Next he takes a folded sheet of paper from his other jacket pocket, unfolds it and places it on the desk. It is a poem he is working on.*

Cavafy (*reading the title of the poem*) *An Old Man.* An old man in the noisiest corner of the café. (*He waves his arms, pulls faces and massages his temples as he tries to find inspiration.*)

The two clerks sit dozily at their desk for a moment or two and then **El Said** *nudges* **Mukhtar** *and gets up. Stealthily he goes over to the door of* **Cavafy**'s *office and peeps through the keyhole.* **Mukhtar** *peeps through the keyhole too. They both listen and giggle as* **Cavafy** *undergoes more contortions. Suddenly he stiffens and smiles. He has found the words.*

Cavafy 'He remembers the desires he stifled, the joy he betrayed.' (*He sits still to ponder this idea as the clerks return to their desk.*)

Mukhtar (*imitating* **Cavafy**'s *various contortions*) The words of poetry fell from heaven.

El Said Like the feathers of a chicken.

They giggle softly together.

Blackout.

Cavafy *returns to the bindery table. Scene change for the rest of the stage perhaps with music. When the lights go up on the bindery,* **Cavafy** *is standing there with a small parcel and a letter.*

Cavafy at his bindery table again, still aged 54

Cavafy The post. Excuse me. (*He opens the letter and quickly peruses its contents. He raises his* *eyebrows*.) It's gossip. I love gossip. I'll save that for bedtime. (*He opens the parcel which contains a book and a letter. He looks at the title of the book and then reads the letter out loud.*) 'Honoured Mr Cavafy, may I dedicate my little volume of verses, *The Swirling Sands of Time*, to you?' In other words, 'Honoured Mr Cavafy, may I stand on your head in a vain attempt to reach the first rung of the ladder to Parnassus?' No you may not. The pages are uncut. As they will for ever remain. When I die and my little library is gone through, how many of the living shall I mortify when they discover that their books are uncut and unread? Poets, self-deceivers, who christen a book, *The Swirling Sands of Time*, deserve to die tomorrow.

There is a knock at the door.

(*Not really wanting to be disturbed.*) A visitor. Excuse me.

The lights go up on the inner stage which is now the sitting room of **Cavafy**'s *flat in the Rue Lepsius. It has clearly seen much better days and is faded and dowdy. Some of the furnishings are those we saw in the first scene after the ball, but over the years they have grown tatty. The basic colour of the furnishings is red. There is a chair for* **Cavafy**, *a chair or divan for* **Forster** *and a drinks table with various bottles and red glasses.*

A Literary Acquaintance

Cavafy *is 54 and his guest,* **E. M. Forster**, *38. It is 1917.*

Cavafy *opens the door to admit* **Forster.**

Cavafy My dear Forster. (*Aside to the audience as* **Forster** *freezes.*) Edward Morgan, or EM, author of several well-received novels about English manners. (**Forster** *unfreezes and* **Cavafy** *shakes his hand warmly.*) Come in, come in. (*Aside to the audience.*) Currently engaged in war work here in Alexandria. So commendable.

Forster, *a physically puny man, appears rather shaken.*

Cavafy You look . . .

Forster I feel somewhat . . .

Cavafy Do sit down. Some water? Is it your war work?

Forster Probably, probably.

Cavafy So distressing asking those poor soldiers about their lost comrades.

Forster *sits down and mops his brow.* **Cavafy** *solicitously gives him a glass of water.*

Forster I . . . (*He becomes hysterical and laughs in a high-pitched way. This goes on for some time and* **Cavafy** *stares at him.*)

Cavafy (*confidentially to the audience*) A possibly first-rate author hysterical in my flat. How alarming.

Forster (*struggling to recover his composure*) I . . . tried the wrong door.

Cavafy (*a little acidly*) You mean downstairs.

Forster Downstairs. I struck the door and it swung open.

Cavafy That sort of door generally does swing open. It's in the nature of their business.

Forster I simply stood there looking in. At the girls. And the formidable woman in charge who started bearing down on me like a Dreadnought. I was terrified. (*He giggles.*) I'm most awfully sorry. Shouldn't I laugh?

Cavafy They are always very civil to me, the girls. They may be about the world's business, as some would say, but they bob their heads and give me little smiles.

Forster (*anxious not to appear prudish*) I didn't look contemptuously at them.

Cavafy (*melting a little because he would rather* **Forster** *hadn't discovered the nature of the trade carried on on the ground floor*) Up here is the spirit and down there (*He points to the floor.*) is the flesh.

Forster An instant elevation for me, it would appear. From the body up one flight of stairs to the soul.

Cavafy The two never have communion with each other in this modern world, alas. They make a joke about the name of the street, the Rue Lepsius. They call it the Rue Clapsius. The girls, poor things, have to give themselves to monsters. Nightly. Daily. Though sometimes I have stood on my balcony and seen angels entering that dark doorway. Angels.

Forster It's quite a dear little street, I thought as I walked along.

Cavafy The admirable English tact. Your drink, my dear Forster. (*He goes over to the drinks table.*) Whiskey, ouzo, mastick?

Forster (*spotting the red glasses on the drinks table*) The celebrated red glasses!

Cavafy In what way, 'celebrated'?

Forster Oh dear. I have heard it said . . .

Cavafy You have heard gossip about me. I *hate* to be the cause of gossip.

Forster Oh dear.

Cavafy What have you heard said, please?

Forster That, that you bring out the red glasses only for . . .

Cavafy Only for special friends and honoured guests like you my dear Forster. It's perfectly true. (*They both laugh.*) So what will you choose to drink?

Forster A thimbleful of whiskey, please.

Cavafy Your famous English tact and reticence. I was a British subject for many years, you know. (*He looks questioningly at* **Forster** *who looks awkward and does not reply.*) *Did* you know? (**Forster** *makes a vague gesture.*) Ah, you daren't say, 'Yes,' because it might show that you have been engaged in *more* gossip about me. I'm sorry. I'm being abominably cruel, aren't I? (*He hands* **Forster** *a red glass of whiskey and a plate of Greek mezethes.*) Drink up. Nibble. I spent part of my boyhood in Liverpool and Bayswater.

Forster I feel positively that I ought to slip my handkerchief over my face when you mention these details so that you can't see my expression and whether it's one of, 'I knew that all along, but I must pretend at all costs that I didn't'.

Cavafy Liverpool is like Alexandria in many ways. Water and trade. Great ships.

Forster Brigantines and coasters.

Cavafy (*pointedly*) *Imperial* galleys.

Forster I know Bayswater. The Bayswater bassinets. Nursey pushing her little treasure through Kensington Gardens.

Cavafy My mother was in love with Kensington Gardens. She always inspected all the babies on display.

Forster Little boy babies in petticoats.

Cavafy A peculiarly British custom.

Forster Nursey should never have allowed it. (*Shuddering at the memory.*) There are people alive who remember me in petticoats.

Cavafy There are people alive who observe and remember too many things. I endeavour to slip out of their field of vision whenever I can.

Forster Thousands of ruined Englishmen have been driven abroad by the memory of their petticoats.

Cavafy And I always imagined it was the Union Jack they were waving. Henceforward I shall regard empire builders in an entirely new light.

Forster Childhood and upbringing have a lot to answer for. My mother dressed me girlishly until I was at least five.

Cavafy And my mother yearned for a daughter. All the time she was carrying me, she called her unborn child 'Helen'. Saints Helen and Constantine share name days, but I wouldn't want you to call me Nellie.

Forster We're a couple of weedy specimens aren't we, honestly? A friend of mine once pointed out that I often stand with one foot off the ground and hooked behind the other leg. Like a sort of linen corkscrew. Sometimes I wish I was the sort of person who stands with both feet indisputably on the ground and his jaw jutting forwards.

Cavafy   Leading with your chin.

Forster   Alas, I have no chin.

Cavafy   I solemnly undertake not to patronize your chin as you have not patronized my mis-use of English idiom. I am even accused of speaking Greek with an English accent.

Forster   How . . . quaint.

Cavafy   So, how do you find the Egyptians?

Forster   Generally brown.

Cavafy   Are they *nice* brown people?

Forster   In my limited experience of people anywhere, I have found that brown people are often to be preferred.

Cavafy   You have travelled to India. I have *never* been in the house of an Egyptian.

Forster   You surprise me.

Cavafy   I have never been invited and never sought to be invited. That is a fact, not quite a policy. Perhaps you have not been in Alexandria long enough to see how all the races practise a kind of incest. The Greeks were invited by Mohammed Ali after 1830 to trade, not to commingle. We have our own hospital at the end of this street and the church which buries us across the way. The Egyptians *are* modern Egypt and we Greeks are a necessary change purse they carry.

Forster   Not to mention the presence of the British. Let us *not* mention the British! But here I am on your divan, sipping your whisky and eating my Greek titbits and I have not said what a delight I found the folder of poems you sent me.

Cavafy   Ah, 'delight'. How would you explain the word 'delight' to a man who had not experienced it?

Forster   I might explain that once I thought Alexandria dull and provincial and given over entirely to commerce, but encountering the poetry of Mr Cavafy transfigured it.

Cavafy   It *is* dull and provincial and given over to cotton and wheat. You were quite right.

Forster   When I think of you every day polishing a line or selecting a vignette from history – if you only knew how envious I feel. I have written my novels, had my moment of esteem and now my inspiration has evaporated.

Cavafy   If *I* am at odds with the world or my ambitions, such as they are, I often sit and look at a volume of pictures. They can be very calming.

Forster   I am more likely to sit and fret.

Cavafy   Above all, never re-read old letters. (*Pause. A sad smile.*) I was out on my balcony all morning, trying to shake myself free of a sorrow in a letter written twenty years ago. I should never have opened it.

Forster   I ought to make a suitable subject for one of your poems, you know. A failed writer with a dry ink-well for a brain. You could describe me in the most pathetic terms. But, then again, why should you when you have the whole of the remarkable Classical World to sample.

Cavafy   No, no, no, my dear Forster. Not the *Classical* world. The Hellenistic one. Somewhat further East. South by South East of Antioch, you might say. The important figures of Athens or Thebes were too much like precocious English public schoolboys for me. Too sure of themselves, and lacking an understanding of the finer points of irony. They are also too well documented and leave nothing to a poet's imagination. I work from faces on coins and generally ignored footnotes.

Forster   Which of my novels did you like best?

Cavafy I think that I liked them all equally.

Forster (*laughing*) That could be the answer of someone who has never read a word of any of them.

Cavafy Or of someone who has read every word of all of them and likes them all equally. People are always sending me their books. Verses. So many verses.

Forster I have a collection of first novels. Young men commendably putting pen to paper and feeling I ought to be advised of the fact, as if my life would be incomplete without 27 semi-fictional sets of growing pains, generally in Oxbridge. Oh dear.

Cavafy Oxbridge. Clearly no brown people there.

Forster Markedly few. (*He recedes into the background, perhaps at the window.*)

Cavafy (*to the audience*) I gave him my best chair and drinks. How could I tell him that Caesarion the son of Cleopatra – also called Ptolemy the Sixteenth and put to death in 31 BC on the order of Octavian – had been running through my head all day and that I had to return to my writing table before he escaped from the poem. There was also exactly the right adjective to fit King Demetrius The Besieger 337–283 BC. I had been on its trail for three months. To be frustrated by my innate good manners! (*He returns to* **Forster**.)

Forster I have wondered whether, totally out of spite, I ought not to circulate this collection of first novels to all the young men who write them so that they can see how one set of growing pains is very much like another: a crush on an older prefect, intellectual liberation at university – they imagine – discovery of their real selves, finally, through love of the prefect's identical sister, and the achievement of serenity on the other side of the fire. It makes a hideous mirror. Volumes of autobiography masquerading as fiction ought to be burnt before their perpetrator's very eyes like a disembowelling.

Cavafy You are very harsh today.

Forster The sun makes me outrageous from time to time. In other people's first awkward steps one is reminded of one's own. At least these callow youths are still writing.

Cavafy (*to the audience*) An excellent fellow, but would he never go? I was beginning to have less confidence in my adjective by the minute. (*To* **Forster**.) I dread the idea of a stranger, undoubtedly someone unsympathetic to me in every way, writing my life's history, constructing a nonsensical idea of who I was from records of what I said or did. The truths are not in public actions I was forced to make, but in my poems. (*Frantic that he cannot get to his writing table.*) MY POEMS!

Forster The final line of my biography would read, 'He ran out of things to say'.

Cavafy You have not! I feel it in my Eastern bones. (*To the audience.*) A transparent subterfuge this, but would it work?

Forster Are they reliable, these Eastern bones of yours?

Cavafy They never fail. (*He takes some sheets of paper from a drawer.*) As one artist to another, I command you. By the shade of Alexander whose great tomb was pretty near this spot, I conjure you – GO HOME AND WRITE! Write of brown people, corn factors, the dark mystery of a Greek church. A story will come.

Forster You are a good friend, Cavafy, kicking my creative soul in its breeches. I salute you.

Cavafy (*aside*) Then salute me and go. (*To* **Forster**.) When we meet again, which cannot be soon enough, you shall read me these six pages and I shall sit and listen wonderingly.

Forster If I catch the first tram, I may reach my desk before your enthusiasm wears off me. (*Dramatically.*) Farewell! (*He leaves.*)

Cavafy (*calling after him*) Be sure to choose

the right door when you leave! Write a guide book if you can think of nothing else!

Cavafy *takes a deep breath and then rushes excitedly to his bindery table. He picks up a sheet of paper which contains his partly completed poem about Caesarion.*

Cavafy Caesarion! Caesarion! The vision is fading. I see you in . . . No I don't! My adjective! (*He throws down the piece of paper and picks up another. He reads the partly completed poem on it.*) 'When the Macedonians rejected him and stated plainly that they preferred Pyrrhus, King Demetrius took off his golden robes, tossed aside his purple boots and quickly dressed himself in . . . and quickly dressed himself in . . . My adjective! After three months of searching, I had it! King Demetrius dressed himself in . . . (*With enormous satisfaction as at last the words come to him.*) 'clothing of *unaccustomed* simplicity'. (*Triumphantly.*) Aha! (*He claps his hands.*)

Fanfare.

Blackout.

Act Two

With friends in a café, 1918. Cavafy is 55

A cheap café. Seated at a table are **Cavafy**'s *friends:* **Pericles Anastassiades,** *55, and two younger admirers in their twenties –* **Alexander Singopoulos** (**Cavafy**'s *heir and husband of his niece* **Rika**) *and* **Vassili.** *In front of them are glasses and a brandy bottle. They all appear despondent.*

Vassili What shall we tell Constantine?

Pericles The truth. He must hear the truth from us before any busybody whispers a distortion in his ear. He did not expect unqualified applause, in any case.

Alexander He won't mind that people walked out of the lecture. But the treachery of Vrisimitsakis is worthy of murder. I need coffee, not brandy.

Pericles We *all* need brandy. Constantine must not find us despondent.

Alexander Why did Vrisimitsakis try and spoil the lecture? He's a madman. I forbid anyone to mention his name in my presence.

Pericles (*patting his arm*) Drink up. You'll be asking the arch demon – you see, I haven't mentioned his name – to fight a duel with you next.

Alexander I will!

Vassili I thought you sounded impassioned up there on the stage. Many people were nodding their heads. Really.

Pericles Perhaps you ought to publish a pamphlet about 'the offending gentleman', deriding his small-minded envy and his capacity for playing silly tricks. It wasn't the exuberance of youth, it was . . .

Alexander Madness, as I said. I could kick him from here to Cairo.

Vassili We'll all kick him. Shave his head

and chain him naked to the doors of the railway station.

Enter **Cavafy** *looking for his friends' table. He catches their eyes and they look uncomfortable. He walks over to their table and they stand and applaud him.* **Alexander** *rushes to pull a chair from underneath the table for him.* **Cavafy** *stands and surveys them, obviously drawing conclusions. Then he sits down with both hands on his cane.*

Cavafy I appear to have burst in upon the funeral of my poetic ambitions, such as they are. Shall I sit here and imagine the worst or will a kind friend scatter light on my ignorance?

Vassili Alexander delivered the lecture with great passion. People were nodding their heads.

Cavafy Perhaps they were ill. The weather has certainly made *me* feel odd.

Vassili He drew himself up, put his elbow on the lectern and said, 'Ladies and gentlemen, this may be the first time you have attended a public lecture on the poetry of Mr Constantine Cavafy, but hereafter it will surely be a weekly occurrence.' I shall remember it for ever.

Cavafy 'For ever'? How was the . . . *personal* content of the poems received?

Pericles Madame Tsimbouki and her daughter walked out.

Cavafy They are hippopotami. Mother and daughter alike. I have never heard of hippopotami having an ear for poetry. Slime and river weed are more to their liking.

Alexander Others followed their lead.

Cavafy Lesser hippopotami. Were there people left in the Club by the end of the lecture? It was a good lecture. I could almost have written it myself. (*Turning confidentially to the audience.*) I *did* write it myself.

Pericles As a gesture, it probably worked. You, I mean the lecture, stated your case and, I am sure, created interest. There was,

unfortunately, a disgusting act of personal treachery earlier on in the evening which will distress you.

Alexander Vrisimitsakis . . .

Pericles (*interrupting him*) Have some brandy, Constantine, before you hear the story. (*He pours brandy for* **Cavafy**.)

Alexander Vrisimitsakis and some cronies tricked me into a bar about an hour before the lecture. I thought they were simply wishing me well or genuinely trying to help me steady my nerve. I'm not used to addressing crowds. But don't think I was drunk. I was still clear-headed enough to address a parliament. Then they called a cab and asked for The Ptolemy Club. While I was straightening my tie, they whispered alternative instructions to the driver. He whipped his horse and, before I knew it, we were roaring hell-for-leather out of town. When I noticed the wrong scenery, I jumped out and ran to the club. I'm afraid I was late and a little short of breath.

Vassili Not during the lecture. You had the lungs of a whale.

Alexander Are you angry with me?

They gaze at **Cavafy** *who is preoccupied.*

Cavafy Any friend who runs across town (*Slightly pointedly.*), full of drink, for me is a true friend. I am not at all angry with you, Alexander. I was wondering how I could recover my poems from Vrisimitsakis. In the circumstances, I would rather that nothing of mine were in his possession.

Vassili Alexander was impassioned. I've done that word to death, haven't I? (*To himself.*) Have a drink.

Pericles Shall we change the subject now?

Cavafy I am not so sensitive, my dear Pericles. Alexander, tell me, did you end the lecture with a reading of *Candles*?

Alexander I did.

Cavafy I hope it wasn't too 'impassioned'.

(*He looks meaningfully at* **Vassili**.) You should have tried to end on a note of barely restrained anxiety. Our past *is* a line of snuffed candles. What has struck me as poignant, I should like to strike other people as poignant too.

Vassili I have been reading Dante. In translation. What do you think of my writing an article which shows once and for all how he has influenced all other writers?

Pericles I doubt whether he influenced Sophocles or Euripides (*He notices* **Cavafy** *looking a little coldly*.) or Constantine Cavafy.

Cavafy Vassili, my dear enthusiastic, not to say impassioned young man. Every generation produces a pyramid of writings about Dante. Your little article, I regret to say, would become lost in the pile. I have a more practical notion. Why not put pen to paper about a certain Alexandrian poet called Constantine Cavafy? If Alexander here can stand up in front of a thousand people and deliver a lecture, surely you can produce a short monograph. A brilliant and perceptive one, I am sure. You would be given every assistance. Just think. If Mr Cavafy's present reputation is built on the shifting sands of the Egyptian desert, then your monograph will slip into oblivion too. But if Mr Cavafy is afforded a golden chair on the slopes of Parnassus, you, as the author of an early study, will gain a great reputation. *You* spotted him first.

Vassili I see your point.

Cavafy Pericles, you are a friend of long, long standing, so I shall forgive you that disapproving expression.

Pericles It doesn't hurt a young man to swim around in Dante for a bit.

Cavafy Particularly in the Third Circle.

Stephanos *and his empty-headed new friend* **Dimitris** *appear at the edge of the stage.*

Alexander Here's Stephanos and a stranger.

Cavafy *has his back to* **Stephanos** *who is looking around the café for his friends.* **Vassili** *waves.*

Cavafy I don't know this stranger, do I? (*He stiffens his back and looks at his watch and is clearly thinking of leaving.*)

Pericles I don't expect so.

Stephanos *and* **Dimitris** *reach the table.* **Stephanos** *shakes* **Cavafy**'*s hand.*

Stephanos (*in a tone of encouragement mixed with commiseration*) We were at the lecture. (*Pointing to* **Cavafy**.) Mr Constantine Cavafy, this is my friend Dimitris Cacoyannis.

Cavafy *stands up and very formally offers* **Dimitris** *his hand.* **Dimitris** *seizes it with an extravagant gesture which takes* **Cavafy** *aback.*

Stephanos (*by way of explanation*) He's an actor.

Cavafy Ah. So you were at the lecture.

Dimitris (*enthusiastically*) Yes.

Cavafy Somewhat duller than your own theatrical performances, I should imagine.

Dimitris I wouldn't say that.

Cavafy The exit of the hippopotami probably livened up matters. And there was the attempted abduction of the speaker too, I have been told.

Stephanos We're late because I wanted to find someone to take an abusive message to Vrisimitsakis.

Cavafy What would I do without my loyal young friends?

Stephanos Dimitris suggested some very colourful turns of phrase.

Cavafy Then I shall shake his hand again. (*He does so.*) Please, Mr Cacoyannis, let us not stand here stiff and formal when you have sprung to the defence of a poor poet. (*He makes a gesture for* **Stephanos** *and* **Dimitris** *to sit down.*)

Dimitris (*clearly having been primed by*

Stephanos *and anxious to perform well for his friend*) But you are the famous poet who gave us *Ithaca* and *Candles*. (*He luxuriates in the sounds of the titles of the poems.*)

Cavafy Stephanos, your friend would enjoy a glass of brandy, I am sure.

Vassili *is about to pour the brandy, but* **Dimitris***'s faux pas makes him not bother.*

Dimitris And *Waiting for the Heathens*.

Cavafy I beg your pardon?

Alexander *and* **Vassili** *snigger helplessly.*

Dimitris How could I forget, *Waiting for the Heathens*?

Cavafy (*icily*) I do not believe I am familiar with that poem.

Dimitris *is puzzled and looks questioningly at* **Stephanos** *who is embarrassed and annoyed.*

Stephanos Dimitris means your poem, *Waiting for the Barbarians*, of course. He tends to confuse titles.

Cavafy I hope he doesn't confuse the lines of plays too. That could be a considerable disadvantage for an actor.

Cavafy *looks at his watch. He has realised that* **Dimitris** *has probably not read a word of his poems.*

Dimitris Actually, I'm thinking of not being an actor any more. Such an unsettled profession. I have a distant uncle who could find me a permanent job. He deals in currants.

Cavafy So, you are thinking of going to Susa?

Dimitris No. He doesn't have an office there. In fact, I've never heard of the place.

Cavafy I wondered whether you would spot the reference. I paraphrased a line from one of my poems you *haven't* read. Though it's almost as well known as *Waiting for the Heathens*.

Vassili (*enthusiastically*) It's from a wonderful poem called *The Satrapy*, about a young man with artistic leanings who dreams more than anything of being accepted as a poet, but feels it would be safer to go to Susa and be a tedious bureaucrat than starve for his poetry.

Pericles Well done. Susa was the capital of the Persian Empire. The young man is imagined as having lived in the fifth-century, before Christ.

Cavafy Susa was one of *five* capitals of the Achaemenian dynasty. Susa. (*He speaks the name very slowly and stares into the distance. He is obviously about to launch into a performance.*) Ancient capital of the Elamites, whose territories were the southwesterly tip of Mesopotamia, Susa became, together with Babylon, Ecbatana, Pasargadae and Persepolis one of the five capitals of the Persian Empire . . .

Dimitris Mm.

The others glare fiercely at **Dimitris**.

Cavafy And the immense building programme undertaken there by Daryush with cedarwood from Lebanon, gold from Sardis and Bactria, turquoise from Chorasmia, silver and ebony from Egypt, lapis lazuli and cornelian from Sogdiana, ivory from Ethiopia and stone from Elam itself, was justly famous throughout an empire that extended to the Jaxartes, the Nile, the Indus and, less permanently, the Danube.

Dimitris Why, that was all one sentence! Do we applaud?

Stephanos (*hideously mortified*) No!

Cavafy How much more satisfying to be a poet than to count currants in Susa. (*Rising.*) Gentlemen, I am in my 55th year and the figure of Caesarion has been standing just out of my vision all day. I feel that if I sit by candlelight at home he may appear before me and bring about the completion of a poem dedicated to him.

Dimitris (*sincerely*) Give him my regards.

Stephanos *is further embarrassed by this remark.*

Cavafy I am sure he will thank you heartily for your good wishes. (*He raises his hat and leaves.*)

Stephanos (*angrily to* **Dimitris** *who is, gauchely, mostly unaware of his social blunders*) How could you get the name of the poem wrong!

Vassili (*to* **Alexander**) *Waiting for the Gypsies* wasn't it?

Alexander No, silly, *Waiting for the Camel Drivers*.

Vassili I'm sorry. (*Clearly aiming the remark at* **Dimitris**.) I thought it was *Waiting for the Eunuchs*. (*They laugh hysterically*.)

Pericles (*finding their humour tedious*) When I was young, was I *this* young?

Blackout.

Cavafy back at his bindery table, aged 54

The lights go up once more on **Cavafy**. *He points to the folders of poems as he speaks to the audience.*

Cavafy (*confidentially to the audience*) You see, I have to be very careful to whom I send these folders. I know where each poem is in case I suddenly lose faith in it and don't want the world to judge me by it. Alexandrians are so nosey. If I'm sending work abroad, or to an eminent person, I send it to one of their friends by one of *my* friends. Imagine having my correspondence chatted about at the Post Office. There's a little outpost of Susa if you like.

(*He changes his tone.*) Some days, all day long, I swore that when evening came I would sit on my divan cutting the pages of a new book or helping Paul to mend his grey silk waistcoat. I took a sheet of paper and wrote in large letters, 'I swear I won't do *that* again.' (*The* **Young Man** *appears in a pool of dim light at one side of the stage with his back to the audience and*

smoking a cigarette.) Then, as it grew dark, the power of the night made me drop the book with its uncut pages. It whispered such sweet counsel in my ear. My body agreed with every insistent word.

The lights go down on the table and up on the next scene which is a cheap, poorly furnished bedroom. The scene could have happened to **Cavafy** *at any time during his middle-age and the audience do not need, nor are they given, a precise age for him. It can be imagined as happening in 1903, when* **Cavafy** *was 40, as a large number of the erotic poems date from about this period.*

Cavafy's experience of love

A rented room in a backstreet. The furniture consists of a bed with its head towards the audience and a nearby chair. **Cavafy** *sits on the chair watching the* **Young Man** *in his late twenties undressing.*

Cavafy I have seen you about the city. The young man in the cinnamon-brown suit.

Young Man It's my only suit. You've seen *it* each time you've seen me then.

Cavafy It's a fine suit. Cinnamon-brown. You know that the scents from the Spice Islands blew out to sea and bewitched the Portuguese explorers?

The **Young Man** *looks puzzled.*

I was going to make a comparison between the cinnamon-brown suit and the young man in it. Sweet and . . .

Young Man Well, it's my only suit.

Cavafy 'Lulling.' That's the right word.

Young Man I've seen you in cafés and places.

Cavafy Oh, 'Places'. We all end up in 'Places'. Tonight I thought, 'He could be an artist.'

Young Man Me?

Cavafy The colour of your tie. The way you had it knotted under your collar.

Young Man (*in pleasurable and amused disbelief that he could be thought to be an artist*) Me? When could I afford to be an artist?

Cavafy When could I?

Young Man That doesn't mean I'm a... (*He refuses to say the word 'prostitute'.*)

Cavafy Not a...I know.

Young Man All this talk. Does it mean you're not going to pay me? I need to be paid. I'm not a...But I need to be paid.

Cavafy I am conversant with the routine of these...transactions. Don't be alarmed. I'll pay you. I might even pay you beforehand and then you'd be free to leap out of the door.

Young Man (*removing his shirt*) I just wanted to be sure. You can pay me afterwards. All this talking. Why don't you touch me? I want you to. I'm not like them.

Cavafy *embraces him. They kiss.* **Cavafy** *runs his fingers through the* **Young Man**'s *hair. He stands holding a lock of the* **Young Man**'s *hair and looking into his eyes. The* **Young Man** *is puzzled.*

Young Man Are you checking to see if I'm cross-eyed?

Cavafy This hair could have been lifted by an ancient sea wind. Let me show you something.

Cavafy *takes what appear to be photographs out of his inside jacket pocket and shows them to the* **Young Man** *who looks disapproving.*

Young Man I don't like pictures like this. I don't need them. It was my choice to come.

Cavafy Yes, your 'choice'. Thank you. (*Pointing to one of the apparent photographs.*) You could have stolen his hair.

Young Man (*tetchily and not really looking at the photograph*) Who is he? I haven't seen him around. Where's he put his arm?

Cavafy (*amused*) It's a somewhat trimmed and crumpled postcard of a statue in the Museum. He's not a living rival. He hasn't been alive for a long time. He's you two thousand years ago. Here and here. (*He runs his fingers over the* **Young Man**'s *chest and down to his belt. The* **Young Man** *holds* **Cavafy**'s *hand on his stomach and looks strongly at him as if to say, 'I have power over you'.*) Yes, you *do* exert power. Don't you think the sculptor caught the curve of the belly phenomenally well? As for the arm. It was knocked off back there in history. Go and make his acquaintance. Room 16 in the Museum.

Young Man Maybe.

The **Young Man** *sits down on the end of the bed facing the audience and begins to remove his shoes.* **Cavafy** *goes over and picks up the suit jacket which the man has carelessly thrown on the bed behind him. When the* **Young Man** *sees what* **Cavafy** *is doing, he reacts angrily.*

Hands off! (*He snatches the jacket.*)

Cavafy (*startled at first, but then realizing why the* **Young Man** *is alarmed*) I was putting your jacket away so that it doesn't crease. (*The* **Young Man** *still clings to the jacket and glowers.*) You are several times stronger than I am. How could I hope to pick the pockets? (*Pause. Eventually the* **Young Man** *releases the jacket.*) Look, I brush the sleeves, shake it to expel the creases at the elbows and then I hang it over the back of this chair with the shoulders gathered slightly to take the weight. So.

Young Man Have I got to take you for my valet? (*He pronounces the final 't'.*)

Cavafy (*with an exaggeratedly correct pronunciation*) For your valet. (*Coolly.*) No.

The **Young Man** *removes his socks.*

Cavafy (*more warmly now*) You looked hypnotized tonight.

Young Man I wasn't drunk. I'm not drunk now. A few brandies in a café, that's all.

Cavafy A coffee or two, with some backgammon and small bets.

Young Man (*smiling*) Are you writing my life history?

Cavafy I watch the world as it . . .

Young Man As it what?

Cavafy Oh, as it slips into the night, having had seductive words whispered in its ear. You looked five years younger than I think you probably are and hypnotized with pleasure, with love.

Young Man Pleasure I can give you. Not love. I don't like it when the conversation gets round to love.

Cavafy I never decry the wonders of the pleasures of the body. The discovery of pleasure is as important in life as being born itself. When you are young and surrounded by the family who want you to be good, you timidly imagine what it would be like if your whole body burned with these sensations that parts of you are beginning to recognize. Then, suddenly, you are old enough to stay out. Your family think, 'Boys will be boys.' But it's boys *having* boys!

Young Man (*laughing*) You know a lot about all this, don't you?

Cavafy Or boys saying 'No' all evening long and then standing outside a lighted tobacco shop window pretending to be interested in pipes and saying, 'Yes, I will accompany you' to a somewhat older boy who is equally uninterested in pipes, but who happens to be standing next to you in front of the same dull tobacco shop window.

Young Man A somewhat older boy who's afraid my jacket will crease and who makes my head spin with his talking, talking, talking.

Cavafy You make me expansive. There is a tide in the affairs of all men, you know. I mean that we all have a prime, a time when we flower. You *must* have been loved or in love.

Young Man Why don't you undress instead of asking the wrong questions?

Cavafy Was there, or is there, a lover?

Young Man Stop! I'll begin it for you. (*He gets up and stands in front of* **Cavafy** *and undoes some of his waistcoat buttons.*) He's an old story now, in any case.

Cavafy Share him with me.

Young Man 'Share'?

Cavafy Tell me about him. People can find it very irritating when I try to burden my every word with significance. I meant tell me about the person you chose to be special.

Young Man I shall soon be so tired I'll fall asleep standing in my bare feet in the middle of the room.

Cavafy I'll run that risk. Look, I'm taking off my jacket. (*He makes a great show of shaking and brushing his jacket before hanging it over the back of the chair on top of the* **Young Man**'*s.*)

Young Man (*resigned to telling his story*) Where do you think we met?

Cavafy You wouldn't ask the question if it were somewhere ordinary. (*With sudden inspiration.*) You met at his wedding!

Young Man (*laughing*) It was in the days before I'd given up office work.

Cavafy Your body rebelled against it.

Young Man It wasn't right for me. You work in an office, don't you?

Cavafy (*a little pretentiously*) Sometimes I help my brother at the Stock Exchange.

Young Man That sounds a bit grander.

Cavafy But you're right. I'm pale with office work. You're putting more fire in me, even though it might not show.

Young Man I was walking home, or somewhere, along the Rue . . . (*He chooses not to finish the name.*) There are small shops with cheap goods. I often stand in front of shop windows, thinking, not really staring at what's for sale. I'm that type.

Cavafy Looking into shop windows, tobacconists' windows, for example, can be very rewarding.

Young Man This shop wasn't anything in particular. It was a this and that shop, selling trash to working boys. You know – cigarette cases that fall apart when you try to put the first cigarette in them, and handkerchieves. That's when I saw him at the end of the counter emptying a box of handkerchieves.

Cavafy And you went in.

Young Man I went in and asked to see a lemon handkerchief to match this suit.

Cavafy Lemon?

Young Man He knew I didn't want a handkerchief, lemon or olive or sky blue. His boss was sitting at the back of the shop making lists.

Cavafy So you had to abandon him?

Young Man Not me! I was a stranger. I wasn't going to leave him till the boss pushed his hand in the middle of my back. I asked about the quality of the handkerchieves. If they were silky to touch. 'I don't mind you touching,' he said. The words almost choked me, but I found question after question. Running my hand through the box of handkerchieves and catching his fingers. We were both choking at the thought of what we wanted from each other.

Cavafy While the boss made his lists.

Young Man I'll show you.

Cavafy What?

Young Man Come here. I'll show you. Do you have a handkerchief?

Cavafy (*puzzled*) Yes.

Young Man Well, give it to me then. It's bound to be cleaner than mine. This (*Meaning the bed.*) is the counter with the box of handkerchieves. You're that side, being him, and I'm this side, being me. (*They kneel on either side of the bed.*) I say, 'I want to see a lemon handkerchief.' (*He spreads out the handkerchief on the bed between them.* **Cavafy** *remains silent, uncertain how to play the game.*) Well? Say something.

Cavafy So you want a lemon handkerchief, sir.

Young Man (*exasperated at* **Cavafy**'s *lack of imagination*) I'm glad *he* had more life than that. (*He pauses, overcome by his memories.*) 'More life.' More idea how to play the game. I examine the handkerchief. (*He picks at the handkerchief on the bed.*) Keep your hands there! (*He takes hold of* **Cavafy**'s *hands and makes sure that they are fully under the handkerchief.*) I brush against *your* hands and then you say something and hook your fingers in *mine*.

As they speak the following few lines, they intertwine their hands above and below the handkerchief. **Cavafy** *begins to giggle.*

Cavafy You must have a *look* at the hem.

Young Man These stitches *feel* as if they're coming undone.

Cavafy If you *pull* them, they don't come undone.

Young Man I'll try them and see.

Cavafy (*shocked and delighted by his double entendre*) *Feel* the way it doesn't wrinkle. (*They giggle helplessly, their hands still intertwined.*)

Young Man I'll have a look at these others.

Cavafy (*coming out of character and removing his hands*) There aren't any others.

Young Man This *one* handkerchief has to stand for a whole box of the bloody things! Oh blow your nose with it! (*He stands up.*) You really enter into the spirit of things, don't you? Now I put the handkerchief in my pocket and I keep it.

Cavafy *remains kneeling and looks up at him aghast.*

Young Man You thought I meant that, didn't you!

Cavafy (*distressed and unsure what to say*) No, I . . .

Young Man (*angrily*) You think I'm the sort

who fills his pockets with every cheap thing he sees. Boys like me *are* allowed to tease people from time to time. Who are you to think I can't afford a sense of humour! (*He holds the handkerchief in his clenched fist near* **Cavafy**'*s face. There is a moment of unpleasant tension. The evening may have come to an end.* **Cavafy** *looks distraught. Finally the* **Young Man** *relents. He unfolds the handkerchief and carefully places it on* **Cavafy**'*s head.*) Now you can wear it in the English way as a punishment.

They both laugh with relief now that the unpleasantness is over. **Cavafy** *duly keeps the handkerchief on his head until told to take it off a little later. The* **Young Man** *sits on the bed.* **Cavafy** *remains kneeling.*

Young Man   Where was I in the story? Suddenly the boss bawled from the back of the shop, 'Evangele, speak up when you're answering the customer! Don't be surly.'

Cavafy   Which colour handkerchief did you choose in the end? Was there a scarlet one?

Young Man   I didn't have any money.

Cavafy   Surly Evangele appeared to have lost a customer, then.

Young Man   You mustn't try and share the joke. Sorry. Now that he's gone.

Cavafy   I would have waited in an alleyway all night for him to lock up the shop.

Young Man   You'd have been waiting alongside me, then. I didn't mean to reveal his name.

Cavafy   I've forgotten it already.

Young Man   We had a routine. He'd go from the shop to a café and wait while I did *my* work.

Cavafy   I thought you were trying to tell me you were devoted to each other.

Young Man (*tersely*)   I played cards for money. I didn't like him to watch because it put me off. He'd wait in another café making

a brandy or a coffee last an hour. Reading the papers three times. If I won, we'd have expensive drinks, many, many of them, and then find a clean bedroom. If I didn't win, there were no expensive drinks, but love can lie down anywhere.

Cavafy (*anxious to know more of the story, but not wishing to offend*)   Does he . . . ?

Young Man   Once he left me. His wages had been reduced and I had lost all my luck at cards. 'We'll have to part,' he said. 'When we're absolutely broke like this, life has nothing to offer us.' The despair had got to him. It takes all of us backstreet Greek boys at some time. He'd been writing to some fourteenth cousins in Canada, but they never answered. 'It's no good,' he said. 'We can't afford to go out with each other.' Things had got that bad after my months of bad luck. 'Anyway,' he said, 'someone else is after me. He's promised me two decent suits. And other things.' Evangele was right. I hadn't been able to afford 'other things' for so long. But I put myself through hell getting twenty pounds to win him back. The other man was a bastard. He lied about the suits and only gave Evangele some shoes when he begged and begged. It wasn't the twenty pounds he wanted. He wanted those nights we spent pressed close together. I wish his cousins in Canada had taken trouble with him. I wouldn't have seen him again, but he'd have been alive. (**Cavafy** *is distressed to learn that the friend is dead.*) Egypt killed him. If love doesn't wear you out, this climate does. And the work. We knew of a boy who was so exhausted he didn't notice the mice eating two of his toes as he slept on a pile of sacks.

Cavafy   His toes!

Young Man   You're from a better family. It can't happen to you. Your sort can bribe a servant to ruffle your clean bed and then you slip back there when you've done with us. But the poor boys, the beautiful poor boys. Like blossoms till they're twenty-five and then we bury them. Into the dirt of Alexandria they go. I've ached for so many who now stink. You're a few years older than 25, aren't you?

Cavafy Does it matter?

Young Man No.

Cavafy You're nearly asleep on your feet. Soon you won't notice an older man's caresses.

Young Man You don't need to feel that! I could leap out of the door as you said. I'm here because I said I wanted to come. And take that bloody handkerchief off your head. There's enough humiliation in the world without begging for it. (**Cavafy** *removes the handkerchief and nervously screws it up and puts it in his pocket. The* **Young Man** *has a sudden amusing thought.*) One of the rooms we used to go to has been turned into the office of a very respectable grain merchant.

Cavafy If only the merchant knew.

Young Man Those nights. He must still be able to smell us.

Cavafy An inexplicable whiff of cinnamon, that's all.

Young Man You and your bloody cinnamon. If you don't stop going on about my suit, I'll walk home in my underpants. (*More gently.*) I'll stay till late.

Cavafy I hoped you would.

Young Man But ...

Cavafy But what?

Young Man Let's not leave together.

Cavafy My policy always.

Young Man It's not that I'm ashamed. Of either of us. We all like to pretend we don't have the reputation we deserve. I like walking out of a building alone, my own man. Can you understand that?

Cavafy Why shouldn't we hold our heads up?

The **Young Man** *removes his trousers and holds them out to* **Cavafy.**

Young Man Valet (*The pronunciation is correct this time.*), remove the creases in my cinnamon trousers. Do you mind me joking like that?

Cavafy No. I'll steam press them with my breath.

The **Young Man** *is standing in his baggy, darned underwear. He looks down at it.*

Young Man I won't be walking home in my underwear after all. You can see all the darns, can't you?

Cavafy Not from here.

Young Man Yes you can. They look like scars. But it's clean.

The **Young Man** *slips off his underpants and leaves them on the floor. He gets into bed with his head towards the audience and pulls the coverlet half over him. He turns on his side as if to sleep.* **Cavafy** *stands clutching the cinnamon trousers, watching him.*

Cavafy (*quietly out to the audience*) I weep for beauty. Unashamedly.

Blackout.

A street, 1928. Cavafy is 65

A bare stage except for the bed which is pushed to the back and used for **Sarpedon** *to fall dead on.* **Cavafy** *is now a little hunched and decrepit. He should sound wheezy. Having walked off the set at the end of the last scene, he now walks on again in an old raincoat and hat carrying a cane. The clothes could have been on the hatstand at the side of The Bindery as could the four lengths of silk worn by Cleopatra's children and the fallen emperor.* **Cavafy** *is brightly lit, whereas the rest of the stage is dim.* **Stephanos, Pericles** *and* **Dimitris** *take up unobtrusive positions at the back of the stage. They are dressed as for the café scene but without jackets. We should no longer think of them as having the characters of* **Cavafy**'s *friends.* **Alexander** *and* **Vassili,** *also dressed as for the café scene but jacketless, walk across the stage and jostle* **Cavafy** *without apologizing. They laugh at him and then* *take up positions at the back of the stage. All five actors have their backs to the audience.* **Cavafy** *takes off his hat very ceremoniously to the young men who laughed at him.*

Cavafy   Angels.

Cavafy *walks slowly across the stage and then he notices a figure across the street in the direction of the audience. The figure is to be imagined by the audience.* **Cavafy** *waves his cane to attract the person's attention.*

Cavafy   Mr Lazaridis! Mr Lazaridis! It's Cavafy. What a fortunate meeting. You were wrong about that little historical matter, just as I said you were. (*He walks to the front of the stage to be close to the person.*) Since our discussion when you thought you had got the better of me, I have been busy with my researches. The Empress Zoë, most incontrovertibly, was *not* murdered by her lover Romanus Lecapenus. Shaved bald and shut up in a cloister, yes, but he allowed her life its natural term. No, I insist Mr Lazaridis. I will not be interrupted. Two waiting women made her kneel over a footstool and drew blood as they clipped her hair, but she was not killed. (*He begins to raise his voice querulously.*) Humbled, pummelled, made abject, but not executed. I insist. (*Raising his voice very loud.*) I insist! What's that? Ah, such a shame. I am going in exactly the opposite direction. (*He raises his hat and bows his head. We are to assume that the other man has left.* **Cavafy** *stands watching him, his hat still raised.*)

Cavafy   I raise my hat to you in triumph. Obstinate old man. He's the type I find unbearable.

A female voice is heard over the tannoy.

Voice   Mr Cavafy insists on calling himself 'Middle-aged'. He also frizzes his hair.

Cavafy *touches his face and appears a little self-conscious.*

Voice   He is also believed to dye his hair.

Cavafy (*confidentially to the audience*)   I use a

recipe of my own invention. Oh no, I couldn't possibly give away the secret.

Voice   I find him a disgusting old man.

Cavafy *storms to the front of the stage waving his stick furiously. He then removes his coat and hat and for the rest of the play he reverts to the 54-year-old narrator who has been our guide. There should be a change in his tone and manner to show this.*

Cavafy   A long time ago I asked you to imagine ancient walls. But beware the walls of the heart. The kind you often start building when young. At the suggestion of others. Other people's walls around your heart. That little muscle that beats away here in its tomb beneath your shirt. To the left of the (*He counts the buttons down from the neck.*) third button. It scrapes itself against the stonework others have kindly helped you build. And, as you grow older, the stones grow mouldier. Your epitaph appears, stretching from the third button to the fourth. 'Constantine Cavafy. Here lies the man he dare not be.' *I* daren't come out, but I shall permit you to look in. It's a strange world in here, isn't it? (*He gestures to the dimly lit figures at the back of the stage.*) My poetic concoctions swell from the walls and pass through them like the ghosts they are.

Throughout the rest of this scene, various characters from **Cavafy**'s *poems appear. They are played by his friends, in the clothes they wore in previous scenes, but we should not think of them as actually being his friends. All play several characters.*

Cavafy   No one sees himself as I see him. This is Demetrius Sotir, two centuries before Christ. (**Demetrius** *turns his face briefly to the audience and is spotlit.*) John Katakuzinos, Emperor of the Byzantines. (**John** *turns briefly and is spotlit.*) Ianthis, a Jewish scallywag. (**Ianthis** *turns briefly and is spotlit.*) All such a long time dead. I like to think of the gods themselves weeping at death, Man's eternal disaster.

The stage is suddenly brilliantly lit and we hear the very loud sound of horses neighing. **Horse One** *and* **Horse Two** *come to the front of the stage on* *either side of* **Cavafy.** *They paw the ground and raise and shake their heads with horse-like movements.* **Cavafy** *puts his hands on their shoulders.*

Cavafy What manner of horses are you?

Horse One Remarkable horses.

Horse Two Wonderful horses.

Cavafy From which green plain?

Horse One From no mere grass field.

Horse Two From a god's hand rather.

Horse One Zeus himself fashioned us.

Horse Two As a gift.

Horse One A wonderful gift.

Cavafy Who was worthy of such a gift?

Horse One Do not ask us to remember.

Horse Two Immortal horses should not know how to grieve.

Cavafy Do you grieve for a man's death?

Horse One A man.

Horse Two A beloved man. Patroclus the tent sharer of Achilles.

Horse One Drained of his blood through many wounds.

Horse Two The arms that stroked us are lifeless.

Horse One We do not care to remember.

Cavafy Poor wonderful horses.

The horses return to the back of the stage and stand either side of the bed. **Zeus** *gives a great bellow of grief (mimed to a tape).*

Cavafy Does Zeus himself weep for Patroclus?

Zeus Not for Patroclus! For Sarpedon my mortal son whom Patroclus killed.

Cavafy You are the king of the gods. Had you no power to keep your son alive?

Zeus There are laws greater than Olympus. The laws killed him. Look.

Sarpedon *enters with the cinnamon-coloured jacket of the* **Young Man** *slung loosely over his shoulder.*

Zeus Patroclus confronted him – a fury.

The taped sound of slashing. **Sarpedon** *mimes being the victim of a savage attack with a sword. He falls dead on the bed.*

Zeus The gashes were long and wide. My favourite child torn and dusty. Let Apollo bathe him.

Cavafy (*in great anguish*) Let me! (*He lays* **Sarpedon**'s *cinnamon jacket across his chest and closes his dead eyes.*)

Onlooker One Make free with perfumes.

Onlooker Two Robe him as if a god and bleach the skin.

Cavafy A pearl comb before his journey home to Lycia. (*He smooths* **Sarpedon**'s *hair. Change of tone. To the audience again.*) I travel widely for someone immured, you know. Lycia, Antioch, Jerusalem. Wherever you run, the walls are still there, still lurking behind the third button. Then again, why leave Alexandria herself? The city of philosophy, of Plotinus and Porphyry, of terribly important heresies – Arianism and Monophysism. Do you worry yourself to sleep wondering whether the Monothelists were right? Above all, it was the city of the Ptolemies . . .

Onlooker Two The people are flocking to the Gymnasium.

Onlooker Three They're being crowned . . .

Mad excitement on the stage. **Onlooker Three** *and* **Onlooker Two** *run from side to side jumping up and down from time to time as if trying to see something over the heads of a crowd. They bump into* **Cavafy.** *They repeat their lines three times, during which time* **Pericles, Vassili, Stephanos** *and the* **Young Man** *drape a length of silk across their chests.*

Cavafy Where . . . (*He is bumped in the back*

before he can finish.) Where ... (*He is bumped again.*) What *is* happening! (*To the audience.*) Someone is being crowned. I'll walk quickly and hope I'm not too late. It's my heart you see. The weight of the stone.

Onlooker Three and **Onlooker Two** *retire to the back of the stage.* **Ptolemy** and **Alexander,** *in their silks, come to the front of the stage and kneel down.*

Cavafy (*panting and with his hand on his heart. He points to* **Ptolemy** *and* **Alexander**) Cleopatra's children. She's always flaunting them in some shape or form. Alexander, what has she created you this time?

Alexander (*in a childish voice*) I am Alexander, son of Cleopatra, king of Armenia, Media and the fierce Parthians.

Cavafy Have they ever seen you in those places?

Alexander (*holding his self-important pose for a little while and then relaxing a little*) Of course not.

Cavafy Ptolemy, which part of the map of the world have they given to you?

Ptolemy (*in a childish voice*) I am Ptolemy, son of Cleopatra, king of Cilicia, Syria and Phoenicia.

Cavafy Seaside kingdoms, how nice. You could cruise back to see your family from time to time.

The **Young Man** (*as* **Caesarion**) *comes and stands behind* **Alexander** *and* **Ptolemy.** *He has a length of pink silk across his chest and there should be a trickle of blood from the corner of his mouth.*

Caesarion I am Caesarion, eldest son of Cleopatra and Julius Caesar the Roman.

Cavafy We hadn't forgotten you. How could we? In your pink silk, the hyacinths against your chest, that belt of amethysts and sapphires. (*The flowers and the jewels are to be imagined by the audience.*)

Ptolemy She's given him a *double* row of jewels.

Alexander With white ribbons and pink pearls on his shoes, he ought to look like a girl.

Ptolemy Only he doesn't.

Alexander I know. If *you* had pink pearls, the eunuchs would die laughing.

Ptolemy Who'd want to be king of the Parthians. They smell of cow fat.

Caesarion I am Caesarion. King of Kings.

Cavafy 'King of Kings', yes. (*To the audience.*) It was a beautiful warm afternoon. The Gymnasium was a remarkable building. Look at that statue for instance. (*He points into the air.*) Everyone loves a party. 'King of Kings.' *And nobody believed a word of it.* (*He wipes the blood trickle on* **Caesarion**'*s chin.*) Rome burst the brilliant bubble of the Ptolemies.

Alexander Why did mother let *him* have the best outfit?

Ptolemy You can see almost everything through it.

Alexander That's mother all over.

Ptolemy You can see through his pink silk *all over.*

Caesarion *looks very awkward and slowly places his crossed hands over his loins.* **Alexander** *and* **Ptolemy** *giggle.*

In stalks **Irene.** *She still wears her* **Haricleia** *'Queen Victoria' evening dress but is not thought of as actually being the poet's mother. She carries a Byzantine crown which she hands to* **Cavafy.**

Irene (*looking contemptuously at* **Caesarion**) Pink silk doesn't make a coronation! (*She removes* **Caesarion**'*s pink silk and drapes it around her own shoulders.*)

Cavafy Says the Empress Irene. Consort of John the Sixth, Katacuzinos, fourteenth century. (*He crowns* **Irene**.)

Irene My husband was a real emperor, not a 'King of Kings' with a double belt of amethysts and sapphires.

Caesarion *refuses to acknowledge that she is talking about him.*

Cavafy What she is trying to make clear is that when she and John were crowned, St Sophia's Cathedral was a ruin and there wasn't a penny left in the treasury for coronation robes.

Irene We wore glass. Simple robes hemmed with blue and green and red glass. It caught the light.

Cavafy Defiantly glass.

Irene We were no less royal.

Cavafy No, you were not.

Irene (*referring to* **Caesarion**) Look at him stripped. Nothing of *him* has come down through history.

Caesarion *begins to walk offstage.*

Cavafy My dreams of him.

Caesarion *looks back sadly at* **Cavafy** *and then exits.*

Irene I have an empire to rule.

Cavafy Don't let us keep you.

Irene I wanted to point out that there was more to us than a poignant use of paste jewellery.

Cavafy Naturally, but no one knows it any more.

Irene I will *not* be frozen by your lop-sided gaze.

Cavafy An artist's licence. *His* choice of the telling detail.

Irene We were still married in a palace.

Cavafy Wearing baubles that nowadays we might sew onto a lampshade. Do you know what I mean by the word 'lampshade'?

Irene Write about the love of my subjects. I will have them arrest you.

Cavafy Nothing about kings being successful, please. Leave that to official histories. I prefer failures, leave-takings, the moments when all dreams become dust. My mother was always very fond, now I recall, of a particular green lampshade decorated with squares of glass in the likeness of a feather. Eye-catching but vulgar.

Irene Poet! (*She storms off.*)

Cavafy Describe an empress and you release a dragon.

Dimitris *as the gauche man from Commagene comes to the front of the stage. His speech and manner should be very awkward.*

Man from Commagene I too am Greek!

Cavafy Oh dear, more noise. Sometimes they make my head whirl when they come at me from books.

Man from Commagene A thorough Hellene, I'll have you know.

Cavafy I'm sure.

Snob One (*now playing a language snob*) You have a very funny accent for a Greek.

Snob Two Notice how slowly he speaks. Terrified he'll commit some grammatical howler.

Snob One It's his vowels I find so offensive. Actually, I can't tell whether he's talking or hawking. Any moment now I expect him to gob on the street.

Snob Three Whereabouts in Greece do you come from?

Man from Commagene Nowhere in actual Greece.

Cavafy He means Greek in spirit, perhaps.

Man from Commagene Precisely. Greek in soul.

Snob One I can still only understand one word in three he says.

Snob Two The accent's as impenetrable as that little number I've been chasing for weeks.

Cavafy Where does this Greek soul of yours originate?

Man from Commagene Commagene.

Snob Three Commagene?

Snob Two Come again! (*They laugh at the pun.*)

Snob One It's a dump in Sicily.

Man from Commagene As a matter of fact, it lies to the North West of Syria. A Greek-speaking kingdom small in area but great in heart.

Snob Three Who would want to go there and drop off the edge of the Earth.

Cavafy With your uncouth accent and thin skin, so determined to be part of the Greek world. (*He affectionately straightens the **Man**'s tie.*)

Pericles *removes his length of silk and tiptoes offstage, perhaps to a slow drum beat. They all stare at him.*

Cavafy A toppled king slipping discreetly away, his feet pinched by rough, unaccustomed shoes. (*He emphasizes the adjective for which he had been searching in the **Forster** scene.*)

The lights go down. **Cavafy** *comes forward to talk to the audience. He is spotlit.*

Once I tried to clear my head of them. I exercised the muscles of my forehead and my cheeks, stretching so much that my eyes stared as if I had been hanged. Then I walked towards the sea, not looking at buildings or people, just the sea. I willed my head to remain empty of Byzantines and Seleucids and all the pack of them. 'I shall look at Nature' I said. 'At the waves of the sea. At the sea birds crying their raucous songs that have nothing to do with history.' Within a minute, I was back here talking to the Emperor Julian and asking why he renounced Christianity. It was a luxurious homecoming. To my own people.

Only **Stephanos** *as* **Man One, Alexander** *as*

Man Two *and* **Vassili** *as* **Man Three** *are now left on the stage which is bathed in an eerie blue light. A loud, strange fanfare is heard. They look about them slightly frightened and certainly puzzled.*

Man One The iron tongue of midnight.

Cavafy No, this was sweeter.

The music again – psalteries, sistrums, a haunting, heavenly sound. It should continue softly until **Man One, Man Two** *and* **Man Three** *leave the stage.*

Man Three This is no mortal business, nor no sound that the earth owes.

Cavafy I sense a leave-taking, a farewell. The god himself!

Man One List, list.

Man Two Hark.

Man One Music i' the air.

Man Two Under the earth.

Man Three It signs well, does it not?

Cavafy No, a leave-taking.

Man Two Peace I say!

Man Three What should this mean?

Cavafy 'Tis the god Hercules, whom Antony loves, now leaves the city.

The music dies away as if moving away.

Man One Follow the noise so far as we have quarter.

Man Two Let's see how it will give off.

All except **Cavafy** *leave the stage in pursuit of the music.*

Cavafy (*coming to the front of the stage and speaking very softly to the audience*) When, all of a sudden, at midnight, you hear an invisible procession passing by with wonderful music, voices, don't lament for your luck which is falling away now, your work which has come to nothing, the plans you had for your life which turned out to be delusions. Don't lament for them pointlessly. Be like a man

long ready, courageous, and bid farewell to
her, Alexandria, who is leaving. Above all,
don't deceive yourself. Don't pretend it was a
dream or that your ears were mistaken.
Don't delude yourself with such empty
hopes. Be like a man long ready, courageous,
as befits someone worthy of such a city. Go
resolutely over to the window and listen with
emotion, but not with the pleading or
complaining cowards use. Your last pleasure
is to listen to the sounds, the wonderful
instruments of that mysterious procession.
Then bid her farewell, Alexandria, whom
you are losing.

Cavafy *closes his eyes and reaches out to touch the
imaginary walls of ancient Alexandria.*

Slow fade to Blackout.

A Vision of Love Revealed in Sleep (Part Three)

Neil Bartlett

A spectacle dedicated to the memory of Mr Simeon Solomon

Neil Bartlett works as a performer, director, writer and translator. His previous work for the theatre includes: **Dressing Up** (1983), **Pornography** (1984); **More Bigger Snacks Now** (for Theâtre de Complicité, 1985); **The Magic Flute** (1986); **Miracles** (for Manact, 1987). His television work includes: **Where is Love** (1988); **That's What Friends Are For** (1989); **That's How Strong My Love Is** (1990). His books include: **Who Was That Man?** (Serpent's Tail, 1989) and **Ready to Catch Him Should He Fall** (Serpent's Tail, 1990). His translations include: **Berenice** by Racine (National Theatre, 1990); **School for Wives** by Molière (Derby Playhouse, 1990). He has also devised **Sarrasine**, a new work of music theatre after a text by Balzac (Traverse Theatre, Edinburgh and Third Eye Centre, Glasgow, 1990). Neil Bartlett is a member of *Gloria*.

Preface

No account of gay performance and performances, whether historical or contemporary, which deals only with that kind of theatre which is based on scripts or playtexts can be considered complete or representative. It would, for instance, be very odd to construct a history which omitted all reference to our only two unique British theatrical art forms, the pantomime and pub drag (as opposed to American glamour drag or continental *travestie*), just because neither of those forms can be in any useful way represented by a script. It would be worse than odd to discuss gay performance in the 1980s without including the work of, for instance, Derek Jarman, Terence Davies, Michael Clark, Lloyd Newson or Lindsay Kemp . . . or, for that matter, the work of Bette Bourne or Lily Savage. Not only would such a discussion leave out some of the most innovative, popular and radical contemporary work; it would reinforce the notion that a 'gay theatre' is necessarily synonymous with the literary theatre – wordy, university educated, un-physical, un-visual and tied to the authority of the author and director – and with its shadow and would-be successor, the politicised, small-scale theatre of opposition, the tradition which most of us think of as being epitomised by the achievements of Gay Sweatshop. If by a 'gay theatre' we mean art made by gay people which is created out of distinctively gay imaginations and out of the traditions of gay culture and experience – a theatre which creates gay images and gay language rather than just 'gay characters' – then that gay theatre cannot be adequately represented by a collection of scripts.

The problem is, how do you preserve, disseminate or even talk about this other theatre, since it is the unique property of the artists who make it? It is art generated and made public by the artist themselves, not written down and then realised by someone else. Jarman and Davies are lucky, because their imagery is devised specifically to be recorded, on film. Much dance and performance is now recorded (usually impossibly badly) on video, and occasionally makes it onto television; but is there a record of the original production of Kemp's *Flowers*? Do we have any idea of how, for instance, Douglas Byng played his panto Dame? Of how Ashton and Helpmann danced their original Ugly Sisters? Of what the Vauxhall Kunst Theater wore when they recreated Marlowe's *Dido, Queen of Carthage* at the Oval House Theatre, or why it mattered? Have you ever tried to explain to someone how British pub drag actually works as theatre? Would a script help to explain, to someone who hasn't seen her in full flight, exactly how the visuals, the comedy, the sex and the politics of Lily Savage's act are scrambled together?

The 'script' of **A Vision of Love Revealed in Sleep** attempts to document a piece of devised gay performance; it is not actually a script at all in the conventional sense. It is a transcript of an actual performance – and even then it omits those passages of improvisation which are crucial to the effect of the show but which simply wouldn't make any sense written down.

This script was not written by one person; it was devised by the company, using, as a basis for six weeks of rehearsal, text which had been devised in the rehearsals for two earlier, solo versions of the show created over a two-year period. As is often the case with work as influenced by the working practices of performance art as by theatre, almost all of the material used in the performance is 'found' – historical or personal material stolen, borrowed, reworked and re-placed, spoken with a new meaning. This is indicated in the script by the use of a different typeface. There is very little material in this script which I actually *wrote*, although it bears my name. Much of the text, and all of the structure of the show (a night's journey from fear to revelation, to which a young man is guided by allegorical figures of his own 'soul') is taken from the original **A Vision of Love Revealed in Sleep,** a prose poem published by Simeon Solomon in 1871. Almost everything that is said about Solomon in the show is said in the words of historical accounts, letters, newspapers, documented hearsay. There's text stolen from Dickens, from Marie Lloyd and from the Bible; material from other texts by Solomon and from his letters. The text for the final sequence of the show is taken from an article describing Jewish wedding rituals published alongside some Solomon engravings in the 1860s. There is text culled from newspapers published, and TV and radio programmes broadcast, during the period of the work's devising. There are also passages of text created through discussion, arguments and gossip with and confession to the company; worked on, refined, put into almost audible quotation marks, this material, in the mouths of the particular queens who made this show, although apparently informal, personal and colloquial, becomes as 'textual', as 'historic', as vivid with meaning and allusion and distinctive period rhythm, as anything from the nineteenth century.

Three crucial elements of the performance are not accounted for by the words. Firstly, the whole show was full of music, played onstage from a grand piano. The score was composed by Nicolas Bloomfield using fragments from Kreisler, Rachmaninoff, Schoenberg, Bruch's *Kol Nidrei*, Bloch, Sam M. Lewis and Cole Porter as source material. Again it was devised in the rehearsal room, not imported from elsewhere. The music was especially important in creating the sensual and emotive atmosphere of the piece, and for creating some of the most vivid changes of tone between highest sentiment and lowest, but *lowest* confession and cheap (if long-practised) comedy.

Secondly, the show was dedicated to a painter, Simeon Solomon, and inspired in the first instance by his paintings; the structure of the show was as much visual as conventionally theatrical. Painter Robin Whitmore was collaborator in the creation of the show for four years; not only did he conceive and paint the settings for the three versions of the show, he also influenced the creation of the whole visual language of the piece. The colours (red, gold, powdered flesh and dyed hair), gestural language (all that pre-Raphaelite turning, leaning, draping) and especially the central image of an isolated, naked, shaved, haunted and very sexual male body were all directly derived from a study of Solomon's paintings. In the first two, solo, versions of the piece, Robin created installations – not theatre designs, but environments using the particular qualities of the sites for the show; a two-storey marble staircase painted midnight blue and crowded with stars, night clouds, giant dreaming faces and angels; a freezing cold, half-flooded, semi-derelict warehouse with the faces this time looking as if burnt onto the walls with charcoal. For the theatre vision of the show he placed the red-robed figures of the Three Queens against a giant unfinished gold painting, evoking the image of an artist's studio – something like upstairs at Leighton House – which was in strange contrast with the vulgarities and sentimentality of much of Solomon's imagery, and the poverty of his later life.

Thirdly, the Three Queens themselves. This work was not just made for them, it was made with them. The images and language of the piece are all distinctively theirs, and some of the jokes and inflections of the text are, I assume, unintelligible unless delivered in their voices; it's the way, as they say, they tell them. Each represents a very different kind of London drag. Bette Bourne has created a unique vaudeville style by combining an Old Vic voice and stage technique with years of touring her radical dragsters Bloolips. Regina has created a genuine work of *folie* in the person of HIH Regina Fong, a Romanoff fallen on hard times and now working the London pubs – a real drag character with her own voice, reworked chorus-girl gestures, adoring fans and even wig. Ivan makes his living by looking like a classically (alarmingly) beautiful transvestite when he wants to, and talking like an extremely assured and relaxed late 80s gay man when he wants to – often at the same time. Each of them not only contributed a distinct performance style, but also brought in their own audience and their own relationship with that audience. Together they created a choric voice of the unacceptable face of gay history, and were the perfect foil for the emotive, personal seriousness of my own performance style.

As for the content of the work . . . my fascination with the life and work of Simeon Solomon is easily explained. It is always better to tell your own story by telling someone else's. In dark times, which ours surely are, then you turn to the unlikeliest heroes for moral and spiritual support. And in a time when gay culture seems under such attack, the story of this man seems particularly vivid, not just because of his courage, his defiance and his beautiful paintings, but because that story, although he only died in 1905, has been so completely lost. The piece is about many different kinds of inspiration, many different meanings of the word 'survival'. It is about how I feel when I stand, now, in the centre of the city of London, and look at a Solomon painting.

Neil Bartlett, August 1989

A Vision of Love Revealed in Sleep (Part Three) was first performed at the Drill Hall, London, on 1 March 1989 by Gloria Theatre Company:

Performers:

Neil Bartlett

Bette Bourne

Regina Fong

Ivan

Directed by   Neil Bartlett
Designed by   Robin Whitmore
Music by   Nicolas Bloomfield
Produced by   Gloria

A Vision of Love Revealed in Sleep, Parts One, Two and Three, also performed in Copenhagen, Hamburg, Glasgow, Nottingham, Oxford, Edinburgh and Sheffield. Part Three revived 1990 with Robin Whitman as The Third Queen.

When the audience enters the theatre, the space is dimly lit; smoke fogs the air, and the stage is hidden behind a huge red velvet curtain. Somewhere, unseen, a grand piano is playing; phrases of haunting, melancholy music. The lights on the audience fade to black; the red curtain slowly opens, revealing a wall of black fabric. Onto this are projected a sequence of captions, white letters on a night sky:

VISION

VISION: SOMETHING WHICH IS
APPARENTLY SEEN OTHERWISE THAN BY
ORDINARY SIGHT: PRESENTED TO THE
MIND IN SLEEP OR IN AN ABNORMAL STATE

VISION: A PERSON SEEN IN A DREAM OR
TRANCE

VISION: A PERSON OF UNUSUAL BEAUTY

VISIONARY: I)   ONE TO WHOM UNKNOWN
                 THINGS ARE REVEALED
          II) ONE WHO INDULGES IN
                 FANTASTIC IDEAS; AN
                 UNPRACTICAL ENTHUSIAST
A VISION OF LOVE REVEALED IN SLEEP
a spectacle dedicated to the memory of Mr S Solomon

As soon as this last caption comes onto the black curtain, there is a sweeping, sudden phrase on the piano, to the sound of which the black curtain falls. The stage can only be very dimly seen. The back wall appears to be painted gold; rising to the centre of the wall is a golden staircase. In front of it there are four posing platforms, giving the effect of a grand artist's studio. Also on the stage is a grand piano. The pianist is dressed in black; as he finished the last phrase he lifted his hands as if to continue, but has held them in mid-air, suspended, frozen. Also in the room is a semi-naked man, posed like an artist's model, partially draped in a length of dull red silk. His right hand is clutched to his breast holding something. Silence.

A single naked lightbulb snaps on. In the darkness, the effect is of a bright light turned on too suddenly in a bedroom. The audience can now see all of the shadowy, abandoned artist's studio.

The man has powdered white flesh and dull red hair; the naked bulb is burning very close to his face. He

looks as if he has been woken in the middle of the night; he speaks in the broken, sleepy way you do speak when, for instance, woken by a phone call at half-past-two in the morning.

Neil   What time is it? Is it late?

Upon the waning of the night, at that time when stars are pale, and when dreams wrap us about more closely . . .

Are we alone?

I was sleeping. I was asleep, I must have been dreaming. I had this dream, and when I woke up I could remember three things, and the first thing was,

'I sleep, but my heart waketh;'

and the second thing was

'Many waters cannot quench love;'

and the third thing . . . the third thing was,

'Until the day break, and the shadows flee away.'

And I fell to musing and pondering upon these things and then, behold, there came to me a vision, and I was walking in a strange land that I knew not, and it was filled with a light I had never seen before, and I was dressed as a traveller. And so I set forth, dazed, and wondering, with my eyes cast down upon the ground, and I felt just as one who sets forth on a journey but who knows not yet its goal;

I didn't know where I was supposed to be going. And so . . .

I called upon my spirit to make itself clearer to me, and to show me, as in a glass what it was I sought; to show me what I was supposed to be looking for. *Then the silence of the night was broken, and for a short while I knew nothing . . .* and then I looked up, and there was someone standing there. Standing right there beside me.

Neil *unwraps what he is carrying in his arms and lets the red silk drape fall to the floor. This reveals that he is entirely naked, and that his whole body is* *shaved and powdered. He has been carrying a portrait; this he now shows to the audience.*

Neil This is a picture of Mr Simeon Solomon, born in London in 1840, in the nineteenth century. He died here, in London, in 1905, in the twentieth century, in our century. Mr Solomon was short, fat, thinlegged . . . ugly; everybody said so, ugly. Alcoholic. Redhaired. Bald. Criminal. Homosexual. Jewish – and this night is dedicated to him. Of all the lives I could cry for, tonight it is him I choose to mourn; and of all the men I could choose to follow; it is him I choose to follow tonight, on this night of all nights.

Neil*'s voice suddenly cuts from the elevated, gentle tone of the opening to a common, chatty, sexy conversation with the men in the audience.*

Neil I don't know why I do it. It's just something I do. I follow strange men sometimes. I see some man walking down the street, he gets on the bus, I get on the bus too, it makes me late for work, it gets me into all kinds of trouble, I don't know why I do it –

Mr Solomon earned his living as a painter and this –

Neil *turns and indicates the gold wall at the back of the theatre. It can now be dimly seen in the lights; it is in fact a giant decayed, unfinished canvas, its golden surface covered in fragments of Solomon's paintings and drawings, angels, robed figures and sleeping men. Across the painting, spreading out onto the walls of the theatre in gold script, can be seen the three quotations from* The Song of Solomon *which begin* **Neil***'s first text.*

– this is one of his paintings.

Neil *walks to the painting, and hangs the portrait of Solomon on a nail sticking out of its worn and paint-spattered surface. Quietly, he bends to kiss the portrait on the lips, and murmurs something in its ear which the audience cannot hear. He turns again to face them, walks forward and picks up a small, old red-bound book that has been left lying on the studio floor.*

Neil And he also wrote a book.

And this, this is his book. He called it *A Vision of Love Revealed in Sleep.* And everything I say tonight is true, and everything I say tonight is written here, in this book, and this book was published in 1871.

He begins to read from the book; the phrases of the text are continually supported, punctuated and interrupted by the piano.

And I turned to the one who stood beside me in my dream, lifting up my eyes, the eyes of one who has ever sought, but not found; and I gazed full upon him. And he spake unto me and he said;

The piano stops; **Neil** *looks, but cannot see the person who he has been addressing in his dream. To the audience:*

Neil He couldn't be here tonight.

I invited everyone I knew, anyone who I thought might know him, just hoping he'd come. I suppose I thought somebody might bring him with them. I even invited people I didn't know, as one does. I went up to complete strangers and said excuse me, yes you, I'm sorry, I don't know why I do this, I've been staring at you all evening, I've been looking at you ever since the houselights went down, would you like to spend the evening with me; would you like to spend this night, of all nights, with me – But he isn't here. I went to find his grave but they told me, I'm sorry, we've no idea. We don't even remember his name.

So I put the flowers down on a grave without a name, just hoping it might be his.

I put flowers on his grave but somebody must have stolen them, or cleared them away, I couldn't find them. I sat on his grave and talked to him out loud, there was no one there to hear me, there was no one there whose advice I could ask –

And so I turned to the one who stood beside me in my dream and he looked full upon me, and he said; I know him whom thou seekest, him whom we go forth to find. He only appears to those who grope in the waking

darkness of the world; in visions shall he be seen of thee many times before his full light is shed upon thee, and thy spirit shall be chastened and saddened by what it sees, but it shall not utterly faint. Look upon me, and I will support thee, and in thy hour of need, I will be the one to bear thee up. Come.

And he took hold of my hand, and he led me along the shore of a dim sea lying at ebb beneath a mysterious veil of twilight. I could see that his lips trembled with all the unuttered voices of the past; but he was not crying. He led me forth, and then he turned to me, he looked at me, and he said;

Tell me all about him. What's he like. Go on, tell me about him. What was he wearing? What did he look like? What did he look like — describe his face to me. Tell me his address; did he live near here? You see I don't know. I don't know. I used to know. We all knew. Everyone I knew was quite sure, but now . . . I don't know. I can't be so sure any more . . . I see some man and I'm not sure if I've been to bed with him. I see some man in the street and I know I've been to bed with him, I follow him, but when I touch him on the shoulders, when he turns and says, 'Hello', — I can't remember. I can't remember his name. I can't remember his address. I can't remember anything at all of all the things we said to each other, in the dark. I get a letter and I see from the postmark it was sent two weeks ago and when I'm reading it I think; maybe he's dead now. I read a history book and I think maybe they're lying to me. How would I know?

How would I ever know if he was like me?

Or if, if we met, he'd like me?

What was he wearing?

Tell me all about him.

What should I say when I meet him; how should we talk to each other? I mean, how did men like us talk to each other in those days?

Ladies and Gentlemen, I wanted to ask your advice. What I wanted to ask you was; Is there anyone here who remembers the nineteenth century?

No? Oh well never mind . . .

Neil *improvises a brief talk with the audience, breaks the tension, welcomes any latecomers, has a drink and returns to reading from the book;*

In 1869 Mr Simeon Solomon very helpfully wrote me his autobiography. It is thirteen lines long, and he entitled it

A History of Simeon Solomon From the Cradle to the Grave.

He was pampered. He had a horrid temper; he grew fractious; the family was wealthy; . . .

everything was going to be all right

EVERYTHING WAS GOING TO BE ALL RIGHT

EVERYTHING WAS GOING TO BE ALL RIGHT

Have you heard this story before?

At the age of sixteen young Simeon had already illustrated the Bible. His favourite book in the Bible was, of course, (keep up, keep up!) *The Song of Solomon.*

Neil'*s voice changes into that of a preacher.*

'The Song of Songs which is Solomon's, beginning at the third chapter and the first verse, which is "I sleep, but my heart waketh".'

Neil'*s voice drops into a hushed, sexual whisper; snatching up the red silk from the floor, he plays both Bridegroom and Bride, turning and posing from line to line, echoing Solomon's sequence of drawings to* the *Song of Songs.*

I sleep, but my heart waketh. Listen; my beloved is knocking at the door, and he says, Open the door to me my sister, my dearest, my love, my dove, my undefiled one. My head is drenched with dew, my locks wet with the moisture of the night. And she says; I have stripped off my dress for the evening — do you want me to put it on again? I have washed my feet for the night – do you think I should get them dirty? And then he reaches out his hand – oh, when my Beloved slips his finger into the keyhole, my bowels stir within me. When I rose up and opened up to greet my beloved there was myrrh dripping off my fingers; the liquid ran down off my fingers all over the doorhandle. And I rose up, and I opened up to my beloved, but my beloved had turned away and gone by. I sought him, but I could not find him. I called to him, but he did not answer. Night after night I lay alone on my bed, seeking my true love. I called him, but he must have been out. I wrote to him, but he didn't write back to me. *And so I said, I'll get up, and I'll go out, out through the city at night, through its streets and squares and I sought for him* on Old Street, and on Poland Street, but still I could not find him; I called for him in the Market, in the Vauxhall and even outside the Coleherne at eleven-thirty in the evening God help me, but still he would not answer me. *And the officers, going the rounds of the city walls, they met me, and they surrounded me, and they abused me, and they stripped me of my cloak and I said* Officer, have you seen my lover anywhere? And no sooner had they left me than I found my true love, and I seized him, and I would not let him go, and I took him home, to my mother's house, and I said Mother! Mother, here he is.

Neil *holds up his finger as if it bore a ring.*

Wear me like a seal upon your heart,
Like a ring upon your finger;
For Love is stronger than Death,
Passion more cruel than the Grave.
Love burns up fiercer than any flame;
MANY WATERS CANNOT QUENCH LOVE,
And no Flood can sweep it away.

Everything is going to be all right

Everything is going to be all right

Everything's going to be all right darling you can trust me.

At the age of eighteen he was hated by all of his family – surely that can't be true;

everybody's Mother loves them . . . *At the age of eighteen he was hated by all of his family, and so they sent him away.* To France. Unfortunately history does not record exactly what Simeon spent his time doing on the continent; the pages of his sketch book for that year are quite blank, but we do know that he returned to London in Disgrace, which is always the sign of a good holiday. And so they sent him away again, this time to Italy, to study Art –

Using the silk again, **Neil** *strikes a grand art-historical pose; The Artist's Model. During this sequence he begins to play ventriloquist, the voice moving between his own and that of the nineteenth-century polite society he is conjuring. The effect is of a solitary figure in an empty studio, but a studio crowded with absent people from the past.*

– and in Italy he had sex with . . . one, two, three, four, five, six, seven, eight, nine, ten, eleven, twelve, thirteen boys . . . well he was there for three months. One of the boys had a face he would never forget. Back in London, everybody was talking about young Mr Solomon and his paintings, they said, Oh! *Such a striking face, what's his name? Where on earth did you find him? Tell me all about him.* Some people even bought his pictures and hung them, I suppose in their living rooms. What Simeon liked to paint best was of course boys . . .

Neil *climbs onto one of the posing blocks and runs through a series of poses echoing Solomon's paintings . . .*

Boys draped in silk. Boys dressed up as women. Boys praying to God. Boys with wings. *Tell me all about him. What's his name?* He knew everyone, anyone who was anyone; he knew De Morgan, Morris, Burgess, Swinburne, Pater, Rossetti, Alfred Lord Tennyson. One night he made his entrance into a particularly aristocratic dinner party dressed only in the flowing robes of a Hebrew prophet, reciting a hymn in a language which no one else there could possibly understand. Another night he ran around a house in Chelsea, in Cheyne Walk no less, stark naked, and screaming like a cat. *Aren't you going to introduce me?* He knew everyone, anyone who was anyone, De Morgan, Morris – *Oh Simeon, I see you're not on your own again tonight. Aren't you going to introduce me? What's his name?* Simeon Solomon was very unattractive. Like me. Simeon Soloman had red hair. Just like I do. When he was a young man he shaved off his beard to make himself more attractive to boys, and that made him a very bad Jew, and when he was an old man no one recognised him anymore they didn't even remember his name and he let his beard grow long and filthy and matted and stinking and in fact he looked just like some dirty, old, Jew ... But he knew everyone, anyone who was anyone, he went to all the best parties, no doors were closed to him, he knew everybody's name, and they said to him *O Simeon, and who are you with tonight? Aren't you going to introduce me?*

Tell me all about him.

They said to him, *O Simeon, what would you like to be when you grow up?*

and he said

Drinker, Failure,

Soldier, Sailor,

Old Man, Poor Man,

Beggarman, QUEEN

The music is now rising under **Neil***'s speech. He begins to introduce imaginary guests to the audience; by the end of this speech he has climbed onto one of the posing blocks; he is then caught in a gesture of entreaty, as if he was indeed an artist's model posing for an invisible artist.*

He knew everyone, anyone who was anyone; the studio was full of people; every night he was surrounded. He knew De Morgan, Morris, Burgess, Swinburne, Pater, Rossetti, Alfred Lord Tennyson; may I introduce Sir Frederick Leighton ... Sir Edward Burne Jones ... Lady Burne Jones ... all the little Burne Jones's all of whom, all of whom are

now dead! He knew so many people, he knew so many men, but history does not record their names, I know nothing about them not even their names, I only know the names of two of his lovers and for the rest I know nothing, nothing, I don't recognise their faces, I don't know their addresses, I wrote them a letter but they wouldn't write back to me, I called them on the phone but I couldn't get through, I said I have to talk to you, I want to ask your advice, I want to spend the night with *you and not with anybody else,* I hold out my hand and there's nothing there;

nothing –

nothing –

there's no one there.

At the top of the staircase, in the middle of the picture, a double door slowly opens. We see **Ivan,** **Bette** *and* **Regina,** *posed in a tableaux based on Solomon's painting of the angel in the fiery furnace from the Book of Daniel. They too have red hair and are in red robes; but their hair is in the pre-Raphaelite style of Jane Morris or Lizzie Siddal, and their robes are floor-length, and are of heavy scarlet velvet. They have gold shoes and heavy make-up. Behind them is a scarlet and gold painted heaven of flames and angels. They begin to descend, with music.* **Bette** *leads them, singing Cole Porter's* In The Still of the Night

In the still of the night, as I gaze from my window,
At the moon in its flight, my thoughts all stray
to you –
In the still of the night,
While the world is in slumber
Oh the times without number
Darling, when I say to you, –
Do you love me, as I love you?
Are you my life to be, my dream come true?
Or will this dream of mine fade out of sight,
Like the moon,
Growing dim, on the rim,
of the hill,
in the chill
still of the night.

Neil Tell me all about him. Please tell me. What he was like?

Regina *She was wicked. She was not as other men are. She hath mingled with the ungodly.*

Neil Did you ever meet him?

Ivan Well I just better had because he still owes me that hundred and fifty quid.

Neil Tell me, did you ever talk to him?

Bette It was six o'clock; it must have been getting dark, because the gas was coming on . . . I was walking along Fitzroy Street; he was living at number 12 then. The windows were dark and so I continued down the street.

Ivan I walked down the street to number 46 –

Bette Number 46 Fitzroy Street WC1 where on the evening of August 20th, 1884 Mr Charles Mason was married before 16 witnesses to his lover Mr Alfred Taylor –

Regina Alfred! I wore the black and gold lace, it was beaded to buggery, and then the police burst in and dragged me screaming to Bow Street –

Bette The curtains were drawn. I turned right and right again onto Cleveland Street –

Ivan Number 19 Cleveland Street; loads of soldiers. Last night, I was with the Duke of –

Regina How much d'you get then?

Bette One guinea.

Ivan and he said, 'Jack Saul, call me Duchess' I said, 'Excuse me! Am I going in the right direction?' He said –

Regina Wait a minute, Bette, was the name of that café we used to go to, just off Monmouth Street –

Bette The *As You Like It.*

Bette
Regina } Barry Stacey!!

Bette My dears, sandwiches for ever.

Regina And Quentin Crisp. Eighty-year-old and still tinting! An inspiration to us all –

Bette You know I had lunch with him six weeks ago in New York. He was telling me about the time he came through customs and they said to him, 'Have you anything to declare?' and he said, 'Only my sin . . .' so I walked all the way down Charlotte Street and right onto Percy Street and then I paused and I looked up at the window of number 15 –

Ivan Number 15, Top flat, where in the summer of 1928 Mr Charles Laughton was living with Ms Elsa Lanchester. The police were downstairs with some boy; it was the first time, but not the last time –

Regina Charles sat Elsa down on the sofa in the front room and he said 'Elsa – '

Bette 'Elsa, I have something to tell you . . . are you listening? I have something to tell you . . .

Ivan Are you listening? Anyway, I turned left and crossed the Tottenham Court Road (excuse me for being so specific, but I shouldn't want anyone to get lost) –

Regina My dear, it's enough to confuse anybody

Ivan So I turned onto Gower Street and there he was. Sitting on the pavement; the most beautiful boy in London. I recognised him from the paintings; he was his favourite model; he said to me, 'Go down six doors and turn right onto Chenies Street;' –

Bette I had to ask a policeman, he said to me, 'You must be for number 16,' I said, 'Officer, how can you tell?' –

Regina He said, 'They're all in there – '

Ivan He said, 'You won't be on your own,' –

Regina So what time does this thing start then?

Bette Eight o'clock.

Ivan What time is it now? Are we late?

Regina Eight thirty four.

Bette Oh well here we are. Good evening. Evening Nicolas.

They say hello to the audience.

Neil Tell me how old you are.

Bette Next Question Please.

Neil Tell me, what are your names?

Bette Bette.

Regina Regina.

Ivan Ivan.

Neil No, tell me your real names, I want to know.

Bette 'Bette' 's about as real as I get.

Regina 'Regina' . . .

Ivan *The Book of Daniel, beginning at the first chapter, and the third verse. And the King ordered that they should take certain of the exiles, who were to be young men of good looks, in whom was no blemish, and prepare them that they might stand before the King. Now among these were the children of Judah; Hananiah, Mishael and Azariah; but the master of eunuchs in the palace gave them new names;*

Bette *Unto Hananiah he gave the name of Shadrach,*

Regina *and to Mishael, the name of Meshach,*

Ivan *and to Azariah, of Abed-nego. And to these God gave knowledge and skill in all learning; and the understanding of all visions and dreams.*

Bette *And in the second year of the reign of Nebuchadnezzar, Nebuchadnezzar dreamed dreams, and his spirit was troubled, and his sleep brake from him. And the king called his magicians to him and he said unto them —*

Neil *I have dreamed a dream, and my*

spirit is troubled to know the dream. And the magicians said unto him —

Regina *O king, live forever; tell thy servants the dream, and we will show the interpretation.*

Neil *The King answered; but the dream is gone from me; you must tell me both the dream, and the interpretation. And they said;*

Betty ⎫
Regina ⎬ *Nobody on earth can tell your majesty what you wish to know . . .*
Ivan ⎭

Bette *Then was the secret revealed in a night vision . . .*

The following lines, delivered by the 'angels' posed like a cluster of pre-Raphaelite chorus girls on their golden stairs, run over each other.

O king, this is the dream, and these the visions that came into your head.

A man whom I had already seen came close by me in the dark of the evening, flying swiftly, exhausted, and he said, I have come now to enlighten your understanding

The men that were with me saw not the vision, but they fled to hide themselves. I alone saw the vision; I was alone.

There came one like the appearance of a man, and touched me, and he strengthened me.

He moved towards me, gently lifted by the spirit from the ground, neither running nor flying,

And behold a hand touched me, and pulled me up onto my hands and knees, and he said to me, thou art a man greatly beloved; stand up!

And then one like a man touched my lips; he spoke clearly to me and said;

Bette *The dream is sure, and the interpretation to be trusted.*

Neil *and I opened my mouth to speak, and I said unto him that stood before me,*

O my Lord, by the vision my sorrows are turned upon me, and I have retained no strength, and he said to me,

Regina   *O man greatly beloved, fear not;*

Bette   *Be strong; be strong.*

Neil   So tell me, is he here?

Are we alone?

Neil   Tell me, how have you lived for so long, I don't –

Regina   Well you know it was different in those days –

Ivan   And it came to pass, in those days –

Bette   *And it came to pass, in the fourth year of his reign, that Nebuchadnezzar the King in his rage and fury commanded that they be brought before him; they said:*

Regina   *We have no need to answer you in this matter . . . be it known, O king, we will not worship thy gods.*

Bette   *Then was Nebuchadnezzar full of fury, and he commanded that they should heat the furnace one seven times more than it was wont to be heated; and he commanded the most mighty men in his army to bind Shadrach,*

Ivan   *Meshach*

Regina   *and Abed-nego,*

Bette   *and to cast them into the fiery furnace; and they fell down, bound, into the fiery furnace.*

To the sound of the Kol Nidrei *playing under these speeches, they step down onto the stage and surround* **Neil.**

Bette   *Then Nebuchadnezzar the King was astonished, and said, Did we not cast three men bound into the midst of the fire? Yet I see four men loose, walking in the midst of the fire, and they have no hurt; and the fourth one looks like a god . . . And upon their bodies the fire had no power,*

Regina   *nor was an hair of their head singed,*

Ivan   *neither were their clothes marked,*

Bette   *and they did not even smell of the fire.*

Bette *pulls* **Neil** *towards him and kisses him as if to awake him from a dream.* **Regina** *takes hold of his hand, and with* **Ivan**'s *assistance blindfolds him with a strip of red velvet, spins him around and guides him up onto the posing blocks.*

Regina   *Come, let us go forth! And I will show thee a Vision . . .*

Neil   *He took hold of my hand, dark against the wan air of the dying night and he stood by me and he whispered in my ear*

Regina   (*blindfolding him*)   *It is well thou hast looked upon the Pleasure which is Past, for now with the greater ardour dost thou desire him whom we go forth to find. Canst thou bear to look forward?*

Neil   *And I looked forward, and I saw that the way before us grew dark in the night air,* and I said; I'm scared. I'm scared all the time. I'm scared of losing my nerve, scared of losing my friends, do you know, I've walked this way home for years but now I'm lost. I'm lost . . . I don't know where I'm supposed to be –

Regina   Look again!

Neil   I can't see anything.

Regina   Look again!

Neil   I can't –

Regina   (*sings*)   There he is, can't you see!

Neil   I can't see anything –

Regina   (*speaks*)   There he is, can't you see?

Neil   I can't see –

Regina   (*whipping off the blindfold*)   Look again . . .

Neil   I looked again, and I saw myself in the mirror, he was holding me so tight . . . and then I looked again, I looked up and I saw this man, I'd never seen him before.

As **Neil** *describes the Vision of Love,* **Regina**

leaves him and quietly moves to another of the posing blocks. He averts his eyes and crosses his hands as if they were tied. Lit by matching shafts of light, both **Neil** *and* **Regina** *look like models posed for a Solomon painting.* **Ivan** *and* **Bette** *watch them.*

I lifted up my eyes and I beheld there one whom I knew not seeking shelter in a cleft in the rocks. The Shame which had been done him made dim those thrones of Charity, his eyes, and as the wings of a dove, beaten against a wall, fall, broken and bloodied, so his wings hung drooping about his white and perfect body ... his head was drenched with dew, his locks wet with the moisture of the night. The crown of flowers on his head was broken; he was wounded beyond all hope of healing, crushed by the burden of his so-great tenderness. And I knew that he in whose presence I now stood was Love, dethroned and captive, bound and wounded, his wings broken, and bleeding, and torn. And as he came forth of his sheltering place the light about his head was blown into thin flames by the cruel breath of the sea, and I saw moving beside him there a crowd of all those who had brought this to pass, and the sound of their laughter filled the night air. And I could look no longer, for I beheld in the midst of that company the image of myself. And I knew that the Divine Captive read my inmost thoughts, for there proceeded inaudibly from his lips the words —

Neil *mouths the words as* **Regina** *quietly says them.*

Regina *Thou hast wounded my heart.*

Neil *And then I looked up, and behold, the vision was gone.* And for a long time I stood there motionless, and then I looked up —

Neil *lifts his arms in a gesture of appeal. Then, in silence; he feels first under one armpit and then under the other; then his liver; then the glands of his groin. He is checking his body for signs of HIV infection. Silence.*

Bette *As with the great tenderness of one*

unconquerable, as a mother encircles with her arms a beloved and sorrowing child ... so he pressed his bruised and smitten charge to his breast.

Neil *And then I turned to the one who stood beside me in my dream.*

Neil *turns to* **Regina.**

and I said, I'm sorry. I'm sorry but I need a drink.

He turns away from **Regina** *and there is* **Ivan,** *right there with a glass of red wine which he drinks.* **Ivan** *and* **Neil** *sit on two of the posing blocks and chat. Or rather, they appear to chat; the imagery and effect of this dialogue, and of course the line which closes it, is carefully structured. However,* **Neil** *and* **Ivan** *never conferred as to the actual location or course of the reported conversation, and played the scene as clearly 'improvised', in marked contrast to the formality of the previous speeches. The bar referred to differed from performance to performance depending on which city we were in. In this transcription the bar referred to is a leather bar in East London.*

Neil I went out *again* last night didn't I? I did actually manage to get all the way home after the show but then I thought well I'm not sitting here watching some dreadful James Bond movie, so I called the taxi —

Ivan Don't tell me; Backstreet.

Neil Well it was Friday night.

Ivan And how was Backstreet?

Neil It was quiet, but you know ... interesting.

Ivan I'm sure it was.

Neil I walked in, you turn left into the bar and you know they've got this big mirror over the bar, which means you can see everyone in the club while you're ordering your drink, but they can't see. So I looked up in the mirror.

Ivan And what did you see in the mirror?

Neil Three men all staring at me.

Ivan Anyone you fancied?

Neil There was one.

Ivan And? I suppose you eventually plucked up the courage to go and say something to him?

Neil Well not exactly. I just went over to him and stood next to him in a, you know, casual but significant sort of way.

Ivan Well he must have said something to you.

Neil He did. He put his drink down and turned to me and he said –

Ivan *Thou hast no pity on thyself.*

Neil *puts down his drink and turns to* **Bette**.

Neil And then I turned to the one who stood beside me in my dream and he said –

Bette *It is even so. Thou hast no pity on thyself, thou hast essayed to kill Love, thou hast wounded his heart. Let us go forth, and I will show the history somewhat of his Shame whom thou seekest; I will show thee a vision of that which may yet be averted.*

Bette *takes* **Neil** *by the hand and gently leads him forward; they climb onto two of the posing blocks, so that there is now a row of four models –* **Ivan** *is still sitting on the fourth block.*

Neil *And so we went along and we came there upon a crowd of men . . . All of whom bore different aspects. I chose in that crowd one there to be the image of myself. Some were mocking. Some carried an air of scorn upon them and others of deceit; some feigned mourning, and others were not moved by anything they saw. I approached, weighed down with a great weight of sorrow, and through my tear-stained lashes I looked down and I saw the Vision of one lying there bound and wounded. The voice of his heart was as dead within him. His body lay untended, and no one had clothed him in his last garments. His feet were tied. His white and perfect body was flecked here and there with blood. And I knew that this*

too was a Vision of Love, betrayed and wounded, bound, and helpless, and I sank down and I cradled him in my arms, but then when I looked down the Vision was gone, and so I turned to the one who stood beside me in my dream and he said –

Bette *Be not cast down, lay it as sign upon your heart, wear it as a ring upon your finger, thou shalt not fail, Come.*

As **Bette** *says this, he makes three gestures: placing his hand quietly over his heart; holding up his finger in an echo of the gesture already used by* **Neil** *in the* Song of Solomon *sequence; and extending a hand to the audience. These gestures are echoed throughout the following sequence each time a variant on this line is used, by* **Ivan, Regina** *and by* **Nicolas**, *seated at the piano.*

Neil *And he took me by the hand and led me forth, and I approached, weighed down with a great weight of sorrow and I looked down and I saw there the image of one lying bound and wounded. The voice of his heart was as dead. His body lay untended, no one had clothed him in his last garments,* no one had even bothered to move the body out of the road. He was covered in blood. And I knew that this too was a Vision of Love, wounded and bruised, he was bruised here, on his back, and on the right side of his face where they had kicked him and so I got down on my hands and my knees to throw my arms around him, but when I looked down the Vision was gone and I turned to the one who stood beside me in my dream and he said:

Bette *Be not cast down thou shalt not fail, come.*

Neil And I said I don't think I can –

Neil *turns and goes to leave but* **Ivan** *swiftly takes his hand and leads him back up; all four of them are now standing on the blocks, three in velvet and one naked, all lit in the same dim shafts of light.*

Neil – he took me by the hand and led me forth. I looked down and through my tearstained lashes I saw there the Vision of one lying, bound and wounded. He was lying in the middle of the main street of the town where I grew up, there was a crowd of people all round him but no one was doing anything so I pushed my way through the crowd, everyone was staring at us, and I got down on my hands and knees and threw my arms around him –

Neil *throws open his arms. In an echo of this gesture,* **Bette** *opens his arms, palms to the audience, and begins quietly to sing* For All We Know. *The three elements of this number –* **Neil**'s *speech, the gestures and* **Bette**'s *song – run together.*

Bette
> *For all we know,*
> *We may never meet again;*
> *Before you go,*
> *Make this moment sweet again.*
> *We won't say goodbye until the last*
> *   minute;*
> *I'll hold out my hand and my heart will be*
> *   in it.*
> *For all we know,*
> *This may only be a dream . . .*
> *We come and go like the ripples on a*
> *   stream.*
> *So love me tonight;*
> *Tomorrow was made for some;*
> *Tomorrow may never come,*
> *For all we know . . .*

The song repeats to the end of the number.

Neil and I said I'll call somebody, I'll call somebody, although I didn't know who I was going to call, I said you keep on looking at me, you keep on talking to me it'll be all right, everything will be all right, everything will be all right, everything will be all right you can trust me darling, but then I looked down and the Vision was gone and I turned to the one who stood beside me in my Dream and I said I can't – and he said be not cast down, thou shalt not fail, and in thy hour of need I shall be the one to bear thee up. Come! He took hold of my hand and led me forth, so I approached, weighed down with a great weight of my sorrow, and I looked down, and I saw this man I recognised, I couldn't see his face, he was covered in blood, but I

recognised his body, he looked just like somebody I know, he looked like somebody I'd been to bed with and so I got down and I took my shirt off and I tried to wipe away the blood and then the Vision was gone, I turned to the one who stood beside me in my dream and he said: Wear it like a seal upon thy heart, like a ring upon thy finger. Thou shalt not fail! Come! He took hold of my hand and led me forth. I approached weighed down with a great weight of sorrow and I looked down and I saw one there lying, I thought I recognised him, he looked just like the lover of my best friend I said please, wait, and he said, I shall be the one to bear thee up, thou shalt not fail! Come! And he took hold of my hand, and I looked down, and he was lying there naked, he was covered in blood and I said please, don't do it to him. You can do it to me; you can do it to anyone here, I don't care, but please don't do it to him, I said, do you know how old he is and I turned to the one who stood beside me in my dream and I said, I think we're running out of time, I don't see why you ask us to wait and be happy and I said **and the sob burst forth from my lips up out of my heart, inaudibly I cried –**

The gestures and the song stop dead.

Regina	
Bette	(*very quietly*) Oh that the day would break, and the shadows flee away.
Ivan	
Neil	

Neil I said, I don't think you know how much I want this night to end, and the morning to come. And then he reached out his hand,

All five reach out their hands to the audience.

Neil and he put his finger on my lips

All five place their fingers on their lips. Silence. Pause.

Neil *begins to talk very quietly, using a very dead, quiet, ordinary voice.*

Neil The other night I was walking home from the club. It was one thirty in the morning; I was on my own. Where I live the buses stop at about midnight and it was Sunday night, I'd run out of money and so I couldn't afford a cab and anyway I think if you want to walk home on your own these days then you just have to practise. I was on my own there was no one with me I couldn't hear anyone else on the street and then I heard the sound of a car slowing down behind me and I thought oh no not again not tonight but I didn't stop I didn't look round because I wanted to get home and because I think if you want to walk home on your own these days then you just have to practise not being frightened so I kept on walking and eventually the car pulled up right beside me and stopped and so I thought OK let's get it over with so I stopped and turned and I looked at the woman who was driving the car and she leant across the passenger seat, she wound down the window and she said excuse me are you gay because if you are you are going to die of AIDS you wanker and so I kept on walking because it was nearly two o'clock and I wanted to get home and because I think if you practise not being frightened then it does get easier and I have often wondered what she was thinking about, I have often wondered just how she felt, I kept on walking because I wanted to get home it was one forty-five in the morning on the way to where I live there is a low wall on the left hand side and on the wall it said GAY and I thought that's nice so I stopped to read it it said GAY, Got Aids Yet?, and I thought that's terrible I wonder who'd want to write a thing like that I hope it's no one I know I hope it isn't my neighbours I hope it isn't the man in number forty-five and so I kept on walking because I wanted to get home on the way to where I live there's a low wall on the right hand side and on the wall was written AIDS I thought I won't stop to read that I've read that one before it says Arse Injected Death Sentence and underneath that is written Queer Today, Gone Tomorrow and underneath that is written One Man's Meat is another Man's Poison. I wanted to get home it was almost two o'clock I live on the fifth floor of my building as I was going up the stairs there was this man coming down it wasn't anyone I know he wasn't one of my neighbours and as I was posing he said under his breath you fucking queer, and so I got home, it was two o'clock in the morning, I got home and I shut my front door behind me. It was two o'clock in the morning, but I decided to fix myself dinner, because I think that when you live on your own, you have to take really good care of yourself.

I decided to fix myself dinner.

I decided to fix myself dinner,

Action: **Ivan, Regina** *and* **Bette** *calmly climb down, open up the lids of their posing blocks and produce cutlery, a table cloth, a lighted cigarette, an ashtray, a plate . . . everything which one needs for dinner. In the space of three lines, they lay a table for* **Neil**; *every time he holds out his hand for a drink or cigarette, it is there. The place setting is in red and gold, and the cutlery on the table includes a hammer.*

Neil   and even though it was the middle of the night I decided to lay the table because I think if you are going to do these things then you should do them with some style. And I think you should always have one of these in the house. (*A bottle of red wine.*) Because you never know just exactly when you're going to need it. And while I was laying the table I listened to the messages on my answering machine. I don't know about you but it's usually the first thing I do when I get in and the first message said

Regina   *Oh Neil, I hope you're OK, listen I'm in a phone box. It's about this guy I met on Saturday, he says he knows you, and he wants to – o shit the money's run out, I'll try and catch you later, hope you're all right, 'bye.*

Neil   Yes I'm all right. And the second message said –

Ivan   *Oh Hi Neil it's Ivan. How are you? I just wanted to see if you were OK after last night. What sort of time were you having, I was having a fucking awful time. Anyway I hope you're OK. I'll call you later. 'Bye.*

Neil Yes I'm OK. And the third message said –

Bette *Oh. Er . . . Hope you're all right. Listen, there's something I have to talk to you about. Could you ring me? 'Bye.*

Neil The thing is, I was expecting a message from my fourth friend and he hadn't called and I know it's stupid to worry about people when you can't actually see them, I know, but I was worried about him.

So I decided to fix myself dinner, because I think when you live on your own you have to take really good care of yourself. And I think this helps. (*Pours himself a glass of red wine. The Three Queens and the pianist also raise glasses of wine to the audience.*) And I would just like to say, I would just like to say to all the other gay people here with me tonight, I would just like to say, cheers.

They all drink.

Then they all step forward for a second toast.

All And we would just like to say, we would just like to say to everyone here tonight, to all of you, and boy do we mean it –

They toast the audience in silence – unless the audience itself responds, as sometimes happens.

So it was two-fifteen and I decided to fix myself dinner using fresh, healthy ingredients just like we're all supposed to do these days, and I don't know if this ever happens to you, but I ended up chain smoking. And then I thought well I must eat something, but why is it that at two o'clock there's only ever spaghetti, so I put the water on to boil and while the water was boiling I read the paper because I hadn't had a chance to read it yet and the paper said;

Why be afraid, why be afraid, why be afraid to say it sodomy and sleeping around are wrong and ninety percent of homosexuals should be put in the gas chamber and thank goodness some people have made their position quite clear and have come up with standards of conduct which mean that our

people don't have to be subjected to this kind of thing –

Regina *stops him by giving him a glass of wine to drink.*

Regina Neil, Neil, Neil . . . As a dear friend of mine always says: don't buy into the paranoia. All right darling?

Neil So I put down the paper. It was three-thirty in the morning, I had to speak to someone, it was that time when you think I'll just call someone, oh no, I can't.

So I turned on the radio, and the radio said:

I was horrified. I was horrified –

Regina Horrified? My dears I was shocked to the core!

Neil *I turned it off when my daughter came in the living room, and if attempts are made to deliberately suggest that the homosexual way of life is just as good as ordinary married life, then that is a basic problem, Government Health Warning: Warning! Smoking can give you AIDS. Just two puffs and you've had it –*

Regina And too many poufs spoil the duvet, and as my mother used to say: Always take the butt out of your mouth before the next pouf!

Neil I must have been drunk because I had to laugh. I had to, *please don't get me wrong, some of my best friends are gay people but there are you know more gay places than straight places these days and you know that woman who called to say they should all be put up against the wall well I have to say that I do think that's a bit extreme OK but something has to be done –*

Bette Something has to be done.

Neil *Something has to be done to stamp out this terrible killer disease because I don't want to be walking down the street with my wife in one hand –*

Neil *is holding* **Ivan**'s *hand.*

Neil *and my little baby daughter in the other and to see two blokes kissing and holding hands but you know that kind of thing is beginning to happen –*

and so I turned off the radio and I had to talk to somebody and so I called up this friend of mine well he's not such a close friend really, I hadn't seen him for weeks and he said

Regina *Are you on your own, listen, I'm afraid I've got some more really bad news –*

Neil And so I put the phone down. But I had to talk to somebody so I phoned up this friend of mine he's in New York now. It was late when I called so when he picked up the phone I said, I'm sorry, I'm sorry I'm calling you so late but I have to talk to somebody, and he said –

Bette *It's all right, dear. It's still tea-time here. Listen, you know little Gary, the two Garys? Yeah. Well we were going to take big Gary upstate for a rest . . . he died. Hello? . . . Hello?*

Neil And I said, I can't think of anything to say. I don't think there is anything to say.

The Three Queens are standing close around **Neil***;* **Bette** *is standing right behind him and holding him tight. During the next speech* **Neil** *slowly and deliberately raises a hammer above his head. When the speech ends, he brings it down on the golden plate in front of him, sending broken china across the stage.*

And then I called my sister who I love dearly in a strange kind of way and she said Oh Neil it must be so terrible for you . . . and then I went to bed I have this dream. I must have been dreaming I am lying in my bed and my Father is sitting by the side of the bed weeping which I've never heard him do because somebody is forcing him to watch me die and why don't you tell me what I should say to him why don't you tell me!

Nicolas *begins to play very beautiful music.* **Regina** *takes the hammer from* **Neil***'s hand; he pulls the tablecloth deliberately from the table so that cloth, cutlery, glass and china all fall into the spilt*

wine on the floor. The table is packed away. **Ivan** *slowly moves across the front of the stage; picking up in turn each of the five glasses used to toast the audience he drains each glass of wine and then smashes it by hurling it to the floor. Broken glass covers the stage. Only the bottle of red wine is saved. The lights are very dim as, at the end of the sequence,* **Ivan** *takes* **Neil** *in his arms. The music ends.*

Bette At ten-past-seven on the evening of February the 11th 1873, Mr Simeon Solomon was in a public toilet in Christopher Place, WC1 – that's right dear it's still there isn't it? Just off Oxford Street round the back of Selfridges. He was with one Mr George Roberts, aged 60. I'll just say that again, George Roberts aged 60; there is hope for us all, girls. Unfortunately history does not record exactly who was doing what to whom.

Regina We don't know if George was sucking off Simeon –

Ivan Or if Simeon was sucking off George.

Regina We don't know if a few moments earlier, perhaps, there was a young man in there, a young man in there . . . watching; possibly a barrow-boy from Berwick Street market. That would have been very nice. But how could I know? I wasn't there.

Ivan Perhaps Mr Solomon was feeling just a little bit desperate. Perhaps he'd wandered round every single cottage in the West End for hours, and he couldn't find anyone, just some old man wanking himself off, and perhaps he thought, oh well, never mind, maybe he'll be wearing false teeth and take them out. But how could I know what that feels like? I wasn't there.

Bette Perhaps he imagined he was somewhere else. Perhaps he imagined he was at home, in bed, and there was a knock on the door and a young man came in – a man 15 years younger than he, who said, Do you think I could get into bed with you? But how would I know? How could I possibly know what a moment like that feels like?

Regina They were arrested. Mr Simeon

Solomon, who came from a wealthy and respected family, was fined one hundred pounds. And Mr George Roberts, who was an unemployed stableman –

Bette I'll just say that again, Mr George Roberts who was an unemployed stableman, George could read but not write, he could read, but not write –

Ivan Mr George Roberts was sentenced to 18 months hard labour in the house of correction.

Regina You do surprise me. What a surprise that was. D'you think it killed him?

Bette Simeon Solomon never apologised for what he'd done. He didn't hang his head in shame. He didn't even have the good manners to leave town.

Regina Of course she left town dear! She vanished for three months.

Ivan Unfortunately history does not record exactly what Simeon did for those three months. The next we hear of him, he resurfaced, in, of all the God awful places in the world to resurface, in North Devon. Ah yes we've all been there! And it was in North Devon no less that Mr Solomon began a new and glittering career giving public readings from the works of Mr Charles Dickens.

Bette Of course he didn't actually say they were the works of Mr Charles Dickens, he in fact claimed that they were his own original works which seems to me to be

Bette⎫
Regina⎪ ENTIRELY REASONABLE
Ivan⎬ BEHAVIOUR!
Neil⎭

Bette Come on girls it's frock time . . .

Bette, Ivan and Regina open the lids of their posing blocks and produce masses of black feathers, tulle, bedspreads, binliners etc; artfully knotting, tucking and draping, they swiftly transform themselves into three Victorian women – vulturine mourners, recreating the original illustrations to the Dickens text wheich they are about to massacre.

During this dragging up, the text is liable to go a little astray . . .

Bette Oh it's taken so long! D'you know people say to me Bette, Bette, Bette, they say –

Regina What d'they say Bette, what d'they say?

Bette They say why, why, why, why, why, why do you go on wearing frocks? I mean, surely there must be an easier way of making a living. And I say . . . No!

Ivan Perhaps, Bette, like Mr Solomon, you just feel the need to speak your mind.

Regina Perhaps Mr Solomon just felt the need to flee to Devon and put on a frock!!

Ivan Well I think in the circumstances, considering all the dreadful things that had happened to him – why I think even I might have felt like fleeing to Devon and putting on a frock.

Bette Even thou, dear, even thou . . . Perhaps he chose to read, in those dark and difficult months of 198 – I mean, 1873, perhaps he chose to read from that laughable masterpiece of mid-nineteenth-century nastiness, entitled, Regina?

Regina *Martin Chuzzlewit!*

Regina's announcement of the charade's title is indeed unintelligible, though impressively loud. Bette tries again . . .

Bette I don't think they quite got that, would you just do it again dear?

Regina (*with accompanying piano*)
MARTINCHUZZLEWITCHARLESDICKENS 1834 ITHANKYOU!

Bette Which text features in its fifty-first chapter a celebrated confession . . . and let us suppose, let us just suppose Ladies and Gentlemen that it was this deathbed confession, this cry in the night that Mr Simeon Solomon chose to express his feelings at that particular moment of history. Ladies and Gentlemen, I ask you to a fading of the

lights . . . (cue fifteen, David, thank you) a
man dying . . . (music I think, Nicolas, thank
you . . .

*The Three Queens are now composed in a tableaux;
three rustling and overdressed vultures around a
naked corpse,* **Neil** *stretched backwards and upside
down across one of the blocks. Although the piano is
now playing a sombre, melodramatic version of
Schoenberg's* Transfigured Night, *and the text is
funereal, the tone is grimly cheerful and, as they say,
'Dickensian'.*

Bette . . . *and gathered here around the
deathbed; Mrs 'Arris . . . an entirely
imaginary character —*

Regina *And Mrs 'Arris's bestest friend,
Mrs Sarah Gamp — Gamp is my name, and
Gamp my Nature — Professional Nurse.*

Ivan *Ably assisted by her dear friend, that
sweetest and best of women, Mrs Betsey
Prig, professional nurse also.*

Bette *It is the night; they are alone together
now. It is one of those silent nights, when
people sit at windows, listening for the
thunder that they know will shortly break.
But the storm, gathering swiftly, has not yet
come.*

Regina *Ah, he'd make a lovely corpse.*

Regina *utters a sigh of pleasure. Looks at the
audience to see who else is gathered around the
deathbed . . . Mrs Gamp and Mrs Prig drink
throughout the scene.*

Regina *Now ain't we rich in beauty here
this joyful evening I'm sure.*

Ivan *Years and our trials, Mrs Gamp, set
marks upon us all.*

Regina *Changes, Mrs Prig . . . changes.*

Ivan *More changes too to come afore we've
done with changes.*

Regina *I could never keep myself up but for
a little drain of the spirits, never knowing
what may happen next, and the world being
so uncertain.*

Ivan *Your countenance, Sairey Gamp, is
quite an angel's.*

Regina *Betsey, I will now propose a toast.
My frequent partner, Betsey Prig!*

Ivan *Which, altering the name to Sairey
Gamp, I drink, with love and tenderness.*

Ivan *Sairy Gamp, you do amaze me.*

Regina *Why so, Betsey Prig? Give it a
name, I beg.*

Ivan *Never did I think, until I know'd you,
as any woman could live on the little that you
takes to drink.*

Regina *Betsey Prig, none of us knows what
we can do until we tries.*

*The Patient stirs. Great expressions of sympathy
from the nurses.*

Bette *Everything that money can do, was
done.*

Ivan *And what can do more, Mrs 'Arris?*

Regina *Nothing in the world, my girlies.
Nothing in the world.*

Ivan *Is he quite collected in his mind? I
mean, is he quite the full shilling?*

Regina *Oh, bless you, no! Excuge me if I
makes remark, which no offence is meant
and none being took I hope ladies and
gentlemen, as I knows there are people here
tonight mourning the dead, but I speaks as I
find, and we never knows what is hidden in
each other's breasts; and if we did we'd have
glass bosoms, and if we had glass bosoms
we'd put the curtains up I do assure you —*

Ivan *But you don't mean to say —*

Regina *No I don't Betsey Prig, there you
are always putting something in my mouth
when I least expect it. Even the tortoise from
the Spanish Imposition shouldn't make me
own I did and as I said to our Maudie, I
said, Maudie! I said, Maudie! Maudie
Littlehampton I'll have a pennorth of gin, a
pennorth of gin she says, I says a pennorth of
gin —*

Regina *is by now shrieking like a demented hen, the body has been forgotten and the text is in shreds.* **Bette** *intervenes to rescue the proceedings.*

Bette *It was very dark!*

Regina *Oh well oblige me Mrs 'Arris I'm sure.*

Bette *It was very dark, and in the murky sky there shone a lurid light.*

Regina *Very lurid I'm sure.*

Bette *A very few large drops of rain began to fall. Thunder began. The thunder rolled; the rain poured down like Heaven's wrath. The lightning flashed, and in a trembling instant everything was clear and plain!*

The Patient/Corpse starts into life, and the melodrama begins in earnest.

Neil *Oh God!*

Regina *So there you are. Still in the land of the living?*

Neil *I cannot bear it; I cannot!*

Ivan *None of us knows what we can do till we tries.*

Neil *I cannot bear it —*

Regina *I never see a poor dear creature took so queer —*

Neil *I cannot, Oh! God!!*

Regina *There! That's the way he's been conducting himself. Instead of being grateful.*

Ivan *Oh fie, for shame sir, fie, for shame, Not Grateful?*

Bette *Not Grateful?*

Regina *Not Grateful!*

Ivan *He should be grateful! He should be grateful!*

Regina *You rouge yourself Sir! Rouge yourself!*

Bette *What was it he had found? What was it that he knew?*

Neil *I have something very particular and strange to say to you. Something frightful to think of —*

Regina *Who denies it?*

Ivan *Who denies it?*

Regina *Not me, Betsey Prig!*

Ivan *Nobody if you doesn't Sairey Gamp! Poor dear! He's all of a tremble!*

Regina *And no wonder, I am sure, considering the things that have been said!*

Ivan *He's as mad as a March hare.*

Regina *Madder!!*

Ivan *A great deal madder! A great deal madder Mrs Gamp!*

Regina *Not only mad —*

All *BUT REALLY MAD!!*

Neil *It is enough to make me mad, considering the things that I have seen. I never would have spoken; but sometimes I have it all before me in a dream! Oh is there such a dream? Sometimes I almost think I hear him; but he's dead!!*

Ivan *Such a Darlin'!*

Neil *He's dead!*

Regina *Well I've had a lovely ev'nin'.*

Neil *He's dead!*

Regina *Well we'd better bury him then —*

Neil *Dead!*

Ivan *Lambs could not forgive!*

Neil *Dead!!*

Ivan *Nor worms forget!*

Neil *Oh why, why, why didn't he live? They don't tell you — But I have sat watching night and day . . . many a night I have been ready . . . now I can speak and I must speak. Jury, Judge and Hangman could have done no more, and can do nothing now!*

Bette *He's dead!*

Ivan *Dead!*

Regina *Dead!!*

Neil *Oh!!!...God!!!!*

Without pausing **Neil** *breaks from his climactic cry of anguish to a simple note of pleasure. The tableau breaks and the Queens disrobe.*

Neil ... Bette, I feel so much better when we've done that bit.

Bette I'm sure you do dear.

Neil Do you know the feeling?

Bette I invented the feeling.

Neil You see, Ladies and Gentlemen, my problem is, I just can't control myself. Not any more. I just can't control myself. I'm walking down the street and I say to myself oh Neil you're doing so well, you haven't cried in public all week, and then I realise that I'm walking down the street and I'm crying.

Bette You dress for hours, the whole thing's done by hand, you spend at least half an hour putting on your face and then you sit down and you have a really good cry. You let yourself go.

Neil And then I'm walking down the street and I realise that I'm biting my lip so hard that there's actually blood running down my chin.

Bette And then what do you do? You change your outfit, you repair your face, and you do it again.

Neil And then I get on the bus, and somebody behind me says Ha! It smells as though somebody in here has shit themselves, and then I look down and I see I've spilt my drink.

Bette And then what do you do? You pack up your frocks, you get in a taxi, and you're ready to do it again.

Neil And this happens to me sometimes, I'd just come, and I must have been crying because I could see the tears falling on his back.

Bette And you do it again.

Neil And then I looked down, and I thought, Oh, I must have haemorrhaged, because I was crying tears of blood, that's what happens.

Bette And you do it again.

Neil And I looked down and I saw there was come all over my hand.

Bette You do it again.

Neil And I looked down and I saw there was shit all over my cock.

Bette You do it again.

Neil And I looked down and I saw that I was bleeding;

Bette You do it again.

Neil And I looked down and I saw that I was bleeding;

Bette You do it as long as you have to dear.

Neil And I looked down and I saw that *the way before us grew dim beneath the fading light of the stars, and that the still pools to the left of us and to the right gave forth their dim reflections, and this whole night seemed to me to be a figure of my years gone by and I turned to the one who led me in my dream and I said –*

I said, please, just put your arms around me.

I said

before you go, do you think you could tell me a story?

During the next sequence **Neil** *sits alone, holding the bottle of red wine.*

Regina *A History of Simeon Solomon from the Gutter to the Grave.* **Mr Solomon died of a massive heart attack, induced by chronic alcoholism, in May 1905.**

Bette *He died alone.*

Ivan *He died alone and friendless, surely regretting the squalid vices which had destroyed his once considerable talent.*

Bette *'I can't believe the poor unhappy fellow has actually done such things. I do think in a case such as this, a man is bound to consider the consequences to all his friends.'*

Neil *begins slowly to pour the red wine out onto the floor.*

Regina *Why have I never heard of him?*

Bette *Why* have *I never heard of him?*

Ivan *Have you heard anything about that poor Miss Solomon? I try not to talk about it for the sake of the family. For my part, I hope I never see him again.*

He never painted again.

The wine is now all spilt and the bottle is empty. The Three Queens slowly turn their backs, move to the staircase and ascend. At the top of the stairs they pause for a last farewell look to **Neil**. *They turn once more as if to leave, then* **Ivan** *suddenly shouts.*

Ivan It isn't true!!

They return to the stage and sweep up onto their posing blocks again as **Neil** *mops up the red wine with the length of red silk, which he then drapes around himself, dripping, so that all four of them are now standing very proudly and very scarlet before the audience.*

Bette They put it in the papers, but it isn't true.

Regina Yes, he was always drunk, and it didn't kill him, not for years. Yes, he was always broke, always, and it didn't kill him. And yes, he kept on falling in love with handsome young men and that didn't kill him either. He lived till he was 65.

Ivan For another 32 years, 32, and for each of those 32 years he drew and he painted . . . he drew on paper and on pieces of cardboard, and if he had to he got down on his hands and his knees and he worked as a pavement artist on the Brompton Road and he never, never, never, never, never, never, not once in 32 years, from 1873 to 1905, he never apologised for what he'd done.

Bette And his friends came to him and they asked him to come back and he said NO!

Regina and his uncles came to him and they asked him to come back and he said NO, *I have*

not been all that I might have been, he said NO, *I am not as other men are*.

Ivan and his family asked him to come back and he said NO! *I cannot possibly ask you to forgive me. My behaviour has been perfectly disgraceful.* Do you know how sorry I am? I am *that* fucking sorry.

Regina He sold matches on the Mile End Road, he slept in the gutter, he slept underneath the arches.

Bette His family got him put in the workhouse, the one at St Giles, you know, where Centre Point is now, and at the end of his life a journalist came to interview him and he said 'Oh Mr Solomon, it must be so terrible for you, an artist, it must be so terrible for you living here with these kind of people', and he said *well actually I like it here. You see, it's so central.*

Ivan Very handy for Chelsea, for in the winter of '87 he was invited to tea by none other than Sir Edward Burne Jones, in Chelsea, and so he got up off his hands and his knees and he dusted himself off and he went and had tea with Sir Edward Burne Jones, in Chelsea, and they found him in the kitchen, trying to get out of the kitchen window with the silver; Lady Burne Jones called the police, but Sir Edward paid them to go away again.

Bette In the winter his uncles bought him a new suit of clothes, they said it was to keep him warm but, of course, it was to make him look respectable; and, of course, he sold them at once.

The Three Queens have opened their boxes once again, and have produced four shabby old overcoats, which **Regina, Neil, Bette** *and* **Ivan** *now put on, making a picture of four tramps.*

Regina In the winter of '87 he just couldn't keep warm, he wore all his clothes at once but he just couldn't keep warm . . . so he'd go into the National Gallery, because it was free, and he'd sit there, for hours, just staring at the pictures . . .

The lights have changed until all the theatre is dark except for the giant painting which is now shining gold behind the silhouetted figures of the four black tramps, with their backs to the audience, looking at the picture. **Neil** *turns and whispers to the audience.*

Neil This picture is an allegory of Love.

He then leaps up, changes his posture and voice and assumes the role of a particularly unpleasant upper-middle-class, closeted, English art expert giving a lecture in the National Gallery. This section of the text is largely improvised in its details, especially with regard to the obscenity of the backchat to other gay men in the audience and the depths of abuse this character directs at black people, foreigners, disabled people and unemployed people in the audience. The monologue is relentless, hilarious and deeply hostile to the character portrayed.

Neil This picture is, of course, Ladies and Gentlemen, the famous *Allegory of Love* painted by Agnolo de Bronzino for Cosimo de Medici at the height of the Italian Renaissance the Quattro Cento. And *welcome* to the National Gallery – and just before we begin this evening's tour I would just like to say how super it is to have so many people here tonight to share art with me. Because I do believe that art is for sharing. And I can't help noticing that there are one or two black people here tonight which I think is lovely, and I'm quite sure that there are some unemployed people at the back there which is also quite thrilling. No disabled people – we build them a ramp and still they don't come and I think it's a shame. It's a shame. I think it's a shame because I do believe that art is for sharing. Welcome to the National Gallery. Well here we are, here we are in room number 642 featuring the famous Allegory of – I'm sorry? . . . I would just like to say Ladies and Gentlemen that if you do have a foreign person sitting next to you tonight – if you could just explain British culture to them as we go along, that would be super, thank you. An allegory . . . well, an allegory, it means that although this appears to be a picture of one thing it is in fact a picture of something else entirely.

And this particular allegory, Ladies and Gentlemen, has of course been the subject of in-depth discussion by the world's leading Art Historical Experts, and yet its precise significance remains obscure. Especially the precise significance of this particular allegorical detail here, this rather handsome young man, with his back to the camera. I couldn't help noticing that you Sir were rather intrigued by that particular detail. Are you two together? Are you? Well that's very modern. Welcome to the National Gallery. I believe that art is for everybody . . . And this particular allegory does remain completely open, completely open to interpretation.

And so we move on, to room number 7,657, featuring the works of none other (I think if we could not blow our nose in the presence of High Art, that would make the evening much easier for all of us don't you? Thank you), Room number 7,657, featuring the works of none other than Mr Leonardo da Vinci, hhmmm, hhmmm!! Mr Leonardo da Vinci. And this is of course the famous *Virgin on the Rocks* – there she is in the middle, completely on the rocks, poor darling. And as we gaze upon the face of Leonardo's angels I am sure that we are all reminded of the famous comment by that Famous Art Critic, Mr Walter Pater, hmm, hmmmn!! who remarked upon the particular androgynous quality . . . I'm sorry? Androgynous? Well, it means, it does mean that this is a picture of a group of, of a group of h . . . h . . . h . . . ho . . . ho . . mo . . seckshuals. And so we move on.

We move on, to room number 1,062, featuring a recently acquired work by none other than Sir Frederick Lord Leighton (hm, hm, hm, hm . . .) Sir Frederick Lord Leighton who of course built that lovely lovely Leighton House just adjacent to Holland Park Walk, good evening sir. And this picture is entitled *The Desolation of Andromache*, there she is in the middle in blue, completely desolate poor love. And this picture too is an Allegory of Love, an

llegory of Love, Ladies and Gentlemen, but
f Love amongst Rich People; you will of
ourse notice those rather attractive and
xpensive High Victorian draperies. And I
vould like you to know, Ladies and
Gentlemen, I would just like you to know
hat recent X-rays have revealed that
eneath those draperies that naughty
aughty Sir Frederick Leighton did in fact
aint all the figures in this composition
ntirely naked – entirely naked! – well they
vere Greek – and then at a later date he
overed them. Except you will notice, yes sir
'm sure will notice, that he could not bring
imself to cover this particular figure, this
oung man here, whose back he has merely
Iraped . . . with . . . with a leather strap . . .
nd so we move on!
Ve move on to the penultimate picture
vhich we shall be looking at in tonight's tour,
lovely little German altarpiece from the
arly sixteen hundreds, *die sexhundt yahr
undert*, featuring the Martyrdom of Saint
Sebastian. Saint Sebastian!! You will of
ourse notice that the Saint is completely tied
ip. Completely tied up. And you will notice
hat the arrows there, the arrows are
enetrating his flesh. They are . . .
enetrating it. Those were the days! And this
icture, Ladies and Gentlemen, this picture
s also an allegory, of Spiritual Fortitude,
lthough I must say I also find it rather
noving . . . in a personal sort of way.

And so we move on, on to the last picture
vhich we will be looking at in today's tour,
nd before we do I would just like to say how
uper it has been having so many people here
vith me tonight, none of you disabled as I say
ut some of you black, which is lovely. And
now this is a personal favourite of mine, a
ather lovely little work by a rather lovely
ittle late Victorian painter, Mr Simeon
Solomon – no, I never met him . . . And you
:an't quite see the details in this one which is
a shame because I particularly wanted you to
see the details . . . So I shall just bring this
particular work a little closer for your
nspection, Ladies and Gentlemen, because
:his picture –

Neil *comes forward with the portrait of Solomon in
his hands. As he does so the other three 'tramps' turn,
and join him. He turns the portrait over to reveal the
reverse, which is a sheet of gold glass in a gilt frame.
Each of the four is now holding a blank, golden
picture, each picture shining in a beam of light; the
rest of the stage is in darkness. Music.*

Neil This picture is, in fact, a picture of . . .

Ivan This picture is an early work by Mr
Simeon Solomon, one of a series illustrating
scenes from normal family life. It is a picture
of a Jewish wedding; here is a young man and
here an old man. The older man is gazing at
the boy and the boy . . . is staring right at you.

Bette And this is a picture of the Passover;
this young boy is speaking to his father, and
he is saying 'Wherefore is this night
distinguished from all other nights?'

Ivan And this is a late work by Mr Simeon
Solomon, one of a series depicting scenes
from a dream –

Bette scenes he must have imagined late at
night –

Regina scenes he must have imagined when
he was drunk –

Ivan scenes that he cannot possibly have
witnessed, scenes depicting events which
cannot possibly have occurred.

Bette This is a picture of a young man
holding another young man to his breast,
and this picture is entitled *Night and Dawn*.

Regina and this picture is entitled *Sleep and
Death* – and this picture is entitled *David and
Saul* –

Bette and this picture, which is the same
picture, is entitled *The Bridegroom and the
Bride*, and beneath the picture is written
'When you find my Beloved, will you not tell
him, that I am faint with love?'

Ivan And this picture is entitled 'The one
that sleeps and the one that watches' – the
older man has flowers in his hair; and the
young man is dressed in a faded robe of violet

silk. His left hand clutches at his heart; his hair is dyed, his eyes are closed, but he is not crying—

Regina and in all of these pictures the two men are gazing at each other, as if—

Bette They are looking into each other's eyes, but not quite—

Ivan as if they can see something which you cannot yet see; as if they are about to kiss—

Bette as if they are about to . . .

Ivan And this picture has been destroyed. This picture was drawn on the pavement outside the Brompton Oratory and it was destroyed by the feet of people shopping.

Bette This picture has faded, there's almost nothing left of it.

Regina You'll have to look very closely.

Ivan WHAT IS THIS A PICTURE OF?

Pause.

Neil And I looked down and there he was, on his hands and his knees, on the pavement, making some kind of a drawing, and I said, my God, I never thought I would meet you like this. I looked down at his hat with the fifty-pence pieces in it and, well, I said to Steven when I got home, I said, listen love, there but for the Grace of . . . and I'm sorry, I reached into my wallet and, well, I gave him a fiver . . .

Neil *lets a five-pound note fall through a beam of light onto the stage; the Three Queens repeat this gesture.*

Bette I would like you all to know that this is a real fiver.

Ivan Well, all right, I will give you a fiver but you must try and pay me back as soon as possible.

Regina I often wonder which of us are going to end up like he did.

Neil I mean, which of us are going to be as happy as he was.

Lights up, the coats are shed; for each of the next three speeches the queen who is speaking is caught in a single spotlight.

Ivan On my sixty-fifth birthday I shan't be falling over dead drunk and dying in the street of a heart attack. I'm going to hold a party. Everyone I know will be there, everyone. And, just for old times' sake, just to show I can do it, I'll be dressed to kill, flirting with all the boys in my white Balenciagia ballgown. I shall arrive late and leave early; but unlike Cinderella, I won't be leaving anything behind. I shall be walking down the street with my arms full of flowers, getting my taxi—you can travel on the Tube looking like this, believe me, I've done it, but it's not for the fainthearted let me tell you—with so many flowers that I shall hardly be able to carry them all—but I will. And of course the taxi driver will be completely overwhelmed. Stunned. He'll say to me, where on earth did you get all of those flowers? Well I could say, it's funny you should ask me that—because they don't always talk to you do they, not when you look like this—I could say actually I'm just about to ask you to drive me all the way to Willesden Jewish cemetery at four in the morning to lay them on the grave of a man I never met but whom I respect; but then he'd think I was totally insane; so I might say, Darling, they're for you, but they're not, they're for me, and anyway that would sound like I was trying to pick him up and I do think trying to pick up the cab driver at four in the morning is just a little bit tacky . . . so what I'd say is, these are my flowers; it's my birthday. I'm 65. These are my flowers; these are my shoes. This is my dress. This is my hair. This is my face, my make-up, so why don't you just stop the cab, get in beside me, and . . .

Regina D'you know I met him? No, I did, I actually met Simeon Solomon. And I can tell you exactly when it was. I'd just come back from Russia, visiting my estates, and the troika was waiting for me outside the stage door of the Black Cap public house, Camden Town, NW1. I was Russian down the

Steppes . . . I was rushing down the steps and I tripped, there was a couple of bottles of vodka caught in the hem of my Schiaparelli gown, how they got there I'll never know. I pushed my way through the adoring throng of fans, Dimitri handed me up into the troika, I flung the sables round me and we were off! off into the crisp night air, the bells jangling, the horses' hooves striking up sparks from the frozen ground, the chill wind making my cheeks flame like those of a seventeen-year-old. Seventeen. And as we hurtled down Kentish Town High Road, NW5, there he was! Pissed out of her screech with her head in dustbin! I said, Dimitri! Dimitri! Stop the troika! We skidded to a halt. I leapt up, threw the sables from my shoulders, and with what was left of the vodka in one hand and a very funny looking woodbine in the other, the wind was whipping my hair into a frenzy, our eyes met, and I screamed out at the top of my fucking voice . . .

Bette Once in everybody's life. (Once, who am I trying to kid?) Once in everybody's life, you get hurt. And that ain't nothing to be ashamed of, because, you know, that's just the way life is. Ladies and Gentlemen, I feel . . . another song coming on. I feel . . . well, let's face it; on a night like this night – after a year like last year – in a city like this city . . . And this song is dedicated to everybody here tonight who's ever been hurt – it's all right darlin', you don't have to lie to me, we've never even met; your mother hurt you, your lover hurt you . . . actually in my case it was my father. Look at me, standing 'ere, I'm 50, 50, and it still hurts me. It hurts. It hurts so badly you can hardly walk anymore; and you know, it's not the heels that are killing you . . . and this is what Mr Simeon Solomon had to say in 1869, this is what she said girls, *The hurt that has been done them passes by; they are made whole, for Love slowly, but surely, heals them; in his arms the broken of spirit are cherished, and when he holds the hearts that are cleft to his breast* . . . Ladies and Gentlemen, this song is most respectfully dedicated to the woman who first sang it one hot August night in 1886, Miss Marie Lloyd!

The lids on the posing blocks fly open once more . . . using several metres of pink tulle and a spare pair of gold stilettoes for **Neil,** *the four queens – for there are now four, since* **Neil** *is in heels too – deck themselves in music hall bows, sashes and hats.*

Bette Miss Marie Lloyd, who said –

Regina What'd she say Bette? What she say?

Bette Miss Marie Lloyd who said, 'Every performance I give, every fucking performance I give, is a command performance, by command of the –

Bette ⎫
Neil   ⎬ . . . Great! . . . British . . .
Regina ⎬ Public!!!
Ivan   ⎭

Neil Thank you Nicolas.

Music. With **Neil** *as MC, they perform Marie Lloyd's greatest hits.* **Bette***'s style is grand, aggressive vaudeville;* **Regina***'s number is delivered with manic vulgarity and much footwork;* **Ivan***'s with maximum sentiment, quiet sincerity and legs for ever.*

Neil (*intro over music*) You could see her in Hoxton at eight and in Shoreditch at nine; she was all over town; she was all over the place; and just when you thought you'd got rid of her, there she was, in the middle of town, in the middle of the night!

Bette
I'm very, very fond of ruins,
Ruins I love to scan;
You'd say I'm very fond of ruins if you saw
    my old man.
We went out in the country
For a stroll the other day
I love to study history . . .
And pubs along the way.
We came upon an Abbey,
It was crumbled all to bits
It looked a relic of a bygone day.
A gentleman said, what is this?
I said, excuse me Sir,
I'll tell you all about it if I may . . . you
    fucker.

*It's one of the ruins that Cromwell
    knocked about a bit;
One that Oliver Cromwell knocked about
    a bit.
In the gay old days there used to be some
    doings
No wonder that the poor old Abbey fell
    to ruins.
Those who study 'Istry sing and shout
    of it;
And you can bet your life there ain't no
    doubt of it;
Outside the Oliver Cromwell last
    Saturday night,
I was one of the ruins that Cromwell
    knocked about a bit.*

Neil (*intro over music*) She worked so long,
she worked so hard. She said: somebody call
me cab! Somebody get me out of here! Am I
too late! And I said, I said, well, it's never too
late . . .

Regina
*Oh we had to move away, 'cause the rent
    we couldn't pay,
The moving van came round just after
    dark.
There was me and this young man,
    shoving things inside the van,
Which we'd often done before, let me
    remark.
We packed all we could, round the front
    and round the back,
And we shoved inside all we could shove
    inside;
Then we packed all we could pack on the
    tailboard at the back,
'Til there wasn't any room for me to
    ride . . .*

*So, this young man
Said: Get in the van,
I'll drop at the Oval on the way.
Off went the van with me stuffed in it,
He said, I've got to take a leak dear,
It won't take a minute,
But he dillied, he dallied,
He dallied and he dillied,
He lost his way, his hands began to
    roam!!*

*Then . . .
We stopped off at the Vauxhall for a large
    gin and tonic,
Now we can't find our way home
(I don't mean rhinestones)
We can't find our way home.*

Neil (*intro over music*) Everybody *loved* her.
They were waiting for her in the gallery; they
were waiting for her in the wings; they were
waiting for her outside the stagedoor at three
o'clock in the morning, they'd say, I've been
waiting here all night, I've been waiting just
to meet . . . *you.*

Ivan
*Now . . .
If I were a Duchess, and I had a lot of
    money,
I'd give it to the Boy who's going to marry
    me;
But I haven't got a penny, so we'll live on
    love and kisses,
And be just as happy as the birds in the
    tree.
The Boy I love is up in the gallery;
The Boy I love is looking down at me.
There he is;
Can't you see?
Waving of his handkerchief,
As merry as a Robin that sings on a tree.*

*All four deliver a triumphant repeat of the chorus as
the footlights blaze. The piano is working full tilt.
Then* **Bette** *and* **Ivan** *repeat chorus again while*
Regina *and* **Neil** *freestyle over the top of it; as the
singing breaks apart the text gathers force and builds
towards the climax of the show. The tulle and shoes
are discarded, and as* **Neil** *delivers the final* Vision
of Love *speech all their joined hands are raised in
unison and all the lights in the theatre come on
together.*

Regina
    The Boy I love
    Is looking down at me,
    And I love him
    And he loves me
    We love each other . . .

Neil
There he is!
Can't you see!
He's waving at me!

Regina   There he is!

Neil   Such a charming man!

Regina   Can't you see? He could charm the drink out of a bottle –

Bette   He could charm the money out of your wallet –

Regina   And even when he was 60 he could charm a boy up an alleyway –

Bette   And YES he was lonely –

Regina   YES he drank too much –

Ivan   YES he smelled bad, YES he insulted each and every friend who ever stood by him –

Neil   and I said well THAT AIN'T NOTHING TO BE AFRAID OF, BECAUSE

Ivan⎫
Neil⎭   THAT'S JUST THE WAY LIFE IS! –

Bette   and nobody wanted to spend the night with him and I said well why don't you come with me, I'll walk you home, you'll be all right with me dear –

Ivan   AND I LOOKED DOWN –

Regina   AND I LOOKED DOWN –

Bette   I LOOKED DOWN –

Neil   I LOOKED DOWN . . . and I saw The Vision of Love, *and he was no longer wounded and no longer bleeding, and upon his face hovered the half-formed smile of a sleeping child, and I knew that this was Love Oppressed, Love Put Away, and as I watched his limbs
stirred in readiness to depart, his wings beat the morning air and with one hand he cast aside the mantle that restrained him –*

Bette   *and I saw many there whom I knew,*

Regina   *many faces that I had seen in dreams,*

Ivan   *and one face in that Company beloved of me above all the rest and I knew –*

Bette   *I knew –*

Regina   *I knew –*

All   *I knew!*

Neil   *that good things were about to happen, for when the sun rises on the outcast who can tell? But I did not know –* I didn't know, I didn't know what was going to happen next!

Music cuts.

Ivan   And the voice said, I think you're ready now . . .

All   Come!

The lights fade to black, leaving **Neil** *in a single shaft of light.*

Neil   *And I was borne along. And I was borne up. And there arose before me the image of one sleeping. And his arms were wound about his head. His lashes were no longer moist with tears, and his face shone. And he was naked. And I looked at him . . . and I looked at him . . . and as if I was both the bridegroom and the bride; as if I were both the beloved and the lover; as the crown of flowers is placed upon the head of the bridegroom, and upon the head of the bride, so Love was the light about us and the crown upon our heads, and the flame of love fell upon my heart.*

The lights rise on the three queens; they are now wearing gold, not scarlet robes. Each holds in his hands a glass of red wine and a red silk handkerchief. **Bette** *gives* **Neil** *a glass and handkerchief.*

Neil   *And the bride and the groom shall drink a glass of wine, and this glass, it is said, is the emblem of their joy.*

They all drink.

Regina   *and they shall exchange rings;*

They all hold up their ring fingers.

Bette *and they shall make their vows.*

They all place their fingers on their lips.

Ivan *And they shall then drink another glass of wine, for one is the emblem of joy, and the other is the emblem of grief; the one of salvation, and the other of consolation, since we must participate alike in all the circumstances of their lives.*

They drink again.

Neil *And then the groom shall take the glass, and wrap it in a handkerchief.*

Each wraps his glass.

Neil And this handkerchief is the handkerchief with which I wipe away the tears from my eyes.

Regina And when I get home I just have a tonic because I'm too tired to get the vodka out, and with this handkerchief—

Ivan With this handkerchief I clean my face.

Bette And I climb into bed, trying not to wake him—

Neil And this handkerchief is warm from his body.

Bette And this handkerchief is wet with my grief—

Ivan My joy, and my anger,

Regina My courage,

Neil My loss of nerve.

Ivan My confusion in the night.

Regina My dear friends.

Bette My farewell . . .

Neil My goodbye . . .

Bette Goodbye!

As at a Jewish wedding, they all tread on the glasses and break them. Music.

Neil *And this is done to bear witness, and*

that our thoughts shall be devoutly intent upon our future state.

And then I looked up, and it was morning, and I couldn't see the stars any more, and I was walking home on my own at four o'clock in the morning, and I said, I said out loud I'm going to keep on doing this,

Ivan Until the day break, and the shadows flee away.

Regina Until the day break, and the shadows flee away.

Bette Until the day break, and the shadows flee away.

Neil *Until the Day break, until the shadows flee away.*

Regina, **Bette** *and* **Ivan** *ascend the stairs, pausing half way up.* **Bette** *turns and gives* **Neil** *an envelope.* **Neil** *opens it, and reads the letter to the audience.*

Neil Simeon Solomon wrote me a letter. And this is what he said: *My Dear Boy, . . . Thank you so much for sending me your photograph. You're not quite what I was expecting, but I must say that I think you are very attractive. I can't help, however, wishing that you were just a year or two younger. Since I last wrote to you, it seems, things have got worse. Please, try not to be too frightened. And tell me darling, because it's what I'd really like to know, are you on your own? Are you alone?*

I'm very sorry I can't be with you tonight.

Lots of love . . . lots of love.

Neil *kisses the paper, and then shows it to the audience. It is completely blank. He holds the paper up in the last of the light.*

Fifteen seconds.

Blackout.

Wild Blue

a collection of short gay plays

1. Uncle Chick
2. Pony Ride
3. Rules of Love
4. Seymour in the Very Heart of Winter
5. The Real Dark Night of the Soul
6. Rex
7. Rosen's Son
8. Lenten Puddings

Joe Pintauro

Joe Pintauro is a playwright, novelist and poet. He is best known for works such as *Raft of the Medusa, Beside Herself, Cacciatore* and *Men's Lives*. The entire collection of his twenty-two one-act plays was published by Broadway Publishing in New York in 1989 under the title *Plays by Joe Pintauro*. Other plays have been published in various collections, including *Gay Plays: Five* by Methuen. *The Dead Boy*, soon to be produced in New York, was given a public workshop by Stephen Daldry at the Royal Court in 1992. Pintauro has written several novels including *Cold Hands* and *State of Grace*, and several award-winning books of poetry. He is currently working on a new novel and a three-part play in collaboration with Lanford Wilson and Terrence McNally.

Preface

A playwright observing the entire history of the world might note that there are few plays with so-called 'gay' themes. Perhaps the theatre hasn't caught up with recent history, which includes the various liberations: gay, feminist, ethnic. We can go back to alter plays (which we have no right to do) and make **Hamlet**'s Ophelia a fellow or Blanche Dubois the gay brother-in-law, which might be no more interesting than putting a dress on a man. But who knows?

I for one would enjoy seeing such things in the hopes of unexpected, unpredictable revelations. I did such a thing with some of my short plays, in fact, when they were works in progress, and found that it unleashed energy that otherwise would have remained covert. My first draft of **Rosen's Son,** for example, was about the daughter of an Orthodox Jew. Her father confronts his son-in-law after her death and punishes him for a quick re-marriage. When I made the daughter a son who died of AIDS, a new play emerged with more excitement and much more moral weight. **Rules of Love** became outrageous, **Seymour in The Very Heart of Winter** became much funnier when the couple became two men, and **Rex** turned hilarious. When these were combined with the other plays, written as gay from the onset, we discovered **Wild Blue,** an evening so successful its production extended beyond its limits to become the longest running play of mine to date. Hopefully, as the theatre takes more risks more such surprises will be in store for audiences.

Joe Pintauro, January 1990

Wild Blue was first at The Glines, New York in July 1987 with the following cast:

Uncle Chick
Uncle Chick   Roscoe Born
Nicky   Tom Calabro

Pony Ride
Zeke   Tom Calabro
Wendell   Dana Bate
Ellie   Park Overall

Rules of Love
Priest   Tom Calabro
Penitent   Roscoe Born

Seymour in the Very Heart of Winter
Tony   Tom Calabro
Victor   Dana Bate
Waitress   Park Overall

The Real Dark Night of the Soul
Sal   Roscoe Born
Farnsworth   Dana Bate
Calaste   Park Overall
The Caller   Tom Calabro

Rex
Eric   Roscoe Born
John   Tom Calabro

Rosen's Son
Mr Rosen   Dana Bate
Eddie   Roscoe Born
Harrison   Tom Calabro

Lenten Puddings
Uncle Wayne   Dana Bate
Megan   Park Overall

Directed by   Robert Fuhrmann
Lighting and Set Design by   Jeffrey Schissler
Costumes by   Charlie Catanese
Sound   Donald Lovelace

Note: In performance the first four plays made up Act One before the interval, with the final four as Act Two.

Uncle Chick

At rise: **Chick** *is packing cartons, going through old letters.*

Nicky *is softly knocking at the partly opened apartment door.*

Nicky (*enters*) Uncle Chick.

Chick What the hell you doin' here?

Nicky I came to visit you.

Chick (*stuffs letters into a carton and goes to door to greet* **Nicky**) Just like that you came ... at midnight?

Nicky I was down here.

Chick Your father know?

Nicky I don't live home any more, Uncle Chick.

Chick Down here doin' what?

Nicky I bought coffee from the Greek place. This gatorade's for me. (*Hands* **Chick** *a container of coffee and moves past him into apartment.*) Nice apartment. What's in the boxes?

Chick Books, records.

Nicky (*picks up a book and reads title*) *The Savage Hunters of the Labrador Peninsula*, by Frank Speck?

Chick Want it?

Nicky Is it interesting?

Chick It's not my book.

Nicky Then how can you give it to me?

Chick Nicky—

Nicky What's the story? You movin'?

Chick They belong to somebody else.

Nicky Who?

Chick How's my brother?

Nicky Fine. And I hear Johnnyboy's

makin' money like crazy, man. He's in music. Records, cassettes, you know. He goes to L.A., Puerto Rico, and London to present stuff. Somethin'. And Aunt Rosemary? She won a trip to Hawaii.

Chick When's she goin'?

Nicky Never. When could you get Aunt Rosemary to leave Passaic?

Chick What's gonna happen to the ticket?

Nicky She gave it back to the nuns. They're gonna run the raffle all over again.

Chick How *you* doin'?

Nicky How do I look?

Chick Older. How'd you find me, Nicky?

Nicky Tonight I was with this guy ...

Chick Yeah?

Nicky Says he knows you.

Chick Who?

Nicky A Steve?

Chick I know a hundred Steves.

Nicky An architect from Tribeca?

Chick Oh. That asshole.

Nicky He was.

Chick How'd you run into him?

Nicky At Uncle Charlie's.

Chick In Bayonne?

Nicky Uncle Charlie's the bar.

Chick A gay bar? (**Nicky** *shrugs, smiles.*) Shit.

Nicky It was good enough for you.

Chick It was not good enough for me. I never stepped foot into one of those joints.

Nicky Okay, where should I go?

Chick If you had any sense you'd go back to New Jersey. (*Turns to a carton and resumes packing.*)

Nicky You want me to be a hockey star like my brother.

Chick I don't interfere with my brother's kids.

Nicky You're supposed to interfere with me. I'm your godchild. You're supposed to take care of my soul.

Chick You got a job?

Nicky Pastry chef. Got my own apartment.

Chick Where?

Nicky Hell's Kitchen. Eleventh Avenue.

Chick Jesus!

Nicky I'm okay there. So... How... What was it with you and this Steve, the architect?

Chick Did you do anything with that scuz bag?

Nicky I don't use my mouth for anything except talk. And after that I say toodle-oo.

Chick When did you come out?

Nicky When I was five or six.

Chick Five or six?

Nicky At Rockaway. You took me in the ocean on your shoulders. I had two fists of your hair like this, and, baby, you had hair down to here 'cause it was the sixties. Granma was alive, and you took us. You taught me to eat clams on the half shell that day.

Chick You spit them all out.

Nicky I didn't swallow them, but I liked them.

Chick This is bad, Nicky.

Nicky I came to visit you.

Chick You *call* people first.

Nicky You wouldn'ta let me up.

Chick What do you want?

Nicky To look at you.

Chick And whatd'ya see?

Nicky I see my father's brother 'cept you're much cuter than him.

Chick Don't assume you can talk any way you like here.

Nicky I always wondered who these women were you use'ta sleep with.

Chick What women?

Nicky 'Why isn't he married?' Aunt Fanny use'ta say. 'He's got a hundred girlfriends' my father'd say. I always imagined the Miss America contest in this apartment.

Chick Your father... There's a case.

Nicky Him too?

Chick What're you crazy?

Nicky You ever do anything with him?

Chick *What?!*

Nicky I could handle it.

Chick He's straight, you little jerk. What is this? What you wanna see me for?

Nicky What are you, Dracula? You got a beautiful face. I came to see my Uncle Chick. Am I makin' you uncomfortable?

Chick Yes. Very.

Nicky Why?

Chick What do you think? I'm embarrassed.

Nicky I was thrilled, man, from the minute that Steve spit it out. He said you were a hot man.

Chick Goddam creep.

Nicky And that you were affectionate. Very tender, he said. I must take after you.

Chick Do you?

Nicky I think probably yeah.

Chick There's a lot of disease out there.

Nicky I don't go with people, Chick.

Chick 'Uncle Chick.'

Nicky Come on, be real with me.

Chick God. Geeez. Nicky.

Nicky What?

Chick You.

Nicky So?

Chick I'd rather you were the other way.

Nicky Why?

Chick It's a hard fucking life.

Nicky I like it.

Chick You're young, and life's too long . . .

Nicky Too long? You mean –

Chick Too long. You outlive your little . . . plans. You get small shots. You start over, twice, three times. It's a bitch.

Nicky I go a day at a time.

Chick Day at a time.

Nicky I seen the zoo out there, from the cowboys to the teddy bears. I'm hip to the bullshit. You know, WASPs go crazy for me.

Chick No lover?

Nicky You think I'm gonna let one of them move in with me?

Chick You need something, somebody.

Nicky Some day there'll be a lover. But tonight it's me and you.

Chick Don't . . . even . . . breathe it. C'mon, punk, out that door.

Nicky Chick, come on, give me a break here.

Chick Out.

Nicky Steve told me what happened.

Chick Steve knows shit.

Nicky His name was David, and he lived here, and these are his boxes, right?

No answer.

You miss him, don't you?

No answer.

So I thought maybe . . . I just could hold you, just –

Chick You gotta go.

Nicky I use'ta imitate your walk, you know that? Uncle Chick?

Chick No. We're related. We're Catholics.

Nicky They don't want us, the Catholics. They won't even let us go to communion. They want us all to be priests or get married. You're my godfather. *Tell me what I should do.*

Chick You're good. You're real good, you hear?

Nicky Damn right, and I love bein' Nick. I love this city. Gotham, man. At night I look at the lit up buildings, Empire State, man. I love the stink of the streets, the smoke, the colors. I love myself, I love you, and I'm not chicken shit. I'm gonna take care of Nicky, and I can take care of you, too.

Chick You a missionary or something?

Nicky When that architect told me tonight that you were too, I swear I got on fire, Uncle Chick. Oh man, there's like a mirror thing when I look at you. I see me. I have no confusion around you. We're like come out of the same place.

Chick Nicky, Jesus!

Nicky Tonight you sleep under the sheets. I'll sleep on top, with my clothes on. Just your arms out. So we can touch.

Chick No good, Nicky.

Nicky *Hands* is all I'm sayin'.

Chick You'll meet somebody.

Nicky Don't send me out there. It's all strangers out there. I'll make breakfast, okay? Hey, Chick. Let me hold you . . .

Chick *folds his arms, remains frozen.* **Nicky** *turns away.*

Chick Nicky. (*Touches him.* **Nicky** *turns and grabs* **Chick**.)

Nicky Don't worry, Uncle Chick. I'm here . . .

Chick *finds himself caught in* **Nicky**'s *embrace. At first he is merely surprised, but he so needs the tenderness, that at last he yields, his arms coming up slowly, till gratefully, lovingly, he returns the embrace.*

Lights fade.

Pony Ride

Set: a bar with a jukebox and grade school class photos on the walls.

At rise: **Ellie** *is bent over the jukebox.*

Zeke Look at that ass. She ain't wearin' no panties. What the hell somethin' like that doin' in Summerville?

Wendell On her way to Chicago.

Zeke That's her limo out there waitin'?

Wendell She come out of it.

Zeke Chauffeur's gonna get frostbit.

Wendell Told her bring him inside.

Zeke Them's New York plates. You got New York music in that box?

Wendell Supposed to be all kinds in there.

Zeke Well, why ain't she playin' her own kinda music?

Wendell Maybe country's her kind.

Zeke With an ass like that? No, she ain't country. How long's the chauffeur been sittin' out there?

Wendell Two hour so.

Zeke Must'a wasted ten gallons of gas.

Wendell He's warm.

Zeke What's she drinkin'?

Wendell Pepsi.

Zeke Zollo and Charlie show up tonight?

Wendell Just left. Wishbone was here, too.

Zeke Wishbone?

Wendell All left just 'fore you got here.

Zeke You mean Wishbone didn't try to have a little fun with her?

Wendell She spurned 'im.

Zeke Oh, no, sweetheart, you ain't shakin' that ass for yourself.

Wendell She spurned Wishbone flat as a pancake.

Zeke She ain't dancin' 'round here for nothin', Wendell. (*Takes a Pepsi to her.*) Hi.

Ellie (*disinterestedly*) Hi.

Wendell Told ya.

Zeke She give me a hardon worse 'an if she grabbed my balls. What time you closin'?

Wendell Any minute. Can't take no chance and keep open past hours.

Zeke Well, I'll be a mother's monkey. She's waitin' for you, Wendell.

Wendell Git on.

Zeke Can't you tell, man? You gonna get laid, buddy.

Wendell Not from no New York trash.

Zeke (*drinks his drink down and throws a buck on the bar. He buttons up his coat, slips on his hat, and crosses to* **Ellie**) 'Night.

Ellie *yawns. He gives* **Wendell** *a sign like 'you lucky dog' and exits.*

Ellie How come you only got grade school graduation pictures up here?

Wendell Don't wanna insult my customers.

Ellie You got change for the jukebox?

Wendell You gimme dollars, I'll make you quarters till hell freezes. (*He makes change and she crosses to jukebox.*) You in the CIA?

Ellie Yes. (*She puts quarter in jukebox and sits at table.*)

Wendell (*brings her a Pepsi*) This one's on me.

Ellie 'Bout time.

Wendell Tell the truth, what you doin' in this town?

Ellie Breezin' through.

Wendell Breezin' ain't spendin' three hours in my bar.

Ellie Depends on your speedometer.

Wendell What's yours say?

Ellie Says I'm doin' ninety-five. How 'bout you?

Wendell My wagon's still in the garage.

Ellie What's it take to get it out?

Wendell Nothin' much if the time's right.

Ellie What's the time like now?

Wendell It's a funny in between time.

Ellie Oh yeah?

Wendell You a reporter doin' a story on this town?

Ellie What's there to report?

Wendell Zero.

Ellie Would it make sense my reportin' on zero?

Wendell Well, you know, typical America.

Ellie This is typical America? (*Laughs.*) No, honey. You been livin' in your mind.

Wendell That driver of yours must be gettin' mighty cold out there.

Ellie He's got a heater.

Wendell Usin' up a lot of gas. You spendin' the night somewhere in this town?

Ellie Depends.

Wendell That's your last drink. I closed five minutes ago.

Ellie No fair.

Wendell This ain't New York.

Ellie Do you fox trot?

Wendell How 'bout if I turn out these lights? (*Turns off main lights.*) I two-step.

Ellie That's good enough.

They dance.

Wendell You married?

Ellie No. You?

Wendell Been.

Ellie Been married, huh?

Wendell Don't I look like I been? A couple times.

Ellie You look like more'an a couple to me.

Wendell Right. You in one of them graduation pictures?

Ellie Not me.

Wendell You ain't from here 'cept . . .

Ellie 'Cept what?

Wendell I seen you.

Ellie Oh yeah?

Wendell On TV or something. (*His hands move down to her ass. She breaks away.*) You gonna spurn me, too?

Ellie You can touch, but don't squeeze. I'm not a squeeze box.

Wendell Touchin's fine with me. Let's go upstairs.

Ellie What's up there?

Wendell A bed.

Ellie There's chairs down here.

Wendell I ain't no contortionist.

Ellie I can sit on your lap.

Wendell You wanna show me how?

Ellie (*puts a straight back chair in the middle of the floor*) Sit. (*He sits down, folds his feet. She lifts her wide skirt and mounts him as if he were a pony. They laugh, face to face.*) Nice smell on your breath.

Wendell What's that?

Ellie Chesterfields.

Wendell Don't smoke Chesterfields. Smoke Winstons.

Ellie Oh.

Wendell Use'ta smoke Chesterfields.

Ellie Uh huh. Oughta open your belt. (*He laughs shyly, reaching under her skirt to undo his belt.*) Let 'em down. Let 'em down. (*He lets down his jeans.*)

Wendell Easy now.

Ellie Take your time.

Wendell You're tight.

Ellie Be all right in a minute.

Wendell Ouch.

Ellie We're gettin' there.

Wendell Phew.

Ellie There. There it is. Comfy now?

Wendell Not bad.

Ellie Let me get a look in your eyes.

Wendell Whaddya see?

Ellie Real velvety brown.

Wendell You like it?

Ellie Yeah, and crows' feet crinklin' up around 'em.

Wendell Think I'm too old for ya?

Ellie Think I'm too young for you?

Wendell No, no. I'm set on gettin' old fast.

Ellie Why?

Wendell Wanna be like Willie Nelson.

Ellie He bores me.

Wendell Gonna let my hair grow, wear a kerchief 'round it.

Ellie What for?

Wendell Tired of the same thing all my life.

Ellie I like the way you look now.

Wendell Easy. I come fast.

Ellie You jus' bored.

Wendell Yeah, I guess.

Ellie You done it all.

Wendell Twice, three times around.

Ellie You done it this way much?

Wendell Too many times.

Ellie Mind doin' it one more time?

Wendell With you I can do it hundred more times.

Ellie How come?

Wendell Cuz you're a movie star.

Ellie I ain't.

Wendell Yes you are, a singer or somethin'. How come you waited 'round here for me when you had your pick of studs the whole night?

Ellie I had you figured out.

Wendell Yeah?

Ellie For the best kisser.

Wendell Best kisser, huh?

Ellie Kiss me, Wendell. (*He does*).

Wendell Easy. I'm quick as lightnin'.

Ellie Don't be quick.

Wendell You're a talker. I ain't had one of them in a dog's age.

Ellie Talkin's half of it.

Wendell You got blue eyes?

Ellie Uh huh.

Wendell Funny blue.

Ellie Like what?

Wendell Like chicory flowers.

Ellie Nice colour, but they shrivel up if you pick 'em.

Wendell You're a country girl.

Ellie Everybody knows chicory shrivels up.

Wendell Half the world don't know what a chicory flower *is*. I can't stand this much talk.

Ellie It ain't made you soft.

Wendell Nothin' makes me soft 'cept finishing.

Ellie You wanna finish?

Wendell Wouldn't hurt.

Ellie First let's improvise.

Wendell What the hell is that now?

Ellie You play roles, like I'd be your little baby —

Wendell Yeah?

Ellie And you, you'd be my daddy.

Wendell Well . . . You start it off.

Ellie Daddy, would you . . . would you do something for me?

Wendell I sure would.

Ellie Protect me.

Wendell Protect you how?

Ellie 'Cause I'm cowld.

Wendell (*envelops her with his arms*) How's this? You warmin' up? Huh, my sweetie pie?

Ellie Pwotect me from everything bad.

Wendell I'm doin' that right now, honey bunch.

Ellie How?

Wendell How do you want me to?

Ellie Put me inside your sweater forever.

Wendell Okay. There's my sweater around you.

Ellie Now button it up and carry me 'round with you forever.

Wendell I'd look pregnant.

Ellie You'd have a pot belly.

Wendell Okay, I'll carry you. How'm I doin'?

Ellie And would you keep kissing me without ever stopping?

Wendell Well, I'd have to stop to breathe.

Ellie Just to breathe, but otherwise, all one long kiss lastin' a whole six months, holdin' me in your arms and not letting me down except to tuck me in so you can go buy me a doll and bring it home to surprise me . . .

Wendell A cabbage patch dolly.

Ellie The old kind with the eyes that blink . . .

Wendell Okay then.

Ellie And then wallpaper my room with paper full of tiny roses, and white curtains with pulldown shades that have little crocheted rings. And make me a trellis in the yard with yellow roses all over it . . .

Wendell I made a rose trellis once 'round a whole gate with a fence.

Ellie And fuck me whenever I asked. And spank me if I was bad and bring me candy from Corwins.

Wendell I can't stand no more of this.

Ellie Please, Wendell, just want you to say one more thing.

Wendell Make it fast.

Ellie Say 'I love you'.

Wendell But –

Ellie Like we was actors. You just have to act the words.

Wendell I love you.

Ellie You gotta look in my eyes.

Wendell I love you.

Ellie Not so *flat*. Say it with all your heart. 'I . . .'

Wendell I love you.

Ellie Oh, yes, that was it. Exactly. Do it ten times.

Wendell Oh, come on!

Ellie Ten times, and we're all through.

Wendell Love you, love you, love you –

Ellie Slow, like before.

Wendell Love you. Love you.

Ellie With the 'I'. 'I . . .'

Wendell I . . .

Ellie 'Love you, Ellie.'

Wendell Ellie?

Ellie Yes. Ellie.

Wendell I love you, Ellie.

Ellie In my eyes now. Looka me.

Wendell I love you, Ellie.

Ellie Once more. Once more like that.

Wendell What're you cryin' for?

Ellie Please.

Wendell I love you, Ellie, love you. Don't cry.

Ellie You'll protect me?

Wendell Sure, I'll protect you.

Ellie And buy me a bag of root beer barrel candy from Corwins?

Wendell Corwin's passed away.

Ellie Oh?

Wendell Yeah, it's the laundromat now.

Ellie No store there?

Wendell No more store.

Ellie Corwin's dead?

Wendell You do come from here.

Ellie Oh, don't go soft on me. Kiss me.

Wendell Now wait. (*She kisses him, getting him more and more excited.*) Miss –

Ellie Lemme ride you, Daddy.

Wendell Jesus!

Ellie Ride, Daddy. Oh, yes, ride.

Wendell Slow down or I'll –

Ellie Wendell, I'm ready, ready if you are.

Wendell Christ! I'm ready.

Ellie Let's go together.

Wendell I'm gonna, gonna –

Ellie Together?

Wendell Uh huh.

Ellie Now?

Wendell Now.

Ellie Now?

Overlapping with.

Wendell Oh, God, yes, yes. Aggggh. Aw Aw. Ughhh . . .

Afterward.

Jesus. Oh.

Ellie Stay still.

Wendell Ugh. Ouuuu.

Ellie Easy.

Wendell Ouuuuwheee. Lemme outta this trap.

Ellie Not so fast.

Wendell Just wanna wash.

Ellie There's time.

Wendell Look, I wanna git decent here. (*Pulls up his trousers under her skirt, then tries buttoning them, but she doesn't get off.*) Lorda mercy, will you let me stand up?

Ellie In a minute. Here, let me wipe your brow.

Wendell Who in the fuck are you?

Ellie One last look in the eyes.

Wendell I had enougha this.

Ellie One last kiss. Please. (*He kisses her.*) Another.

Wendell Shit.

Ellie One more. The last. The final. (*He kisses her.*) And one last word. Say 'goodbye'.

Wendell Yeah. Goodbye.

Ellie 'Ellie.' 'Goodbye, Ellie, darling.'

Wendell Goodbye, Ellie.

She dismounts and starts putting on her coat.

Ellie I'm over here in this graduation picture, 1966.

Wendell Yeah?

Ellie Second row, fifth from the left.

Wendell Second row, fifth from the left? (*Checks photo.*) Oh no. That's my son Billy.

Ellie They called me Billy 'round here once.

Wendell Now don't go insultin' my kinfolk.

Ellie I wouldn't insult Billy. I am Billy.

Wendell You get outta here, you weirdo. Get outta my place. (*She throws a quarter into the jukebox.*)

Ellie I was warned about you, Wendell, by one of your old wives. She said to me, 'Billy, you want something from Wendell, you just gonna have to *steal* it 'cause he don't part with shit.' So I stole. And I got.

Wendell You, you –

Ellie You think no man can do what I just did there? All's it takes is a lil' operation.

Wendell You're pullin' something on me.

Ellie Well, you think what you want. I *got* what I want. Now I can go home for real.

Wendell Oh, yeah? And where is that?

Ellie Oh, it ain't a place, Daddy. It's a state of mind.

Wendell Dear Jesus Lord, forgive me. You can't be Billy. Tell me you ain't Billy.

Ellie Second row, fifth from the left. That's me, Wendell. 'Bye.

The song she picked on the jukebox starts to play.
Wendell *stares as she leaves. Lights fade.*

Rules of Love

Priest 'Bless me, father' . . . Hello?

Penitent Bless me, father, for I have sinned. My last confession was two years ago.

Priest Speak louder please.

Penitent My last confession was two years ago.

Priest Okay, two years ago.

Silence.

Are you still there?

Penitent I'm here. I was . . . afraid.

Priest Did you say 'afraid'?

Penitent Yes.

Priest What are you afraid of?

Penitent I've committed a very grave sin, father.

Priest All right.

Penitent And by afraid, I meant I was nervous about coming here.

Priest I'm not going to hurt you.

Penitent I know.

Priest So take your time.

Silence.

Now your sins?

Penitent I . . . I've fallen in love.

Priest That's no sin.

Penitent With a priest.

Priest Even so, that's no sin per se.

Penitent We've had sex 15, maybe 20 times.

*The **Priest** recognizes the voice of the **Penitent**.*

Priest Oh . . . Let me explain something: after a person confesses a sexual sin to a priest, if that priest follows up with an intimate act with that person, the priest cannot be forgiven except by the Pope.

Penitent I know about that.

Priest But it ends the relationship. Don't you understand? And it ties his hands because he can't question you about your personal material, to explain or to stop you from doing something foolish. For God's sake, find another priest to confess to.

Penitent There are no other priests hearing confessions tonight.

Priest Then come back tomorrow.

Penitent I want to confess to you, father. I know what I'm doing.

Priest All right, say what you want to say.

Penitent At times I feel absolutely no guilt whatever for this relationship. I have the purest memories. Other times, the whole thing troubles me deeply. I feel dirty.

Priest You shouldn't.

Penitent Convince me.

Priest (*shifts uncomfortably*) Do you have any other sins to confess?

Penitent Yes, sins against myself. Selling myself cheap. I don't mean literally, though sometimes I did feel like just a piece of meat.

Priest Don't say that.

Penitent Why else would I come here if I didn't feel that way? God if there's one true sin I should confess it's that I tried to get him to leave the priesthood.

Priest Easy.

Penitent If God hates me for that, He has a perfect right to.

Priest There's no hate in God.

Penitent Promise me that?

Priest Yes, I promise.

Penitent I was alone for too long, father . . .

Priest Okay.

Penitent And here was such a beautiful man, worth caring for, and he wanted me. I did *not* go after *him*. I just couldn't resist his attention to me.

Priest Isn't that what most people yearn for?

Penitent It was so damn egotistical.

Priest No it wasn't.

Penitent I thought I could accomplish what God had failed to.

Priest And what was that?

Penitent To get the guy off that ice-cold mountain he was sitting on all alone, like a lost little boy, afraid to love, afraid to touch.

Priest Maybe you succeeded.

Penitent I don't think so.

Priest But don't you realize that I can't give you absolution unless you're prepared to avoid the occasion in the future?

Penitent You mean avoid him?

Priest Precisely.

Penitent I know the rules.

Priest Shouldn't you think about this?

Penitent I got a job in . . . another city. My plane leaves in a couple of hours.

Priest I see. All right then. Do you have any other sins you wish to place before God?

Penitent You're not really going to stand up and fight for me?

Priest What the hell do you mean?

Penitent You're not going to throw over all these cockamamie regulations and grab me and take the both of us out of here?

Priest Shut up. You can't do this.

Penitent *We can do whatever we want!* What do *you* want to do?

Priest (*after a pause*) Do you have any other sins you wish to place before God?

Penitent Shit. I've told you all my sins.

Priest Then for your penance please attend mass and offer it up for the spiritual welfare of this priest and of yourself.

Penitent He needs it more than I . . .

Priest You might remember him often that way.

Penitent I will remember him often. I promise you that.

Priest Thank you.

Penitent Thank you, father.

Priest You're welcome.

Penitent Goodbye, father.

Priest Forgive me?

Penitent *does not answer.*

Now recite your act of contrition.

Raises hand in the absolution blessing, using the Latin form.

Ego te absolvo ob omnibus censuris et peccatis. In nomine patris et filio et spiritu sancto.

Penitent Oh my God I am heartily sorry for having offended Thee, and I detest of all my sins because I dread the loss of Heaven and the pains of Hell, but most of all because I have offended Thee my God, who are all good and deserving of all my love. I firmly resolve with the help of Thy grace to confess my sins, to do penance, and to amend my life. Amen. (*Begins to get up to leave.*)

Priest Wait!

Penitent *kneels.*

Which city?

Penitent Speak louder, father.

Priest Which city?

Penitent Chicago.

Seymour in the Very Heart of Winter

A small, elegant restaurant in Greenwich Village, N.Y. But we see only one table which, presumably, looks out upon the street. The table is beautifully set for Christmas Eve dinner: a small centrepiece made of one red candle in its holder, surrounded by loose sprigs of holly. One salmon dinner is before **Victor,** *untouched, and a plate of pasta is before* **Tony,** *almost totally consumed. A wine bottle is on the table, all but empty.*

Tony *is an Italian-American, good looking, street-wise, much younger than* **Victor** *and worshipfully in love with* **Victor.**

Victor *assumes the superiority and physical grace of a royal public figure. Once a well-known actor, he has been out of work much too long, now past middle age. He is still unquestionably attractive.*

The **Waitress** *is friendly, formal, and impeccably dressed for a function in which she takes pride.*

As the play opens, we see the couple at table, **Tony** *eating hungrily, and* **Victor** *just sitting, wine glass in hand, looking out the window.*

Tony You haven't touched your food. That's a whole baby salmon.

Victor Tell them to give you a doggie bag.

Tony This blows our food money for the week. Victor? You're ignoring me.

Victor I heard you.

Tony What'd I say?

Victor Something about the food.

Tony If I bore you, have the guts to tell me.

Victor Will that change you?

Tony Bastard.

Victor I am a bastard tonight. I am a bitch.

Tony If you're tired of me, spit it out.

Victor All right, I'll have dessert. Will that make you happy?

Tony I'm not your Daddy, Victor.

Victor But I could be yours.

Tony Start in with our ages now, and I'm walkin' outta here.

Victor All right, all right. Tell me.

Tony What?

Victor What I wasn't listening to. (*Closes his eyes as if listening to music.*)

Tony Go to hell. You act like you're alone. I'm talkin', and your eyes are on the waitress, out the window. Everything 'cept me. Now they're closed. Good night, Victor. (*Waves sarcastically.*)

Victor Good wine relaxes me.

Tony Christmas Eve dinner is a big thing for Italians.

Victor All right, I'll have dessert.

Tony We can't afford dessert here. I'll take you to Rocco's, and we'll split a cannoli.

Victor It's raining.

Tony I'll get the limo. You can ride in back.

Victor Let's stay.

Tony Turnin' down a ride in a limo? A famous actor like you?

Victor Don't hurt me.

Tony You're *famous.* I think the waitress recognized you.

Victor I'm not famous. I wouldn't be caught dead in that funeral car of yours if I could afford a taxi cab.

Tony Poor Victor. 'Fraid your friends at unemployment'll think you're a hypocrite?

Victor My friends know very little about me.

Tony They know you're living with a chauffeur.

Victor Temporarily.

Tony It's over two years now, Vic.

Victor I don't want to go into this.

Tony I pay the rent. You sleep with me.

Victor Go flash your tits someplace and hustle yourself some hunk.

Tony Suppose I want you instead?

Victor Don't be ridiculous.

Tony Where will you go when the hunk moves in?

Victor I'll kill myself.

Tony Thanks. You make me hate myself. (*Toasts* **Victor** *sarcastically*.) Merry Christmas. (*There's a painful silence.* **Victor** *sips wine.*) You know you got like this last Christmas, too. Victor? (*Reaches for his hand.*)

Victor What possesses those jerky, frenzied, lunatic Christmas shoppers? It was summer two weeks ago.

Tony You know what you look like in your suit with that tie? Vic? In this soft light?

Victor Oleg Cassini.

Tony Like a cover of G.Q.

Victor The shit's coming out of your ears.

Tony I'm not buyin' it, Victor. You care for me. And I'd die for you . . .

Victor All right, I won't kill myself . . . (*Sees something out the window.*) Look at those nuts, loaded down with packages . . . When I was a kid, I would've cut off my arm for a Christmas tree. I was dying to smell a big spruce in our living room and sleep under it, on that rose-colored rug, looking up at the lights and the ornaments, having a real tree from the forest in our house.

Tony Why didn't you?

Victor My father was funny about Christmas. It was like a political thing. But the smell of those pine trees on the sidewalk in front of the stores at night, dark green giants all around as if you were lost in a forest suddenly. I'd bend down and grab a branch from the sidewalk and hide it inside my coat and sneak it to bed, holding it near my face, smelling the cold forest in the dark, pretending I was far north in a totally sunless country where people live to be two hundred years old . . .

Tony No sun?

Victor No. Just the aurora borealis and starshine . . . and moons so bright you can read a newspaper. But there'd be no newspapers up there, no buses, no motorbikes, no factories, no wars, no cars, no TV . . . just . . . giant pine trees and log cabins and fireplaces. There would be violence. But the holy kind. I mean rabbits and deer hanging dead in the pantries next to the mince pies, not the violence of the subways, you understand? No muggings, just the men having to hunt for the women and children, and total trust, total trust . . . because we'll all be . . . cousins, born and dying in each other's arms, just generations going on and on. And at night during the blizzards we'd all gather in big snow cellars lined with fur where we told stories, all of us buried under the ice with our fur walls and fires, deep . . . in the very heart of winter. That's why I wanted a Christmas tree, so I could sleep under it and dream of that place.

Tony You should'a stood up to your father.

Victor I did once. He got pale. He stood me in front of him and took my hands in his. 'Christmas trees are not for us. We get something else.' And that was all fine, but I still wanted my tree

Tony After they died, why didn't you go out and get one?

Victor I was still only a kid. My aunts were orthodox.

Tony No. I mean later with Seymour.

Victor Seymour?! Are you serious? Enough Christmas. It's the wine.

Waitress (*comes and picks up wine bottle to remove it*) Coffee for monsieur?

Tony We're invited somewhere for coffee.

Waitress The check?

Tony Just the check.

Victor Wait. There's wine left.

Waitress Oh, I am so soree.

Tony Victor, it's empty.

Victor There's more, see? (**Waitress** *pours – a tablespoonful.*) See?

Waitress Monsieur is right. (**Exits with bottle.**)

Tony Do you ever hear from Seymour?

Victor He's teaching in Massachusetts.

Tony Well, does he write to you?

Victor I hear through others.

Tony Him and his . . . you know, girlfriend still together?

Victor He's living with a student, a boy. I heard they're happy.

Tony Boy, does he change his mind.

Victor Please . . .

Tony It impressed me though about your breakup.

Victor What impressed you?

Tony That he left you for a woman and still you said he treated you decent, you know, that he said he'd never stop loving you.

Victor I said he said that?

Tony Um-hum. (*Yes.*)

Victor I only got to know him when we started breaking up.

Tony It makes me laugh, you with a guy named Seymour. That name is what gets me.

Victor Seymour is an English name.

Tony I imagine some fat Jewish kid.

Victor It's not even a Jewish name. It's French, from Maurice, meaning dark-skinned, like a Moor . . .

Tony Okay . . .

Victor Jane Seymour was third queen of Henry the Eighth. The Jews used Seymour to Anglicize the name Shimon, which was a royal name anyway. One of the twelve tribes of Israel.

Tony Slow down.

Victor I'd still be with Seymour Eliot if I hadn't been an idiot. I'd give my right arm to be with him right now. I'd be sipping port and demi-tasse and laughing instead of staring at this shit. (*Throws napkin over his plate.*)

Tony That's twice you cut off your arm.

Victor Can it, Tony.

Tony Once for a Christmas tree –

Victor I'm not listening.

Tony The other arm for Seymour. You got no arms left, Vic.

Victor Don't make fun of me.

Tony How'd you meet this Seymour? I'm serious.

Victor He was the dramatics teacher in my high school.

Tony You made it with your high school teacher?

Victor I used to clean house for my aunts to scrape up ticket money so I could go up to Mr Eliot in the halls and say, 'I went to the theatre last night'. I dyed my hair.

Tony What color?

Victor Blue-black.

Tony You're kiddin'!

Victor It made my eyes stratospheric blue. I wore sweaters with no shirt. Went through Woolite like it was Coca Cola. I joined the Dramatics Society. He made me treasurer and gave the parts to everyone else. Even then I was smarter about the theatre than he was. I hung out in those shady side streets, around the little ticket agencies, the stage doors, hoping to talk to a star. Once I went up to him in the halls: 'I saw Charlton Heston on forty-fourth street.' He looked at me as if I said I saw a fly on a garbage pail. Never told him I saw Julie Harris coming out of Sardi's. I refused to ask for an autograph. Why jinx myself? I'll be her myself someday. I'd take the train home promising myself that I'd become an actor, I'd get involved with Mr Eliot, and pay back my aunts every penny . . . And I did . . . all those things, didn't I? (*His eyes are lost in the movie of his life playing out the window.*)

Tony He noticed your sweaters?

Victor No. Years later, I got a part in *The Orestia* at Circle in the Square, and who do I see in the audience one night?

Tony Woody Allen.

Victor Seymour Eliot and Claudia Simonetti, his friend. They were on their way to Yale for teaching jobs. Claudia was in Physics. So sorry looking, so thin –

Tony Seymour?

Victor He was balding . . . but sexier, his legs crossed and his arms folded as if he were Arthur Miller or somebody. He recognized me and smiled. That minute everything I ever lost was given back to me: my mother, high school, the house in Brooklyn . . . even my father was there in Seymour's forgiving Jewish smile. Nothing ever came close to that thrill.

Tony Like a physical feeling?

Victor A burning here, as if your chest were on fire. The man's eyes. His beautiful eyes were like a threshold to a future world. His face was like a saint's vision.

Tony I've felt that with you, Vic. (**Victor** *is so self-absorbed here, that he doesn't hear.*)

Victor Right there I said to myself: How can I trap this unicorn? How can we be lovers forever? They went off to Yale, and guess what I did?

Tony You followed them.

Victor I sat in on classes. Got a job in the bursar's office, went places with them. Then Claudia switched to MIT, and Seymour asked me to live with him.

Tony Just like that.

Victor Ten years we lived together. I never cheated on him. I did a lot of acting. Met a lot of nice people. One night Seymour has to work and the guys drag me to this jazz restaurant. Older crowd, and he's there. He was supposed to be in rehearsal. I was shocked, you know, because he never went to those places. And who do I see him with?

Tony Claudia's back?

Victor Claudia's back, and she has her arm around my lover, putting a drunken kiss on Seymour's lips. And Seymour looks back at her with this gentle, loving expression, which shocked me more than a canon firing in my face. What a fool I was. I'm walking toward them, headless, blood dripping all over my suit, my hands out to both of them, like 'How nice to see you guys'. Seymour jumps up giving me a hug, pulling up a chair, calling the waiter. 'No' I said. 'Can't sit here. Got to get back to my friends.' I'm walking away like a zombie, jazz playing, people laughing and screaming, and I'm paranoid that everybody *knew*, all along, and maybe even that's why the guys dragged me there, to wake me up, and I hated them . . . I . . .

Tony Ever tasted a St Joseph cake? Victor?

Victor (*dazed, exhausted*) What?

Tony St Joseph's cakes. They're even better than cannolis.

Waitress (*enters*) L'addition?

Tony Just the check.

Victor Port for me.

Tony Uhhh . . . No port.

Victor You're telling me I can't have a port because you want a *cannoli*?

Tony I'm tellin' you Rocco closes soon.

Victor Who wants to sit under fluorescent lights and eat sugar?

Tony Dessert here's six bucks. Coffee, two-fifty.

Victor How dare you. When I was speaking of . . . (*Stands.*) Get me out of here.

Tony Sit down a minute.

Victor *sits. The* **Waitress** *arrives with a glass of port and places it before* **Victor**.

What's that? I said the check.

Waitress Compliments of the house . . . for Monsieur.

Tony Get it outta here. Take it.

Waitress Oui, monsieur. (*Takes the port and exits.*)

Victor You goddam rotten little sonofabitch.

Tony No handouts. I pay. My parents didn't know the difference between Santa Claus and Uncle Sam, okay. To them red and green was traffic lights, and they were Catholic, so what's the difference? After Seymour, what can stupid me give you? A piece of salmon you won't eat? My ass is flat from ridin' in that thing you call a funeral car, even though it saves you cab fares. Twenty bucks for a fish you didn't touch. The past was so great, and today so shitty, you let a goddam fish die on your plate for no reason whatever except you're sad over Christmas trees. What do I give such a guy? Right this minute your socks and jockey shorts are dryin' all over my apartment. My phone bill quadrupled. You owe me for the rent so I give you rubdowns. And still you tell me it's temporary, so you can get the hell away from me the minute the *right* deal comes along, but it's Christmas Eve, for cryin' out tears, and the right thing isn't gonna come along in the next twenty-four hours, so please take your Christmas tree and your Seymour stories and file them under 'tough shit', and let's get outta here and go get a cannoli and a cup of coffee where we can afford the fuckin' things.

Victor Animal. Give me a handkerchief.

Tony Here. (*Throws his napkin at* **Victor**, *accidentally hitting his face.* **Victor** *throws it aside.*) I don't have a handkerchief.

Victor You . . .

Waitress *reappears, upset by what she perceives as* **Tony**'s *insensitivity.*

Tony Let's see. Dollar fifty on every ten . . .

Waitress *pulls out a neatly ironed handkerchief and gives it to* **Victor.**

Victor Merci. (*Wipes his eyes, pats his mouth, and offers it back to* **Waitress**.)

Waitress (*gestures for* **Victor** *to keep it*) No, no, no.

Victor Merci. Vous êtes très très gentille. Bonsoir.

Waitress Bonsoir, Monsieur. Joyeux Noël.

Victor Merci.

Waitress (*to* **Tony**) Monsieur. (*Gathers the many bills on the table and exits.*)

Tony (*moves to* **Victor**'s *side*) If you die before me, I'll never love anyone else.

Victor What good will that do me?

Tony Who knows? I may go before you.

Victor (*reaches up and touches* **Tony**'s *cheek*) No. Don't.

Tony The wine did this to you tonight.

Victor It's not the wine, Tony. The wine is innocent. Only the wine is innocent.

Allows **Tony** *to help him stand, and they begin to exit.*

The Real Dark Night of the Soul

Sal, *a newspaper reporter, enters his apartment with a newspaper, his briefcase, and a six-pack of beer in a brown paper bag. He drops newspaper and briefcase, pulls off his tie and takes shirt out of pants. Then he opens a beer and punches replay button on his answering machine.* SFX: *tape rewinding. Silence. Then beep.*

Farnsworth (*on tape*) Sal, it's Farnsworth. Midnight. Yeah. You left here a half-hour ago, and you're probably at Celeste's or some gin mill, relaxing, but I just read your copy, and Jesus, this is the quality of writing I've been begging for to put this goddam newspaper back into shape. When more writers like you hang around this office till midnight to get it right, then not only this rag but this whole country will fall back into place. Sal, I don't know how to repay you.

Sal With a decent salary, you silly motherfucker.

Farnsworth (*on tape*) See you at nine a.m., fella.

SFX: *beep.*

Celeste (*on tape*) Sal, it's Celeste. Are you crazy running out of here at one in the morning? All I said is to rethink our relationship. This isn't easy for me, you know. I want you to call me when you get in. It's one-fifteen. Don't let me wait up.

Sal Bitch.

SFX: *beep.*

Celeste (*on tape*) Sal, it's one-thirty, and I know you're there.

Sal Fuck you.

Celeste (*on tape*) Sal? Pick up, or I'll just let the goddam tape run out . . . Maybe you're at some bar. I'll wait one half-hour. If you don't call me by then, I'll know what you're trying to tell me.

Sal Go to bed.

SFX: *beep.*

Celeste (*on tape*) Sal, it's 2 a.m. and I'm not thrilled with this. I know you're there. Are you there? Sal, don't make me worry. Now call, you hear?

Sal Sure, baby.

SFX: *beep.*

Celeste (*on tape*) I'm through, Sal. It's 3 a.m. and I'm not going to be the guilty one. I'm going to bed and putting my machine on, okay? If I don't hear from you, well, I'll assume we're dead.

Sal Jerk.

Gets up to turn off the machine, and just as he is about to, SFX: *phone ring in the room, then beep.*

The Caller 'In the real dark night of the soul it's always 3 a.m.' You know who said that? F. Scott Fitzgerald. Hey, Dave, pick up. C'mon, don't let the beep cut us off. Take your hand away and breathe, you sonofabitch. Jesus, do you hear that music in the background? It's the music of hell. I'm at the port of entry with two hundred faceless orphans, and we're drowning in dance and drink and terror 'cause it's easier than going home to our empty lives. I miss you so much. 'He's whining again.' Isn't that what you're thinking? Big Dave wouldn't do that. Dave's a real he-man. Where's the beep? You fuck. When I heal from what you've done to me, I'll probably be turned to stone just like you. The whining – you hear, motherfucker? – is because I'm alive and tender and I hurt, and I'm proud of it. You can't hurt. Not while you're inside your 2000 dollar suit. You can only pray that someone like me will kill himself over you so you can own his gift of love with no repayment. But remember, I was the one who was happily married. And you, you fell on your knees that night in your kitchen and begged me to stay 'cause only *I* could *save* you. 'Just be my friend. Nothing sexual. No, no. Just look into my eyes without turning away. Just touch fingers ever so lightly. It's a natural physical feeling.' I felt it. I did. Yeah, it was magnetic, and I admitted it. I admitted it, so I got scared, and I cried. You leapt up and held onto me and said, 'Don't you ever be afraid. I'll be here forever to help you.' What happened to forever, Dave? Huh? What the fuck happened to *forever*? I opened up a grave . . . exhumed such old feelings, my father, my brothers, feelings I had buried in that grave, and when you promised not to trick me like they did, well, I just lifted the cadaver, stood it on its feet, and it blinked. It moved. Its name was Love. My monster was brought back to life, but it scared Big Dave, and now Big Dave won't talk to me, but I know you're listening, you poor handmade-shoes, pole-up-his-ass ex-friend. You know what I'm going to do? Tonight I'll answer your prayers. I'm going to lead my monster back to its grave, shoot it in the brain, and cover it up forever . . .

Sal (*grabs phone*) Don't shoot your monster. Do you hear me?

The Caller Who . . . who is this?

Sal My name's Sal.

The Caller Sal who?

Sal You dialed 242-9664.

The Caller I dialed 9644.

Sal 9664.

The Caller Why'd you let me go on?

Sal Look, I'm straight, but I have the same monster. My girl threw me out tonight.

The Caller I'm sorry.

Sal I'm sorry about this bastard Dave.

The Caller It's okay.

Sal It fucking stinks. Look, you've got my number now. I'm available. I mean, purely for a drink, a talk . . . Hello?

The Caller I'm here.

Sal Well you've got the number.

The Caller You're some character.

Sal Hey, you got a drink in your hand?

The Caller Yeah.

Sal Want to toast?

The Caller Who?

Sal Our monsters. Should we?

The Caller I don't know.

Sal Let's go. Lift your glass.

They lift their glasses.

Here's to monsters – yours, mine, everybody's.

They drink. **The Caller** *hangs up.* **Sal** *looks into the phone speaker, then slowly, sadly, puts it down.*

Rex

An apartment in SoHo. A dinner table is set for two.
At rise, **John,** *the younger of the men, is finishing*
setting the table.

Eric (*enters*) Spend the day at the gym?

John I drove out to the country.

Eric How was the house?

John Survived the winter.

Eric Plumber turn the water on?

John Yeah. Rosario was cleaning when I left.

Eric Why didn't you stay?

John I had to make it back.

Eric Georgette Klinger?

John No.

Eric Tai chi?

John No.

Eric You went to the Zen Center?

John I wanted to chat with the new priest.

Eric The cute young priest.

John I had a minor moral question.

Eric Cut the crap.

John It had to do with the food on this table.

Eric Had enough macro? (*Lifting a plate. Smelling.*) Tofu with scallions. What's the sauce?

John Sesame oil.

Eric Out of a bottle.

John I didn't say I *slaved* over it.

Eric And this is what? (*Lifts plate, pushes chair back in horror.*) God, what *is* that?

John Okay, just hear me out.

Eric It's some sort of meat.

John Eric, we must eat flesh tonight.

Eric Eat flesh? Have you gone crazy?

John It's organic.

Eric Of course it's organic. It's flesh.

John I mean no steroids or antibiotics.

Eric Who guaranteed you that?

John Eric, the bird is from the wild.

Eric Bird?! It looks like tuna fish salad with a chicken leg stuck in the middle.

John I had to shred the creature.

Eric Why didn't you shred the leg?

John The leg was intact, so I left it intact.

Eric I'm not eating that fucking thing.

John We've got to. I killed it.

Eric You what?

John I ran it over with the Mercedes.

Eric A chicken?

John No. A pheasant.

Eric Call our nutritionist.

John It's a higher matter than that.

Eric Call your therapist.

John For a massage?

Eric Not your massage therapist. Your analyst.

John She'd only want to know what *we* think about it. The Zen priest said if we take it into our own bodies, it'll re-enter the lifestream.

Eric It'll turn to shit!

John Oh, fuck you.

Eric Nothing in Buddhism says you have to eat it because you killed it. Murderers would have to eat their victims. This is obscene.

John Are you classifying me with . . .

Eric You didn't murder it. I didn't say you murdered it. But you did kill it.

John *I* killed it.

Eric You said you killed it. Okay, you ran over it. And as a result . . . What am I saying? You *killed* it.

John I did not murder this bird.

Eric I said you only killed it.

John I tried to save the fucking thing.

Eric Okay, take it easy.

John It was flopping around in the road, limping, dizzy.

Eric Dear God.

John I lifted it by its wing and threw it into the back seat and nearly killed *myself* driving to the vet.

Eric You went to the veterinarian with this . . . ?

John He worked on it for an hour.

Eric On this?

John It died in his hands.

Eric This is an expensive little dish.

John He didn't charge, but it cost us sixty bucks for the container.

Eric What container?

John *brings pet casket to the table.*

Eric That's a little casket.

John The whole thing is made of pressed oatmeal, so it's bio-degradable.

Eric Get that fucking thing off my dinner table.

John They were going to incinerate it.

Eric Isn't that what you did?

John I roasted it.

Eric Oh my God, this boy's gone over the falls. Should we eat every mosquito we slam?

John You rotten . . .

Eric We'd gag on the cockroaches we put away in our lifetimes, you and I. Jesus!

John What do you want me to *do*, you sonofabitch?

Eric Throw the fucking bird in the garbage.

John That's not right.

Eric Then eat the disgusting thing.

John Okay, you take a bite, and I'll take a bite, and we'll put the rest in here and forget this whole thing.

Eric A casket made of oatmeal?

John Just a pet casket.

Eric Just a pet casket . . .

John It decomposes and makes the animal one with the earth.

Eric It'd be one with the earth if you'd left it on the road.

John The crows would have picked at it.

Eric So 'caw, caw' we're two giant crows at a dinner table in SoHo, picking at a bird run over by a Mercedes Benz in East Hampton. You're getting a part-time job.

John You're freaking me.

Eric I'm freaked! Get that casket off the dinner table.

John Listen to me. I don't know how things got this far, okay? But just end it and put the thing in the oatmeal thing and bury it.

Eric Who bury it? Me bury it? Should we bury our toenail clippings? The hair we have cut? In teeny oatmeal caskets?

John You're scoffing at the dignity of this animal and of human life . . .

Eric I'm going to call Ruth's emergency number.

John Call for yourself, Wimpella.

Eric Wimpella? *Wiiimpellaaa?*

John Just taste it. I said taste the goddam thing. For me. Me, your significant other . . . Eric?

Eric *tastes it.*

Well?

Eric What can I tell you? It's not bad.

John Who are you kidding?

Eric You marinated it.

John Olive oil, ginger, lemon, pepper . . .

Eric (*eating more*) Oh, John, remember duck?

John Duck. My God!

Eric Lamb chops. Bacon.

Both (*clutching hands over the table in a harmonic, operatic cry*) Ham Hawaiian!

Eric *bites into something hard.*

John Oh-oh. Don't tell me your tooth.

Eric (*takes small piece of something out of his mouth and drops it on his plate. It clinks like a chunk of lead*) Asphalt. You eat.

John Oh. (*Tastes it. Makes a face.*)

Eric What?

John Meat. Disgusting.

Eric Now swallow. Swallow.

John There. I did it. I feel dizzy.

Eric Now why don't I go down to the dumpster and heave this little heap. No ceremony . . .

John First put it in the . . . that.

Eric (*lifts it cradled in tinfoil*) Tinfoil doesn't decompose, darling.

John Give me. (*Dumps the bird into the oatmeal casket, crumples up the tinfoil.*) Put on the lid. (**Eric** *does.*) Thank God. Now let's not look at it. I'll get our tea. I have lemon tarts for dessert.

Eric No tarts. No tea. Tonight we fast.

John Thanks for understanding this silliness.

Eric Can you handle the truth?

John What?

Eric I understand none of this. Now you just sit there and mourn, and when I get back, we'll watch a movie.

John Say a prayer for it.

Eric I'll think of something.

John His name is Rex.

Eric It has a name?

John It's a male. When it was flopping in the back of the car, I had to talk to him, and—

Eric Rex. Fine. Now mourn quietly till I get back, and then we forget Rex forever. You got that?

John Yeah.

Eric No matter how much wine we drink at a dinner party, we never tell this story.

John I swear.

Eric See you in a few minutes. (*Exits.*)

John *stares.*

John Goodbye, Rex.

Music: Rex Tremendae, *chorus from the Mozart Requiem. Lights fade to black.*

Rosen's Son

Two men, one old enough to be the father of the other, are lying on the floor of an apartment foyer. There is quiet in the foyer although we are aware that something awful has preceded it. The older man wears a raincoat. His umbrella is next to him. The younger man is in a tuxedo. There is a coatrack with the hats and coats of dinner guests.

Mr Rosen Forgive me, Eddie.

Eddie Shhh.

Mr Rosen Do you forgive me?

Eddie I think so.

Mr Rosen Where's the gun?

Eddie I've got it.

Mr Rosen Did I hurt you?

Eddie My lip's cut.

Mr Rosen I'm sorry.

Eddie Just take it easy. Relax.

Mr Rosen I've gone crazy. I miss my boy.

Eddie I miss him too, Mr Rosen.

Mr Rosen So you get involved two months after he dies?

Eddie Your son was sick a long time.

Mr Rosen So you celebrate his death by moving a stranger in here to live with you?

Eddie He's no stranger.

Mr Rosen You call me 'Mr Rosen'?

Eddie All right. Ziggy. Take it easy.

Mr Rosen Strangers' coats in my son's foyer.

Eddie Just shut up.

Harrison (*off*) Ed?

Eddie Yeah?

Harrison (*off*) Who buzzed?

Eddie I'm taking care of it.

Harrison (*enters speaking*) Our guests are waiting. Who is this man?

Eddie Ben's father. (*To* **Mr Rosen**.) This is Harrison.

Harrison Mr Rosen?

Mr Rosen What else?

Harrison My deepest sympathies . . . for your recent trouble. Would you care to join us? (*Indicates dining room.*)

Eddie No, Harrison.

Mr Rosen I come here with a gun, he invites me to dinner.

Harrison Does he have a *gun*?

Eddie I took it from him.

Mr Rosen Does he know who allows him to stand here in this foyer? My son. Because of his death you stand here. Is that true, Eddie? I would vomit on that table in there.

Harrison He's off his rocker.

Eddie This is not him.

Mr Rosen Young people, you have no hearts, no memory, but wait. You'll get yours. Just lemme outta this death oven.

Eddie I'll call you later.

Mr Rosen Call nothing. Which way out of this hell?

Eddie (*getting his coat. To* **Harrison**) I've got to go with him.

Harrison You're *going*?

Eddie To see him home.

Mr Rosen Are you crazy? For me what is home?

Harrison Eddie, you can't just leave our dinner guests.

Eddie Shut up, will you, Harrison?

Harrison Are you aware of the tone you just used with me?

Eddie I said shut up.

Harrison I'm calling the police. He's threatened us.

Eddie Do that, Harrison, and I'll leave you. I swear to Christ.

Harrison Did you say you'll leave me?

Mr Rosen Easy come, easy go.

Harrison (*pointing at* **Rosen**) You are trespassing, and it's criminal.

Mr Rosen Bite your tongue, cutie. Who do you think you are to get your bloomers in such an uproar over me? What do you see standing before you? An old man in a raincoat. One wife. One child. Both dead. Both dead. Him I put in the diamond business. For you, you bastard.

Harrison Does he mean me?

Mr Rosen Who do I mean, this umbrella? You start living with a man two months after his lover dies – are you the blessed Virgin?

Harrison I knew Eddie a year.

Mr Rosen (*to* **Eddie**) While my son was sick, you fooled around, you pig in a tuxedo.

Eddie He worked in our office.

Harrison You're wrong, Mr Rosen.

Mr Rosen Drop in a hole, the two of you. Young people, you replace other people like spark plugs. Half your age I said goodbyes that would make you sweat blood. I cut the tattooed numbers off my wrist with a kitchen knife, then worried: without my numbers how will they find me, my mother, my sister? Don't worry. You. I tried to teach you, but only diamonds you learned, only money so you could have Mr Bloomingdale's here, who tells me I trespass my son's apartment. *Mazel tov.* Give me at least back my gun.

Harrison Don't give it to him.

Mr Rosen Afraid to die so young, Mr Bloomingdale's? My boy was not afraid. He smiled. Relax, Mr Bloomingdale's, the gun was for my head, not yours or his, though you are pigs enough to be slaughtered . . .

Eddie Ziggy, please.

Mr Rosen Shame on people who eat with candles, not for God, but to hide pimples and wrinkles. Young people who live together not for love but only for sex, boff, boff, like pistons, machines. You never get bored? (*To* **Harrison**.) What are you smiling at?

Eddie Harrison, go now.

Harrison *starts off*.

Mr Rosen Not so fast, cutie. You wanna make a deal? You change places?

Harrison With who?

Mr Rosen My boy.

Harrison Oh, Eddie.

Mr Rosen You crawl into his grave and send my son home to his father.

Harrison I'm so sorry for you, Mr Rosen.

Eddie Harrison's a good person.

Mr Rosen Young people living in a magazine. Did you show him a picture of my boy? (*Takes out his wallet.*)

Eddie Jesus!

Harrison I'm not afraid. I'd like to see him.

Mr Rosen (*showing him photo*) Look at a handsome face, eh?

Harrison Very nice.

Mr Rosen You . . . (*To* **Eddie**.) What's his name?

Harrison ⎫
Eddie ⎭ Harrison.

Mr Rosen (*to* **Eddie**) Goyisha? (**Eddie** *nods.*) Where do they get these names?

Harrison It's a family name.

Mr Rosen Your nose is a fortune cookie next to my son. I'm serious.

Eddie Okay, Ziggy, let's call it quits.

Mr Rosen A basketball is your neck. It's my way of speaking. You play an instrument?

Harrison I've always regretted not . . .

Mr Rosen The flute, my son. Avery Fisher Hall. Clippings to drown in.

Harrison (*handing back the photo*) He's extraordinary. He's beautiful. Eddie, our guests are waiting.

Mr Rosen I came here to splash my brains onto your table. That's what the gun was for, to put out your candles with my blood.

Harrison Please . . .

Mr Rosen But I changed my mind. In the river throw the gun. Me, I'll do like the elephants: go to Miami. The sun will polish my bones. For a little fee, a lawyer will send you my tusks. They'll go nice here, either side of your door. Speaking of doors, kindly point how the hell a person gets out of here.

Harrison May I be excused please?

Mr Rosen Leave. *Mazel tov.* (**Harrison** *exits.*) You forgot the summers at the lake, the canoe, you and me? The dinners, the holidays, birthdays? I had to accept you, didn't I? I had to swallow it, and I did, and you just forgot those days?

Eddie I didn't forget any of it.

Mr Rosen Was we really a family?

Eddie I thought we were.

Mr Rosen I thought so, too. I thought so . . . (**Eddie** *puts on his coat.*) Where you goin'?

Eddie To help you get a taxi.

Mr Rosen No taxi.

Eddie Then I'll call you later to see you got home safe.

Mr Rosen Never dare you call me again in your life. You're nothing to me.

Eddie Don't say that.

Mr Rosen Liar. You want I should disappear so bad.

Eddie No.

Mr Rosen Look at his face. Such a liar. After this minute, never, never again will you see this face of your 'Mr Rosen'. But before I go, I want you should tell me a truth so perfect as you never before spoke the truth to anyone in your life, and I'll give you the freedom of a thousand doves set loose on the mountaintops.

Eddie Ask me.

Mr Rosen Do you love that one in there? The truth, before God.

Eddie I'm trying to love him. I'm the kind of man who has to have somebody. I'm trying very hard . . .

Mr Rosen Does he love you like –

Eddie He's different.

Mr Rosen Like my boy used to? Remember –

Eddie Different.

Mr Rosen Like you were God on earth?

Eddie No.

Mr Rosen Does he laugh with those same funny brown eyes?

Eddie Of course not.

Mr Rosen Bake bread like he used to?

Eddie No.

Mr Rosen Play the flute on Sunday while you read the paper?

Eddie No.

Mr Rosen The truth, before God.

Eddie (*shouts*) It'll never be the same for me again! Never!

Mr Rosen This is true?

Eddie What do you think? (*Weeps.*) You bastard. You awful man.

Mr Rosen Good, you cry. Now I'm happy. Goodbye, Eddie. Don't follow me. Don't call me. God bless you. You were my son. Really. You were. My other son.

Lenten Puddings

Uncle Wayne *is craggy, rural, yet intelligence and breeding are apparent.* **Megan** *is richly dressed, wearing a diamond ring. They are out of doors in crisp spring air, on* **Uncle Wayne***'s deck.*

Uncle Wayne I was just not strong enough to make the thirty-six lenten puddings this year. The mailing became too expensive, and some of you don't even send thank you's.

Megan Then why do you refuse to give us the recipe?

Uncle Wayne The recipe will go to the grave with me.

Megan You just can't keep that recipe secret any longer. Now I drove eighty miles today. I tried to make one by guesswork last week. It didn't last three days.

Uncle Wayne All eaten?

Megan No. It went rancid. Tasted like rotten oranges baked in rubber. Then rigor mortis set in. I don't know why my mother never learned to make them. How could you have been brother and sister?

Uncle Wayne It always beat me. My lenten puddings last over five years in the refrigerator.

Megan Well, I poured rum all over my stone. It did soften . . .

Uncle Wayne But tasted like fruit cake.

Megan God, worse than fruit cake.

Uncle Wayne Rum is disgusting in lenten puddings.

Megan How hostile of you to keep this secret from the entire family. I just want to pass on my grandmother's recipe to my children. Don't I deserve that?

Uncle Wayne You speak of deserving with that diamond ring you're wearing? You're drowning in your husband's greed. Like malformed kittens, you should all be put into a bag with a rock and thrown in Lake Babcock. And you drive eighty miles for the recipe you *deserve*.

Megan My grandmother's recipe.

Uncle Wayne Something money can't buy.

Megan This was my grandmother's summer house . . .

Uncle Wayne My *mother*, don't forget. And she was just like you. I never was particularly proud of her. Your mother was like her, too. You were all hot-house bred. A fresh wind would wither you in seconds.

Megan I spent summers here as a child. Had you died before my mother this place would be mine.

Uncle Wayne So the old bachelor didn't deserve an inheritance? Which niece or nephew will he leave it to when he kicks off, as he seems to be ready to do? Are there rumors, Megan?

Megan No one wants this sad little place.

Uncle Wayne Just the recipe to lenten puddings because this is the first year one didn't arrive on every doorstep. For twenty years I cooked up in this shack, from New Year's to Ash Wednesday, to keep warm, to put a pleasant smell in the house, to nourish the children of my brothers and sisters because I'm the last of all the aunts and uncles. Thirty-six puddings take a whole winter, honey. This year I was too tired, and there was no goose this past Christmas . . .

Megan What on earth has a goose to do with it?

Uncle Wayne Wouldn't you just love to know! . . . Well, they won me over finally. They'll get your two sons. It's the young they want . . . Imagine a robin forgetting how to build her nest. That's what's coming to this country . . .

Megan You should have married.

Uncle Wayne You think I don't know what love is?

Megan What have my poor sons done to you? You've never even met them.

Uncle Wayne How dangerous that would have been. Why was I punished by you. Even though I presented you year after year with my penitential pie like a puppy begging to be forgiven. But, no . . .

Megan You can't believe that *I* was punishing you. Why, I . . .

Uncle Wayne It's too late now to melt me. There'll be no thaw for Uncle Wayne this spring. Oh, just go. Leave me my privacy.

Megan Uncle Wayne . . . (*She rises.*) Be happy, darling. I'll go if you like.

Uncle Wayne Enjoy your drive.

Megan (*starts to exit then stops at the door looking out*) When I was a girl, this property seemed a continent. It's so small now, such a tiny garden. What happened to the cedar gazebo?

Uncle Wayne Wisteria pulled that down twenty years ago.

Megan A little house that let in the sun and the rain. I remember that gardener loved to sit in there behind the drooping purple blossoms, hiding from his work. Was he Yugoslavian?

Uncle Wayne We never had a gardener.

Megan He'd sit inside the gazebo on that yellow wicker chair of Uncle Edward's. What happened to that chair?

Uncle Wayne It's still there on the porch.

Megan That tiny green thing on the porch?

Uncle Wayne It was yellow. I painted it white. Was white twenty years. Now it's green.

Megan Did the oaks stop growing?

Uncle Wayne Unlike chairs, trees grow. The oaks grew with you, that's all, Megan.

Megan So the trees remained my friends.

Uncle Wayne It *was* wisteria that pulled down your cherished gazebo.

Megan They shared a fate, the gazebo and the wisteria. It was inevitable, like marriage.

Uncle Wayne A form of strangulation I wouldn't know about.

Megan I remember the Yugoslavian sitting there, resting, fanning himself with his straw hat, hiding behind the purple blossoms. How they drooped sadly blooming all around him.

Uncle Wayne Paul was never sad, nor did he ever hide from work.

Megan He'd be sweating in his overalls and his workshirt. He'd roll up his sleeves, and they'd be so tight above his muscles I worried about his circulation. Such blue eyes and brown skin and yellow hair that glowed even in the shade . . .

Uncle Wayne You do remember him.

Megan There's such sadness in foliage that hangs. Charles wouldn't allow willows on our property . . .

Uncle Wayne Your grandmother planted those willows, and when her sister, my Aunt Margaret, came, she'd say, 'For God's sake, plant trees that'll hold up their heads like this child of yours'.

Megan Who was the child?

Uncle Wayne I was the child.

Megan You were your aunt's favorite?

Uncle Wayne Yes. She was an old maid. She taught me the recipe for those lenten pies. Not your grandmother. Your grandmother had a cook. Your mother learned to cook from a poor Scots woman.

Megan I missed my legacy entirely, didn't I?

Uncle Wayne The lenten puddings never were your legacy.

Megan I must have broken fences when I followed you about up here, adoringly, everywhere. That was my downfall, wasn't it? Wasn't it? Following you about?

Uncle Wayne Say what you mean.

Megan What I saw that day in the gazebo. You thought I told the family about it, and I never had the courage to assure you that I wouldn't. I didn't tell a soul. I didn't breathe . . .

Uncle Wayne They all found out about it anyway.

Megan Not from me. I swear it to you. Uncle Wayne, I was so afraid for you . . .

Uncle Wayne Were you?

Megan What happened to Paul?

Uncle Wayne He lives nearby, with his wife. His daughter's in college.

Megan You see him.

Uncle Wayne He comes to work in the garden now and then.

Megan He still works in the garden?

Uncle Wayne Once a week he prunes and putters around while I make him lunch. We don't charge each other.

Megan I imagine he has a great deal of love for you.

Uncle Wayne We have kept faithful in our ways.

Megan I envy him.

Uncle Wayne Do you?

Megan I think you are a very strong, very beautiful man to have had such a friend. I had hoped to marry someone like you, but obviously I wasn't that lucky.

Uncle Wayne Who are we? We think we know in one decade, then it passes, and we're asking the question again.

Megan If you become worse, I mean ill, would Paul take care of you?

Uncle Wayne Yes, he would. Paul will always be here.

Megan Well, then . . . (*Leaving.*)

Uncle Wayne   Here! Sit down before you run out of here. (*She sits.*) Per pudding: one tablespoon of goose fat, one orange rind, one cup Cognac . . .

She pulls a pad and pencil frantically out of her bag and writes.